Lake Chapala through the ages

an anthology of travellers' tales

Canadian Cataloguing in Publication Data
Burton, Tony, 1953-
Lake Chapala through the ages: an anthology of travellers' tales
/ Tony Burton
Includes translations from Spanish, French and German
Includes bibliographical references and index
ISBN 978-0-9735191-2-9

1. Chapala, Lake, Region (Mexico)—History. 2. Chapala, Lake
Region (Mexico)—Description and travel. I Title.

F1254.B87 2008   972.2/35   C2008-904743-5

ISBN 978-0-9735191-2-9
First edition 2008 2nd printing 2022
Commentary, translations and map © 2008 by Tony Burton,
illustrations © 2008 by Rosemary Chan, unless otherwise credited.

Cover design, incorporating photo of Villa Reynera: Rosana Sánchez

Sombrero Books, P. O. Box 4, Ladysmith B .C. V9G 1A1, Canada

Lake Chapala
through the ages

an anthology of travellers' tales

TONY BURTON

Illustrated by
Rosemary Chan

SB

SOMBRERO BOOKS, B.C., CANADA

For Gwen

Contents

Boxes

Copyright and credits

Every reasonable effort has been taken to ensure that any pre-existing copyright has been respected in compiling this book. Any infringement of copyright is entirely unintentional, and the publishers would be grateful if it could be reported for correction in any future edition.

Thanks are extended to Ms. Margo C. Mitchell of Plover Press for her kind permission to reprint, in chapter 41, parts of *Notes of a Villager,* the translation by John Mitchell and Ruth Mitchell de Aguilar of José Ruben Romero's *Apuntes de un lugareño.*

The translation used in chapter 13 is by John Black; that used in chapter 16 by Brigitte and Bob Plummer; that used in chapter 33 by Marianne Davey, and that used in chapter 55 by Marie-Josée Bayeur. Translations used in other chapters are by the author.

The support of the Lake Chapala Review, which published part of chapter 33 in vol.6 #2, April 15, 2004, and of Mexico Connect e-zine (www.mexconnect.com) which published parts of chapters 5, 6, 24, 32 and 35 previously, is also hereby acknowledged.

A note on style

Square brackets [xxx] are reserved for editorial comments and clarifications. Other parentheses are as in the original. In the interests of clarity, paragraphing and place names have sometimes been modernized.

Introduction

This book includes extracts from every published book that could be located which makes more than a passing mention of Lake Chapala, and which was written (originally) prior to 1910. Most are first hand accounts. A small number of magazine and newspaper pieces are also included where they offer additional material of interest.

Why 1910? Because that marks the end of Chapala's first tourist boom. It is the year when President Porfirio Díaz visited the shores of the lake for the final time, staying in Ocotlán, rather than in Chapala itself. Later that year the Mexican Revolution erupted. Mexico, including the Lake Chapala region, was thrown into chaos for more than a decade.

The building of the railway branch line in 1920 meant that visitors could travel, for the first time, from Mexico City or the U.S. to Chapala entirely by train. Though the railway was short lived (it closed in 1926), this allowed a group of European and American intellectuals, including distinguished writers such as D. H. Lawrence, to rediscover the delights of the village. The more adventurous also discovered neighboring Ajijic. The volume of writing about, or undertaken at, the lake increased exponentially. This period really began a second major boom in Chapala's tourist fortunes, the details of which are best left for another occasion.

Many of the early historical accounts were written by Franciscan friars. While in no way impugning their motives, it is inevitable that these accounts reflect a somewhat Eurocentric view and pro-Catholic standpoint, which may have distorted the indigenous reality. The character and status of the writer plays a large part in these narratives and should be bourne in mind when reading them. Partly for this reason, as well as to satisfy the curious, a brief biographical sketch of each author is included.

Inevitably, given the relative levels of investment and development, coverage of the northen shore of Lake Chapala is somewhat more comprehensive than coverage of the southern shore.

I hope that this modest introduction to the history and development of the Chapala region will encourage readers to further explore the dozens of fascinating sub-plots scattered throughout the region's history.

The Lake Chapala Region

Legend:

Lakes (circa 2007)

Area of lake shown on Narváez's map of 1816-17 but drained after 1906

Former wetlands (now mainly farmland)

C. Grande   Prominent hill (C = Cerro)

Present day village or town

Site of 16th century Franciscan friary

Hacienda

Railway (completed in 1888)

Highway (excludes toll roads)

kilometers
0   10   20

The 16ᵗʰ century

Invasion! The Aztec Empire was invaded by Hernán Cortés in 1519, and Cortés gained control of the Aztec capital city Mexico-Tenochtitlan on August 13, 1521. Over the next few years, a series of expeditions set off to continue the exploration of the New World. Early expeditions took conquistadors to the Pacific coast. Colima, for instance, was originally founded in 1523 on the coast, but relocated inland in 1527.

Two well-placed brothers, cousins of Hernan Cortés—Fernando (or possibly Hernando) de Saavedra and Alonso de Ávalos— are central to the history of Lake Chapala. The details are sketchy, and the precise dates still debated, but in 1523, it seems that Hernan Cortés granted Fernando de Saavedra, who had previously accompanied an expedition to the Colima area, the *encomienda* (the right to collect tributes and labor from Indians) for an area of land (and mines) which extended from Tamazula to the shores of Lake Chapala.

Alonso de Ávalos, Fernando's younger brother, arrived in New Spain in 1523 and participated the following year in the conquest of Xaliso (Nayarit). When Cortés asked Fernando de Saavedra to return to Mexico City and accompany him on a military campaign to Higueras (Honduras), Alonso was left in charge of the encomienda. By 1528, the brothers were in control of a sizeable portion of western Mexico, which became known as the Province of Ávalos, administered from Sayula, stretching from present-day Tamazula, and Tapalpa to Tizapán el Alto, Jocotepec, Ajijic and Chapala. The Province of Ávalos was subject to the Audiencia of New Spain (based in Mexico City). As a result, for much of the 16ᵗʰ century, Lake Chapala was effectively divided between the Audiencia of New Spain and the Audiencia of New Galicia (founded in 1547 and based in Guadalajara), with the latter only gradually acquiring control over the northern and western shores of the lake. In 1550, for instance, Ajijic belonged to the Audiencia of New Spain, but by 1572 or so, it was firmly inside the Audiencia of New Galicia.

Most historians concur that the Spanish occupation of the Province of Ávalos was a relatively peaceful process, which enabled many indigenous customs to survive largely unchanged into much more recent times. The Indians in most places were encouraged to take Spanish names, to congregate into larger groups (this made them easier to control, and also freed up potential farmland) and they were then resettled. The first lakeside town to be refounded in this way appears to have been Jocotepec on November 20, 1529. The document, signed by Hernan Cortés and Miguel Triudoy, the Royal scribe, lists the "first Indian founders (already rechristened) of Xocotepec as: Santiago Jacobo, Luis Cupertino, Graciano Concepción, Jorge Simeón, Pedro Tadeo, Salvador Hesperito, Lorenzo Antonio, Lorenzo

Sebastián, Bartolo Jacobo, Andrés Joseph, Juan de los Reyes, Pablo Roque, together with their families."

The Spanish occupation of the Province of Ávalos may have been a relatively peaceful process, but things changed dramatically in 1530. This was the year when Nuño de Guzmán marched into the picture. There was no love lost between Nuño de Guzmán and Hernán Cortés. Guzmán had a reputation for unbridled cruelty. He was president of the first Audiencia, the administrative body overseeing New Spain, which was the equivalent of a Supreme Court, council, executive and (in part) legislature, all rolled into one. Guzmán took advantage of this power to lead a brutal expedition to conquer areas to the west and north of Mexico City. What drove Guzmán on? One of his slaves had mentioned the existence of seven cities, rich in gold and overflowing with jewels. The cities were rumored to lie far to the north and to be as big as Mexico City. Several years later, in 1536, some of Guzmán's companions heard a similar tale about a city called Quivira. Greed prompted several serious attempts to find these fabulous cities, one of the century's most famous legends.

Early in 1530, Guzmán's forces reached the northeastern corner of Lake Chapala and took the native village of Cuitzeo. On this expedition was Juan de Sámano (see chapter 1) who has bequeathed us a valuable eye-witness account of the conquest of New Galicia.

Nuño de Guzmán tried everything he could to snatch parts of the Province of Ávalos, awarding land grants in direct conflict with those made earlier by Cortés, and even creating a fictitious land title in order to support his claim to have been the true pacifier of Sayula. However, his efforts to rewrite the history of the Province of Ávalos failed, presumably because Cortés and Alonso de Ávalos still enjoyed ample support in Spain.

The conflicts between the two powerful groups, headed respectively by Guzmán and Cortés, were resolved only when Guzmán was sent back to Spain in 1536 (he died there in1544) and after the death of Cortés in 1547. Over the next few generations, intermarriage between their feuding supporters ended the enmity between the groups. The complex genealogy of this period has been brilliantly reconstructed by historian Rodolfo Fernández in *Latifundios y Grupos Dominantes en la Historia de la Provincia de Ávalos*.

In summary, the south shore of the lake had been incorporated into colonial New Spain relatively peacefully; the north-eastern shore had been incorporated by brute force. In the 16th century, Lake Chapala was, by turns, an administrative frontier zone—between the Audiencias of New Spain and New Galicia,—an ecclesiastical frontier zone—between the ecclesiastical dioceses of Guadalajara and Valladolid (Morelia)—and a geopolitical frontier zone—the scene of the intense rivalry between two of New Spain's most powerful individuals: Hernán Cortés and Nuño de Guzmán.

1

Conquistadors describe the lake
1530
Juan de Sámano

Accompanying Nuño de Guzmán in 1530 was Juan de Sámano, the son of Spanish King Charles I's private secretary. Juan de Sámano was an experienced soldier who had fought for the Spanish army against the French prior to being sent across the Atlantic to serve the first Audiencia. He was a captain, victualer and scribe in Nuño de Guzmán's band of about three hundred conquistadors, and was an eye-witness to the conquest (1530-31) of New Galicia, the western part of New Spain.

A few years later, Juan de Sámano was back in Mexico City, where he was appointed a senior judge in the second Audiencia. In a curious twist of fate, he was responsible for overseeing the return to Spain of his former leader Nuño de Guzmán, when the King ordered that he be sent back to answer serious charges.

In return for his part in the conquest, Juan de Sámano was granted the right (*encomienda*) to collect tribute and labor from Indians in the Zinacantepec area, near Toluca.

It is from the expedition led by Guzmán in 1530 that we have an early description of Lake Chapala. Guzmán's precise route is not known for certain, but soon after leaving Tzintzuntzan, in Michoacán, he reached the River Santiago, close to present-day Ocotlán. Across the river, on the western side, was the native village of Cuitzeo. It was late February or early March of 1530.

In order to cross the river, Guzmán's motley crew of Mexico City-dwelling Spanish adventurers, still seeking their fortunes, and hundreds of Indian followers, built rafts and captured local canoes. In the absence of any informers providing advance information about the region, Guzmán sent his scouts a day or so ahead of the main party on several exploratory trips. From one of these trips, came the first report of Lake Chapala. In Juan de Sámano's words:

And on the other side of the mountains was a very large lake. The governor sent a scout to the top of these mountains to come back and rejoin him at the end of them, where the Río Grande de Nuestra Señora, which enters the lake from the foothills and goes through the lake for what seems to be about three or four leagues, leaves it again without any hindrance. The scout, going over the mountains found himself in a village called Chapala and in other places whose names were not known at that time, and ended by crossing the mountains again, hard work for the horses, thereby returning to where the governor was.

A league is a variable measure of distance, from 4,180 meters to 6,687 meters, depending on the region. To add to the imprecision, it is also sometimes used to represent the typical distance that could be covered in an hour on foot, a distance which depended on the nature of the terrain.

These early conquistadors were far more interested in minerals (gold and silver) and large expanses of rich, fertile agricultural land, than they were in natural beauty. The lake offered them nothing of any great significance. Guzmán's forces quickly pushed on towards Tonalá. On March 26, 1530, they divided into two, and the main group followed the course of the Santiago river towards the Pacific Ocean, before heading northwards along the coastal plain to Sinaloa.

Where the conquistadors saw no reason to dally in the Chapala region, the Franciscan missionaries who followed closely behind encountered plenty of native people whose souls they could save. The Franciscans rapidly established missions (friaries) in several places, including Ajijic (1531)—the first to be established in New Galicia after Guadalajara—Poncitlán (1533-4) and Chapala (1548). Among other things, the friars also introduced many crops, animals and agricultural techniques from the Old World (Spain) to the New. The decade following 1530 was a defining time in this region.

Sámano, Juan de c.1530 *Relación de la Conquista de los teules chichimecas.*

2

Indian chieftains and Franciscan friars
Mid-16th century
Father Antonio Tello

The illustrious Franciscan chronicler Fray Antonio Tello was born in 1567 in the province of León in Spain. He became a Franciscan friar in 1611 and arrived in New Galicia in about 1619, where he was the Secretary to the Provincial Minister of Santiago, Jalisco. He served as guardian of various Franciscan monasteries, in Autlán, Zacoalco, Cocula, Tecolotlán and Guadalajara. He began writing his account of the evangelical work of the Franciscans in 1637, and completed his work in about 1653, shortly before his death in 1654. As we shall see, there are some inconsistencies in his work, possibly on account of his age when he began writing it, coupled with the length of time it took to complete.

Tello is thought to have done much of his writing while guardian of Zacoalco friary, originally founded in 1550. A later guardian of this friary, Francisco Mariano de Torres, also left us his own version of the region's history.

Crónica miscelánea de la sancta provincia de Xalisco *is one of the seminal works of the 17th century, despite not being published at the time. The six volumes were the earliest attempt at a comprehensive history of the region. Tello's aim was to extol the evangelical work of the Franciscans in New Galicia, Spain and the world. Of the original six volumes, only four now remain.*

Tello's work is full of details and surprises. Among the many curiosities is the detail he provides about different kinds of mosquitoes, distinguishing between cínifes *or* zancudos, *"numerous, very large and troublesome";* jejenes, *"which are half the size and only slightly similar"; and* rodadores, *"which are found in dense masses like smoke".*

The extracts in this chapter are not a first-hand account but were written in the 17th century to describe events that had unfolded in the mid-16th century.

In Book II, Tello describes the Lerma River:

... following a roundabout route it enters the beautiful lake of Chapalac, which is more than thirty leagues in length and seventy around, and which has abundant fish in its fresh, crystalline waters. It leaves from there very gently, so it hardly seems to be moving. It runs for thirteen or fourteen leagues until it reaches a precipice, two or three leagues from Guadalajara, over which it falls with great noise into a very deep canyon...

Tello then refers to the 20,000 head of sheep that come to graze season-ally on the pastures near the lake each year, before describing a "Great event on Lake Chapala":

This year [1540] Lake Chapala overflowed. Its waters rose more than an infantry lance in height, until they covered a split rock that is on the way to San Juan Cosalá, and the water turned very green.

Writing so long after the events, Tello makes several errors relating to dates. Some historians date this catastrophe to 1539, not 1540. The precise height indicated by an infantry lance is uncertain, but is believed to be equivalent to about four meters. Only a decade after the lake has been "discovered" by the Spanish conquistadors, this is the earliest date given in the literature for any post-conquest flood of the lake. The lake flooded with some regularity until the mid-20th century.

Tello also relates the history of Ocotlán and Cuitzeo, and how the Indians encountered by the conquistadors were unhelpful. He describes how the Spaniards made rafts to allow the soldiers to cross the (Santiago) river, leading to a bloody battle where the river met the lake. The conquistadors eventually won, taking possession of the Indian canoes.

Soon after the Spaniards took control of the region, the Franciscan priests began their work. Tello provides us with a lengthy and richly detailed account of happenings in one important location:

The village of San Juan Cutzalán [San Juan Cosalá] was a large settle-ment next to Lake Chapala, in which lived many heathen Indians. As a result the men, like the women, went about naked, with nothing covered except their private parts. Because the Indians were so numerous that they no longer had enough space, with the permission of their chief and lord, some left, taking with them their idols, to found other small villages such as Tomatlán, Axixic, Xocotepec and Tzapotitlán, which is now called San Cristóbal. The chief who governed them was called Xitomatl, also known as Tzacuaco, because he was a man with large projecting eyes.

The Franciscans

The Franciscan Order was founded in Europe in the early 13th century. Three Flemish Franciscans were the first to arrive in New Spain in 1522. On June 24, 1524, twelve more Franciscans, the "Apostolic Twelve", led by Fray Martín de Valencia, arrived to join them.

The Franciscans embraced chastity and poverty. They saw the New World as an opportunity, not only to convert the pagan masses of native Indians to Christianity, but also to put their idealistic ideas of utopian society into practice, and demonstrate that natives and Europeans could live in peaceful and productive co-existence.

The early friars were men of vision. They were tireless, hard-working and entirely devoted to what they saw as their duty. Their Order was politically well-connected, and quickly became firmly established in the geo-political structure of the times. During the second half of the 16th century, the friars began to encourage the "congregation" of Indians into villages and towns, in order to make it easier to minister to their needs. Unfortunately, this served also to encourage epidemics.

The friars had been granted broad powers by a papal decree in 1522 to administer sacraments, organize religious life and expedite the evangelization. They were practical men, and interpreted this as a license to baptize; confirm; conduct marriages; say Mass; preach; teach religion, crafts and agriculture; heal the sick and bury the dead. The friars came to be viewed as the best protectors of the native Indians against the violent or unjust excesses of conquistadors and local administrators. Indeed, they essentially replaced the native priests as the natural leaders in Indian society.

In the eloquent words of historian Lesley Byrd Simpson, "This admirable band of men, armed with nothing but goodwill and faith, set about their conquest of New Spain with an energy, daring and intelligence equal to those of Cortés himself. *And their Conquest endured."* (emphasis as in original)

He alone and his family possessed an idol that was the main one, called Huitzilopoch, which means Itztlacateotl in Nahuatl, and "hidden god" in Spanish. He ordered his subjects to have an idol in each barrio [district], and since there were many barrios, there were also many idols that they worshiped, so that their names were not known; to them, and in particular to the hidden god, they sacrificed many boys and girls, as well as all the captives they took in the wars they fought against the Tarascan nation, which was their enemy. When they had cut them open and removed their hearts, they were offered with great shouting, celebration, dancing and joy. They bathed their bodies with the blood of those thus sacrificed, saying that by that means they would be made strong and invincible (an obvious trick of the devil, as they generally experienced). For the idol of the said chief, which he had in his hut, they made a fire every night, keeping it alight until the morning.

This chieftain had five women, who were those that his subjects could maintain, paying tributes of lots of fish, ears of tender corn, and squash and other products of the ground, which offered, and still offers, neither gold nor silver.

He went always with one of the women until she was made pregnant. Once being so, he left her and took up with another, and in this way with all the others; when they all were, he replaced them more often. His subjects had two or three, more or less, according to their means. The devil commands them, speaking to them through their idols, so that each one makes a little clay pot or jug and then, by scratching their ears, places a drop of blood in it. When they bathe, they throw the little pot or jug with the blood into the lake, the devil persuading them to believe by so doing that they gain immortality."

In the year of 1531, when Nuño de Guzmán and his army were conquering Culiacán, there arrived from the province and kingdom of Mechoacán to the multitudes of this great village of Cutzalán, the blessed and holy father Fray Martín de Jesús or de la Coruña, of our seraphic religion and son of the most holy province of Santiago. Raising the pennants and banners of the faith, and beginning to preach to the said chief and his leaders, he pointed out to them with apostolic jealousy the tricks and lies with which the devil, father of both, had cheated them, and that all the idols they worshiped were not gods but devils, and that there was only one living God, the true creator and lord of everything, and that he was the one who should be worshiped, because without faith and belief in him, no-one could be saved.

The chieftain, hearing these and other reasons that were said for that purpose, consulted with his leaders, and since everything that the blessed father preached to them and said seemed to them to be good and in accordance with reason, God shone upon them, they then managed to assume the faith without any contradiction, and with them all their subjects; seeing how well things were going, the first thing the holy father did was to take away from the chief his idol Itztlacateotl or Huitzilopoch; and with this all the idols in the village, and smashing them into pieces, he threw them into the lagoon. He also told them that it was necessary that they be baptized, each choosing one of the women they had, whoever seemed best, to marry and to remain with them until death, because Christian law did not allow the taking of more than one wife and others had to be left, and having said the same to the other Indians they quickly obeyed. This done, the holy Fray Martín made a small chapel out of tree branches, and dedicated it to the glorious forerunner Saint John the Baptist, the name it keeps to today. Later it was replaced by a building which remains, and the village, called San Juan Cutzalán, beginning to serve the Lord in doing the work of the true apostle. And the first to receive the Holy Baptism, and to take a wife, forsaking all other women, was the chief, who gave up his heathen name of Xitomatl or Tzacuaco, and took that of Andrés, being named Don Andrés Carlos after his baptism, in honor of the most triumphant emperor Charles V, King of Spain, recognizing him as his lord, as did all his subjects without opposition.

The holy father later decided to make the temple more spacious and a proper friary in which Our Lord God could be worshiped and served, and in which the clerics could be taught to administer the holy sacraments. He discussed this with Don Andrés Carlos and his leaders, who seemed to believe that since there was no water there, it should be founded where there was water. Therefore, the holy Fray Martín, Don Andrés and the leaders moved to a place called Axixic, where there was much water. There they began to found the friary which remains to this day; Don Andrés and those who went with him built new houses, remaining there without more ado to foster the work of the friary, which began in the year of 1531.

While work was taking place on it, so that the holy baptism could continue, the very holy father built a small chapel, which was not finished that quickly, dedicated to the glorious Assumption of the Mother of God, in a place called Tomatlán. And then the Indians celebrated here their fiesta in which mass was said and baptisms carried out, first taking away from them their idols and doing to them what Don Andrés had done. This chapel stood for only a very short time, because one day such a large hurricane came that it was demolished and destroyed, leaving little trace that it had been there. They made another temporary one, a little higher, where it was called Tecolotlán, and in this one administered the Holy Sacraments, until the said friary was completed in the year mentioned, retaining the name of Axixic to this day, always with friars of our Holy Order of San Francisco. The dedication in the beginning was to San Francisco, until a cleric arrived who was called Fray Andrés, in honor of the apostle. He removed the original title and gave it the name of the apostle San Andrés, and from then on it has been called San Andrés de Axixic.

In Book IV, Tello provides chapter and verse about the friaries in Ajijic and Chapala.

In the year of 1564, the Guardian of Axixic was Father Sebastián de Verlenga. In 1567, two springs of hot water burst out in San Juan Cusatlan next to the lake and boiled with such strength that they raised the water very high and made a lot of noise, on account of which the natives were shocked and scared. Being only recently converted, and still not firm in the faith, the devil spoke to them, when they consulted him, or he appeared to them, and said that if they wanted to see the water pacified, they should throw five children into it. Having thrown them in, they perished, burnt alive, and the water abated. Since children in the Mexican language are known as pipiltotonti, the hot springs and the site where they are called to this day Pipiltitlan, which means place of children. Much of this is recorded in the History [Book II].

From the beginning of the conquest and their conversion until today, these Indians have always been served by clergy of Our Father San Francisco.

The friary has a church with one large and very spacious nave, with its choir, baptistery and sacristy; ornaments, choir capes, and two silver crosses, one large and one small, for processions, thurible and navicula, chalices and patens, and everything needed for divine worship and the administration of the Holy Sacraments in the villages of visitation: San Juan Cuzatlan, San Antonio, Jocotepec, San Cristóbal and San Luis. In all those villages there are hospitals where the sick are attended and shelter is provided for the traveling poor.

Several chapters later, Tello's attention is focused on the founding of the friary in Chapala, which took place in 1548.

The village of Chapala is eight leagues [32 kilometers] from the city of Guadalajara, between south and east, at the foot of a very large range of hills which is to the north, and next to the large lagoon called the Chapalac Sea, which is sixty leagues [250 kilometers] around and thirty in length; in praising it, suffice it to say that it is not as famous as those [lagoons] they call Malacayo, or as Maeotis [the ancient name for the Sea of Azov; a body of water connected to the northwestern corner of the Black Sea], or that known as the Sea of Tiberias. It has fresh and pleasant-tasting water and is so clean that the disturbances that water generally creates are not found in it. It has a quantity of white fish and catfish, sufficient to supply the city of Guadalajara (the main town in the Kingdom of Galicia), and many other parts as knowledge spread. The lake takes its name from the village of the same name, since it is assumed to have been the main place even in heathen times, on account of the many people who were congregated in the said village; thus, even though there are several villages on its shores, it was not called anything else but the lagoon of Chapalac, seeing as the principal place was this one of Chapalac. It was first founded, according to oral tradition by many people who were in the village of Ponzitlan, seven leagues away, and with the multitude of people, many families came and began to settle in this place.

Despite the claim of Mota Padilla (1742), repeated in Antonio de Alba (1954) and Casillas (2004), this is not the earliest known description of the lake. Both the Geographic Accounts (1579) and Antonio de Ciudad Real (1585) include descriptions written much earlier.

The most likely explanation of its name being thus, is that its chief and principal person was then an Indian named Chapa, who encouraged the said populace, congregating them under his control; the Indians were never of bad habits nor were they bloodthirsty. Rather, they were formerly very peaceful and domesticated, as came to be seen, since they were not conquered or subjected by the clamor of arms; rather, they, with good disposition, received the Catholic faith and the Holy Gospel. In ancient

---

Chapala's church, friary and hospital

As Father Antonio Tello reports, the first church in Chapala was founded in 1548 by Father Juan de Almolón. The friary was a small house with a single cleric, between the church and the lagoon. The site later became the stables of the Hotel Arzapalo and, later still, the garden of what is now Casa Braniff. Opposite the church, a short distance away, was the Franciscan hospital for the Indians: the Hospital of the Immaculate Concepción (Limpia Concepción de Nuestra Señora). Its site was later occupied by a parish school, then a glass factory, and then a Beer Garden restaurant.

In a much later century, the street where the hot springs were (Calle de Agua Caliente) was renamed Hidalgo, and the street where the Franciscan friary had been was renamed Juárez. The prominent hill where the lay brother lived in a hermitage overlooking Chapala is still known, even today, as *Cerro San Miguel (St. Michael's Hill)*.

It seems clear from Tello's account that not all the Indians became true believers. Some Indians blamed the church for calamities such as the floods which occurred in 1540, and for other natural events. This resulted in the church being burnt down twice in the 16th century: in 1557 and again in 1581.

times they did not have particular gods or idols; rather each one, as they deemed fit, had his own little idol of clay or wood, like those that have still appeared even in these times. The lagoon tends to give up some small clay figures shaped like a man, which must have been thrown into it during those erroneous times, or possibly afterwards, when they emerged from them, having been persuaded by the evangelical clergy who with their Holy preaching showed them the true God they had to obey. The only certain thing is that they worshiped a common idol, which they had placed in a shelter in this village beside a hot water pool, where the others would hold their barbaric and sacrificial ceremonies, not because they were forced by law or obligation, but voluntarily...

Present in this village, at the time of its conversion, were the blessed Fathers Martín de Jesús, Juan de Padilla, Miguel de Bolonia, and other clerics who looked after all the villages which were founded on the shores of the lagoon. In 1548, by which time all had been baptized and converted to Christianity by the aforementioned priests, the church and friary were begun by Father Juan de Almolón.

In the year of 1552, the Visitor Contreras arrived in the said village, and in 1555, another Visitor, called Alonso de Ojeda, came, and the lake rose so much that the village of Chapala was flooded.

In 1557 the church burned down, having been set on fire by an Indian named Juan Tzincayol. In 1562, Father Sebastián de Párraga came to this friary and planted the church's orange trees.

In the year of 1567, on July 15, the lake rose again so far that all the homes in the village fell down, and on December 30 of the same year there was an earth tremor and earthquake which brought down many churches in the province and part of the main chapel in this village... [*this earthquake was almost certainly in 1568—see box, page 17*]

This village has a pool of most excellent hot water, which emerges and flows from a very attractive small hill close by, from the foot of which emerge springs which, collected in two tanks made of stones and lime form two pools. On the summit of the hill is a chapel dedicated to San Miguel. Mass is said in it on his feast day. A lay brother lived in the chapel/hermitage for many years, demonstrating by his retreat, and by not descending to the village, his great virtue and penitence, being content with whatever the natives wanted to provide by way of food. In the lake are two or three small islands, one about a league long, and another smaller one, in front of this village. By tradition, it has been inhabited by a friar of exemplary solitary life, who having once set foot, remained there; only the natives visited from time to time with some of their fresh

Pioneering priests

Father Juan de Padilla was a Spaniard from Andalucia. By 1529, he was established in the Colima area. Always barefoot, he founded numerous churches (including Zapotlán and Tuxpan), as well as friaries in western Mexico. He died in 1542 in what is now New Mexico, becoming the first cleric to die preaching the gospel north of the current Mexico-U.S. border. In 1942, four hundred years after his death, a monument was erected in his honor in Herington, Kansas.

Father Martín de Jesús (or de la Coruña), born in Galicia, Spain, was one of the group of twelve Franciscans to arrive in New Spain in 1524. In early 1526, he founded the monastery at Tzintzuntzan (Michoacán). In 1531, this humble and patient missionary arrived in Cutzalán (San Juan Cosalá), converting the local Indian chief, Xitomatl (or Chacuaco), giving him the post-baptism name of Andrés Carlos. It was with the approval of Andrés Carlos that Martín de Jesús founded the friary in Ajijic.

Father Miguel de Bolonia, born in Flanders, spoke, or understood, nine languages, including several Indian tongues. He traveled widely through northern New Spain, spending time in numerous friaries, including Chapala. This deeply religious, virtuous, penitent friar loved both Indians and Spaniards equally. One of his roles was to resettle groups of Indians, following conversion to Christianity, to found new villages or help develop larger settlements like Guadalajara. Many Jalisco towns owe their origin to him. He died in Chapala in 1580 (July 14); following his burial, a large comet appeared in the sky. He is commemorated today by an inscribed marble stone laid (in 1943) in the presbytery of Chapala's main church.

produce to assist him. The water of the lagoon is very fresh, its waves are normal and very big when disturbed by the wind; it always blows around mid-day, when the wind is southerly; the shores are very clean mud, and their sands very white.

There are some reasons to doubt what the cause is of this lagoon, whether there are secret springs, or if it is the water of the river, that they call in that region the Grande, which has its source in the Toluca valley, close to San Mateo de Atengo, and, running swiftly, because of the water that enters it, flows into this lagoon. It is said that this river, finding at the start of its being, the place, a plain surrounded by mountain ranges, filled it, and caused this lagoon, and beginning to drain, it retained the large amount of water that it has, because although water leaves, it never stops entering. If it did not have anywhere to drain, it would surpass and overflow the tops of the highest hills and mountain ranges. This seems to be so for the water of the lagoon is so extreme with its goodness, and of the same quality as that of the river; but the opposite seems more in conformity with reason, saying that it originates from secret springs, and the reason seems to be because, if the water did not come from springs, the lagoon would be muddy and not clean, and also because in the lagoon a type of fish called whitefish spawns. This does not spawn, and neither has it been seen, in the river. Finally, if the river water were to diminish, the lagoon would lose water if it were fed totally by it. Principally, when its rising has stopped and we see whether the river is bringing little or much water, the lake is always there. There is yet another reason which proves the point, and that is that those who move about it have observed that some parts are very hot and others very cold, and noted that it has hot water springs in places, because the heat which it has is much greater than that which could result from greater or lesser depth. The truth is that with the rising of the river, when it is considerable, it would grow still more.

The pleasantness of this village and its district can readily be understood, since the land, desiring to equal the greatness of the water, produced 368 orange trees in the streets, which surround the church and friary in a wonderful order; they were planted by the hands of Father Sebastián de Párraga, as has been said.

Abundant in this village are native fruits and some from Castile; in this jurisdiction are harvested wheat, corn, beans and other vegetables; many cattle, mares and horses, and some mules; the natives are of the Cazcana nation.

Tello's discussion of the relative merits of river and springs in maintaining the level of the lake was light years ahead of its time. It was to be several centuries before such ideas were further developed. Tello's remarkable prescience has been largely ignored by the scientific community.

Tello, Antonio. 1891, 1942 *Crónica Miscelánea de la Sancta Provincia de Xalisco.*

3

Floods, comets, idols and earth tremors
Mid- and late-16th century
Matias de la Mota Padilla

Born in Guadalajara in 1688, the historian Mota Padilla is thought to have studied in the Augustinian College of San José de Gracia, Guadalajara, prior to completing a law degree in 1711. Between 1713 and 1739 he held various posts. He was then appointed Treasurer of the Audiencia of Guadalajara.

In 1742, he finished the work for which he is now best remembered: *Historia del reino de Nueva Galicia en la América Septentrional.* The

book was undertaken at the request of the King of Spain in order to celebrate the conquest of New Spain. A variety of circumstances conspired to prevent this work reaching Spain until almost fifty years later.

From 1744 to 1748, Mota Padilla was an associate judge of the criminal court. He died in Guadalajara in 1776, having been instrumental in the planning and founding of the University of Guadalajara.

Lawyer and historian Matías de la Mota Padilla wrote his Historia del reino de Nueva Galicia en la América septentrional *(1742) to promote the idea of converting the area, including New Vizcaya, into a new Viceroyalty. His account has clear links and similarities to several earlier works, including those by Father Tello, Mota y Escobar, and Ornelas Mendoza y Valdivia. It is apparent that Mota Padilla relied on these writers for at least some of his information.*

The author describes Europeans' first view of the lake, from a hill above the village of Zula la Vieja (now the city of La Piedad, Michoacán):

...this one, among all the lakes, is entitled to be called the Sea of Chapala. It is very special, its water being fresh and healthy, its sand clear, and it is free from mud and obstacles. In places its beaches are dispersed, and in places the waves beat against cliffs and crags, raising waves that break on rocks and reefs, the currents throwing up shells and snails. It is a little less than thirty leagues in length, with a circumference of more than sixty leagues. It produces catfish, delicious to taste, in abundance, so large that, by hand, they reach one and a half varas [1.26 meters]. The white fish reaches half a vara. It is so healthy that it is not prohibited even for a sick person and there is no fish like it in all the kingdom. The lake is seven leagues across with, in the middle, a small thickly vegetated island, of over four thousand [square] varas, which has been depopulated on account of the difficulty of administering the sacraments to its inhabitants. There are many villages on the lake's edges, which give their name to it, even if its most common name is that of Chapala (named for an Indian chief who held sway over it), since the water crashes against the walls of the main building in the town....

Between east and south, with respect to the city of Guadalajara (in its current location), is the village of Axixic, a guardianship of Franciscan priests, with an adequate friary and number of clergy to help and administer to the Indians in the villages of Cuzalan [San Juan Cosalá], Xocotepec [Jocotepec], San Cristóbal and San Luis. They lie west of Chapala and its lagoon ten leagues from the city. They are in the jurisdiction of Zayula [Sayula], have two thousand Indians, young and old, and five hundred Spaniards and other classes, who work in cultivating the land, which is good for seeds and for raising cattle and horses. In the village of Cuzalan is a spring with water that is so hot that any animal that falls into it is rapidly destroyed....

Chapala is ten leagues from Guadalajara, between east and south, and is the village from which the lake takes its name, perhaps for having been in former days the most populous of those surrounding it, although today has been almost destroyed by several floods of the lake, especially in the years of 1555 and 1577. It has on the shore, opposite the cemetery, more than two hundred leafy orange trees, which Father Sebastián de Párraga planted in 1572. [cf. Tello's more likely date of 1562] Similarly, it has a very healthy pool of hot water next to the church. We saw already how there is a densely vegetated small island in the lake, where a lay brother lived for twelve years. His residence impeded the cult in which the neighboring Indians came to the lake to make offerings to their gods. The idols were of rock, trinkets and clay, which Father Juan de Almolón threw into the lagoon. Each month, the lay brother left and took twenty young men to the island, to whom he taught the faith meticulously, and dispensed the necessary support, which was very fruitful. The usual wind that has been observed on the lake comes from the south. It has also been observed that in some parts of the lake the water is very warm and in other parts very cold....

On December 30, of the year 1567, several comets having given warning, an earthquake followed which ruined various churches. Already, on July 15, Lake Chapala had risen so much that it destroyed all the buildings in its village although, on account of divine providence, not a single person perished, not in Chapala, nor in the other places with the destruction of the churches. It was not like this with the tremor that was experienced on December 27 of the following year, 1568, in which the church of Cocula collapsed, wretchedly taking Father Esteban de Fuente Obejuna, its founder. On the same day, the church in Tzacoalco [Zacoalco] fell, and sixty Indians perished, and with them also Father Hernando Pobre, who had founded it. Also so many birds were seen flying that they obscured the sun, and so unusual that they provoked admiration in all who saw them. In the year of 1573, there was a hurricane which lasted three hours in Colima on November 14. At the same time, the earth trembled in such a way that many houses and the church fell down. In the year of 1577, a very large comet was seen in the month of April, and on August 3rd, there was an eclipse, which turned day into night, and then a great plague was experienced, from which an immense number of Indians died.

Mota Padilla, Matias de la. 1742 *Historia del reino de Nueva Galicia en la América Septentrional.*

The 1568 earthquake

Research and comparison of historical records, attempting to unravel inconsistencies in dates, suggests that the Chapala area was seismically active from 1564 to 1568. The largest earthquake, causing the collapse of many churches, houses and friaries, occurred on December 27, 1568. There were widespread reports of damage. The main chapel in Chapala was destroyed.

The pattern of damage suggests that this earthquake had a magnitude of about 7 on the Richter scale. According to one of the Geographic Accounts for the region, landslides dammed the Ameca river for three weeks, and when the river flow resumed, the water was "of a reddish color that made it impossible to drink for many days." Large cracks appeared in the lowlands. The flow of natural springs was changed, and the level of Lake Zacoalco was altered.

The earthquake's epicenter was close to the junction of three major rift valleys, each with its own parallel systems of faults. The first is occupied by Lake Chapala, the second follows the Tepic-Zacoalco depression, and the third includes Sayula and Colima. The movement is part of the gradual splitting of a large triangular block (housing Puerto Vallarta) away from the Mexican mainland.

4

Converting the barbarians
Mid-16th century
Francisco Mariano de Torres

Francisco Mariano de Torres had been guardian of the friary at Zacoalco in about 1740, and held a similar position at Cocula at the time of writing this book in 1755. The original of this Chronicle, as well as the originals of Tello and Ornelas y Valdivar are all housed in the Jalisco State Library in Guadalajara. All three are incomplete. Torres' work was first prepared for publication in 1939.

His Chronicle includes a brief account of the first missionary work in the Chapala area, which is very similar to Tello's:

In Zacoalco the good Fathers separated, Fr. Miguel de Bolonia leaving for Santa Ana Acatlán and Fr. Martín de Jesús climbing the inaccessible slope that went towards the lagoon of Chapalac. The chief of these people had his court in San Juan Cozalán. There he, like all his vassals, men and women, went about naked, and they had many women, which was a great impediment against their conversion, because wearing clothes seemed to them to be very awkward, and having a single woman intolerable. But, just as there is no iron that does not submit to the hammer blows of the divine word and the anvil of patience, with great patience and fervent preaching, our venerable Fr. Martín so dominated those barbarians that he made them do whatever he wished. The first was to take from the chief his idol, called Istlacateotl (which means god of the salt), as well as the idols of the others, and break them into pieces, throwing the fragments into the lake. Then he tried to make a church and friary, where clerics could live, to administer them. Because there was no water in Cutzalán, they chose the place of Axixic, the same chief going there to live to give the work greater passion. But while this was happening, since it would take some time, both the church and friary being large, and with such thick walls that they have lasted to these times, they ordered a church of

branches built in Cutzalán, in the name of Saint John the Baptist, who remains the village's patron today. There, they baptized the chief, changing his name from Xitomatl, which he had, to that of Andrés Carlos, and likewise, they also baptized all his subjects. The man of God Fr. Martín de Jesús, went to live in Axixic, to look after, for a time, the spiritual and material fabric, and to say Mass.

Torres, Francisco Mariano de. 1755 *Crónica de la sancta provincia de Xalisco.*

5

Gathering geographic knowledge
1579-1586

After 1569, several attempts were made by the Council of the Indies in Spain to survey the provinces in the New World. The most successful was the survey ordered in 1577, which became the basis for the Geographic Accounts.

The Viceroy of New Spain, acting on behalf of the King of Spain, instructed the authorities in each administrative center to call a meeting of the "Spaniards in the district, and the other natives", to find out what they could about the area's geography, people and history.

Many of these Geographic Accounts have survived in the archives to the present day, and several transcriptions of them have been published. Unfortunately for us, not all the accounts of the areas bordering Lake Chapala have survived, so our knowledge of what they once contained is incomplete.

The Viceroy wanted the answers to 50 specific questions. Inevitably, the responses from different localities in the same general area sometimes became somewhat repetitive.

We will first examine parts of the response from Xiquilpan (Jiquilpan), on the southern side, as an indication of the style and substance of a typical account. Then, we will look at some significant extracts pertaining to the district of Poncitlán on the other side of the lake.

At this time (the end of the 16th century), the Spaniards saw at least as much potential for the southern side of the lake as the northern side. In later centuries, for a variety of reasons, the northern side became increasingly favored.

The answers from Xiquilpan (Jiquilpan) were signed by Francisco de Medinilla Alvarado, the corregidor (mayor) of the village and province, on June 1, 1579, in the presence of notary Gonzalo Hernández. Nothing more is known about either man.

This settlement is called Xiquilpan, and it is also known in the Tarascan language as Guaninba, which means in Spanish "toasted maize"; Xiquilpan means xiu-quiletl, which is a plant from which the blue die known as indigo is made.

The discoverer of the village was Cristóbal de Olid.

This said village of Xiquilpan is in temperate land, which is more warm than cold, and it is cooler in this village from October to January: it is healthy land, and not humid. A river, which never dries up, passes the village; it carries very little water in summer and, in winter, it rises so much that, many times, it can not be crossed. At less than one league from this village towards the north is a lake called Chapala, which is forty leagues around. They catch in it a lot of white fish and catfish, and another kind of small fish. A large, very full, river, which is called Chicnahuatengo, enters this lake. The winds in the said village are gentle, and come from the north and north-west; in the months of January and February, the winds are somewhat stronger.

The village is settled on flat and very level ground, without hills. It is a land of few rivers: there are some streams of water around it; there is water in abundance for the natives. There are some high hills, of productive woods towards the east, of pine and oak groves; towards the west, there are some hills of higher ground, with few woods. It is very fertile land of many foods; it grows and produces a lot of corn, chile, beans and other seeds that the natives sow; the native fruits are guamúchiles, avocados and guavas; there are lots of figs, pomegranates, quince trees and grapes. It is land which grows anything that is sown.

This village of Xiquilpan has very few Indians: there could be in it about one hundred tributary Indians. They say that before the land was won, there were one thousand two hundred men, and, after the lands had

Animals and crops

Native animals and crops included tobacco, maize (corn), zapotes, avocados, guavas, cacao, peanuts, vanilla, tomatoes, chili peppers, and papayas. Two native dyes also became major items of trade. Cochineal (scarlet) was derived from insects and indigo (blue-purple) from a plant. The Indians in the Lake Chapala region did not have any domesticated animals.

Non-native species, introduced by the Spanish, included pigs, chickens, goats, sheep, cattle, wheat, barley, fruit trees, figs, grapevines and olives (both originally restricted to friaries and monasteries), peaches, quinces, pomegranates, cabbages, lettuce, radishes, as well as many flowers, weeds and rodents.

been won, their number has been diminishing as a result of the many diseases that there have been; in particular, in [15]76 there was a great plague in this village, which was general in all of New Spain, from which a large number of people died. It is a village formed a long time ago. The people are smart. For the most part all of them speak and understand the Mexican language; they have another language which they call zayulteca, which is the native one that they have and speak; there are others who speak the Tarascan language...

The indigenous population in New Spain crashed in the first hundred years following the conquest, largely as a result of smallpox and other European diseases. Estimates of the native population prior to the conquest range from 4 to 30 million; a century later, there were just 1.6 million. Similarly, according to historians Cook and Borah, the population of New Galicia fell from about 169,400 in 1548 to 18,500 in 1650, recovering to 122,000 by 1750.

The village is settled on flat land, as has been said; it is low land. The dwellings are small, covered with straw; the streets run from the east towards the west. There is a plaza in the middle of the village, next to the friary of brothers of the order of San Francisco that is in this village, where there is usually a guardian with a companion....

This village was subject, when it was heathen, to Cazonzi, king of Mechuacan, who ruled over and was in charge of it; he put an Indian chief called Noxti [presumably the pre-Christian Indian name of chief Nox] in this village on his behalf in order to govern and look after them. In those days, they gave corn and chile as tribute to the said Cazonci, which was received by Noxti and sent to Pátzcuaro. At that time, they idolized the Devil, so that he would help them when they went to fight other Indians from neighboring villages. They say that when they caught an Indian, they carried him to a hill next to the village, and there they sacrificed him and offered him to the Devil, and they cut him open and removed his heart, and those who had made the sacrifice ate it. At that time, they did not settle because they were scattered across the hills.

The Indians of this village were formerly at war with the Indians of the province of Avalos and other peoples. They were led by a captain that Cazoncin sent from Pátzcuaro, and other times the said Noxti went with them. The weapons that they fought with were bows and arrows, and some sticks measuring one vara, [0.84 meters] on the ends of which they put a perforated stone, with which they fought. They say that at this time they wore some shawls of joined together sisal, like jackets, without anything else, and cotton breeches, different to what they now wear. Their food was tortillas, tamales, beans, and other wild herbs that they called *quiletes*, [meaning edible herbs or greens in general, such as *Amaranthus* and *Chenopodium*; one common name for several species of the latter, including the frequently used epazote, is *quelite*] and they drank white maguey wine called *tlachiquil* [unfermented pulque]. They say that they used to live longer than now, and that the reason for this could not be ascertained.

The high hill that is to the side of this village is called, in zayulteca language, Huaxuatli, which means "hill of the trees called Vuaxi", which give some pods, similar to carob beans, which are eaten by them.

This village [Xiquilpan] is on healthy ground, and the greatest sicknesses that there are among the natives are pustules and fevers, which they purge with a white root called "of Mechuacan"....

In this village, and its subsidiaries, are some maguey fields, used to great advantage by the natives for their farming and in their meals.

In this village and its subsidiaries, grow pears, figs, pomegranates, grapes, peaches, quinces, nuts, apples, all Castilian fruits; native [plants] are avocados, sweet canes, guavas, capulines (which are local cherries), squash, chile, tomatoes and a lot of corn. It is land where it does not snow, formerly or now. They raise many birds, from Spain, and natives.

In this village grow cabbages, lettuce, onions, radishes, blites, and every kind of vegetable from Spain.

Wheat and barley grow in this village.

Michoacán root

Michoacán root, an *Ipomoea*, or morning glory, became popular in Europe as a cure for innumerable ailments. Reports of the many plants, including Michoacán root, used by indigenous people to treat sickness, convinced King Phillip II to send one of Spain's leading physicians and naturalists, Dr. Francisco Hernández (1515–87) to explore New Spain in 1570. Over the next seven years, Hernández became fluent in Nahuatl and compiled a monumental work on the native plants of central Mexico and their therapeutic benefits. He is considered to be the first trained scientist to have undertaken scientific work in the New World. His book, *The Natural History of New Spain*, written in Latin, and superbly illustrated by indigenous artists, described more than 3,000 different plants, along with many animals and minerals. Michoacán root and many other plants were incorporated into the European pharmacopoeia of the time, such as John Frampton's *Pharmacopoeia Londinensis* (1618). Even in an era of synthetic substitutes, many of the plants continue to be widely used.

There is a wild plant in this village with which those who are crippled are cured: it has leaves like a lettuce; it is so hot that the part where the root is put burns naturally, like a fire. [believed to be a spurge, or *Euphorbia*] There is another, which has a root similar to camote: it is a preventative for everything. They cure with these herbs and with others known to the natives.

The animals that there are in the village are wolves, which breed in some swamps that are in between some reed beds, a quarter of a league from the village. More than eighty thousand sheep come from other parts to pasture seasonally on the edge of this village each year; it is very good land for them and they grow very well, since there some saltpeter deposits around the marsh.

The village has a quarry for stone, stone which becomes reddish: it is very good and light in weight; from it the stone to make the friary of this village has been taken...

There are no salt beds in this village; the natives supply themselves with salt which is brought from Colima, twenty leagues from this village, and from the province called Avalos fifteen leagues away.

The shape and building of the houses of this village are of adobes and barro: only their foundations are made of stone; they are flimsy and covered with straw, and their wood is from mountain pines.

The dealings, contracts and farming that the natives of this village have, and which sustain them, are of quantities of corn, chile, beans and other seeds, that they gather and sow in great amounts; by selling them to other natives who come from other neighboring villages, they make reales, with which they maintain themselves. They pay their tribute to his Majesty in reales. Some of the subjects, living as they do in an area of many woods, are employed making beams, tables, cases and chairs, which they sell to Spaniards and other people, thereby maintaining themselves....

As previously mentioned, this village of Xiquilpan has a friary of monks of the Order of San Francisco; there are two clerics in it: one is the guardian. The founder was Brother Juan de San Miguel, and it was founded about forty years ago for all the clerics that were in this province of Mechuacan.

In this village is a hospital, where the sick are treated, which was begun thirty years ago and founded by a cleric called Brother Alonso de Pineda of the Order of San Francisco. It receives no rents: it is sustained only by the poor, from the alms they beg from the natives.

The Franciscans built many hospital chapels in western Mexico. Many of

The role of sheep

Wool had been a major item of trade in Spain for centuries before the conquistadors arrived in the New World and quickly recognised its potential for large-scale sheep farming.

Elinor Melville explores the consequences of this kind of farming in some detail for one area of central Mexico in her book *A Plague of Sheep, environmental consequences of the conquest of Mexico*. She argues that the introduction of sheep placed great pressure on the land. Their numbers rose rapidly, but then crashed as (over)grazing changed the local environmental conditions.

Sheep farming took off during Phase I (Expansion; 1530-1565) and the Viceroy, Luis de Velasco, became concerned that it might threaten Indian land rights, and also food production. Regulations gradually introduced to control sheep farming included a ban on grazing animals within close proximity to any Indian village.

During Phase II (Consolidation of Pastoralism; 1565-1580), the area used for sheep remained fairly static, but their numbers (and therefore grazing density) increased greatly. By the late 1570s, some pastoralists were moving large flocks (tens of thousands) of sheep from farms in central Mexico to seasonal pastures near Lake Chapala. This practice of grazing on harvested fields or temporary pastures, was known as *agostadero*. The term originally applied to summer grazing in Spain, but was adopted for "dry season" grazing, between December and March, in New Spain.

So important was this annual movement that provision was made in 1574 for the opening of special sheep lanes or *cañadas* along the route, notwithstanding the considerable environmental damage done by migrating flocks. As flock sizes peaked, more than 200,000 sheep made the annual migration by 1579.

By the end of Phase III (The Final Takeover; 1580-1600), most land had been incorporated into the Spanish land tenure system, the Indian population had declined, mainly due to disease, and the sheep population had also dropped dramatically. At the time, the Spanish thought this could be explained by a combination of killing too many animals for just their hides (Spaniards), an excessive consumption of meat (Indians) and by the depletion of flocks by thieves and wild dogs. Melville's research, however, suggests that the main reason for the decline was environmental degradation.

them have survived, relatively unscathed, to this day. The main churches in the same towns were far less lucky; most were modernized, often in the poorest of architectural taste, by successive generations of clergy who considered themselves progressive.

The remainder of the responses in the Jiquilpan Geographic Account have no relevance to Lake Chapala.

The Geographic Account of Poncitlán and Cuiseo del Río (Cuitzeo), on the northern shore of the lake, was ordered in 1584, and is dated March 9, 1586. The reporter was the corregidor Antonio de Medina, and the document was drawn up in the presence of notary Juan Martínez. Nothing else is known about either man.

This account provides many interesting details about local cultures such as that of the Coca Indians, but as René Acuña emphasizes, these geographic accounts should never be considered as truly scientific. They were not eye-witness accounts. Many of their statements were entirely unsupported by any evidence. They often relied on hearsay and on dubious interpretations by a limited number of respondents who were not necessarily in the best position to know or recognize the true facts.

The village of Cuiseo [Cuitzeo] was formerly called Coatlan, for an earthenware vessel they had made, coiled and like a serpent, in which they put pulque, which is a white wine they make from a tree called Mexcal which is a maguey. And they offered this vessel, full of the said wine, to a stone idol dressed with a cloak, that they had in a hut. And the language that the natives speak is called coca...

The way of government, in general, was that no one could be idle, nor could anyone take the woman of another nor steal, under penalty of death, which they would carry out on those found doing the above, by blows with clubs and sticks. After they were dead, the bodies were thrown in the fields for the buzzards...

[The village is] located on the banks of a large, deep river, which is that of The Nine Rivers. It is so deep that it can not be crossed in the rainy season, except in a boat or canoe, nor can it be forded in the dry season except in a few places, downstream towards the west. The said river passes through a large lake [Chapala] (about thirty leagues around), with lots of whitefish and catfish....

The foods they used were tamales, tortillas; mainly they used corn toasted with salt, which they called Izquitl, and atole made of corn, a kind of porridge (a little thinner) to drink hot with powdered chile, broken up and sprinkled on top and cold, beaten with water; and fish, which they had in the river, and some venison or rabbit (which they still use) and the provisions and things of Castile....

A footnote in Acuña (1988) says that Izquitl refers to grains of corn toasted on the comal, and is an early reference to palomitas de maíz *or popcorn.*

Likewise, they harvest chia, huauhtli, cocotl, which is a kind of mustard-like seed which they use, ground up and mixed with corn and water, to make a beverage to drink before and after eating. It is a good food among the natives, and better and healthier than the grain they call cacao (as thick as an olive) from which they similarly make a beverage... It is grown on the coasts where there is damp heat....

The cotton, from which they make their clothes, is brought from Colima and Compostela; ...some cotton is also grown by the natives on the shore of the lagoon.

It is clear from these Geographic Accounts that the respondents recognized the dramatic impact that imported diseases were already having on population numbers. Equally evident from these accounts are the many changes wrought by the rapid introduction of Spanish crops, animals and agricultural techniques. Of particular significance in the Chapala region was the use of agostaderos, *seasonal pastures for animals, principally sheep, on the flat, marshy swampland at the eastern end of the lake.*

Acuña's Nueva Galicia volume includes an image of a map of the region dating from about 1550, which clearly shows several Lakeside settlements, including Jamay, Mezcala, Chapala and Ajijic.

Acuña, R (ed) 1987 *Relaciones geográficas del siglo XVI: Michoacán* and 1988 *Relaciones geográficas del siglo XVI: Nueva Galicia.*

6

Visits to the Lake Chapala friaries
1585-1586
Antonio de Ciudad Real

Antonio de Ciudad Real (1551-1617), the author of this work was born in Spain. He entered the Franciscan friary of San Juan de los Reyes in Toledo in 1566 at the age of 15. In 1572, he was sent as a chorister to the Yucatan to accompany Diego de Landa, who was consecrated as Bishop of Yucatan the following year. He rapidly became fluent in spoken Maya and exhibited considerable curiosity about the life and customs of the region. By 1584, Ciudad Real was back in Texcoco, near Mexico City, convalescing from fevers that had plagued him for three years.

After Father Alonso Ponce arrived in New Spain in September 1584 as Visitor of the Franciscan Provinces, he took Ciudad Real along as his secretary on his tour of inspection of all the missions. Five grueling years later, they returned to Europe (1589). Ciudad Real's account of Ponce's travels was undoubtedly written while in Europe. After Ponce's death, Ciudad Real crossed the Atlantic once more in 1592, and spent most of the remainder of his life in the Yucatan. He passed away on June 5, 1617, in the friary at Merida.

The account of their travels, *Relación breve y verdadera de algunas cosas de las muchas que sucedieron al padre fray Alonso Ponce en las provincias de la Nueva España*, was not published until 1872, in Madrid.

As Visitor of the Franciscan Provinces, Father Alonso Ponce de León visited 166 friaries belonging to the six Franciscan Provinces, as well as several friaries run by other orders (Dominicans, Augustinians and Jesuits). This was a formative period for the missions, when many were mired in conflicts, both internal and external.

Antonio de Ciudad Real's detailed account of Ponce's visits is an outstanding source for the history and geography of the colony in the second half of the 16th century. It includes information about the basic geography, climate, resources and human settlement of the area from as far north as

present-day Nayarit to as far south as Nicaragua.
The depth and nature of descriptions of each place suggest that the author must have been familiar with the questionnaire used to compile the Geographic Accounts a few years earlier. The range of material in the book is extraordinary. Details abound about the flora, fauna, native foods, cooking habits, medicinal plants, salt works, caves, fountains, languages, Indian groups, and dozens of other characteristics of those parts of New Spain that were visited. It is an amazing achievement for the time.
Friar Antonio de Ciudad Real and Father Alonso Ponce visited the south shore of Lake Chapala in 1585, and the northern shore on a separate trip in 1586.
We join them in January 1585, as they are on their way from Jiquilpan towards the southern side of the lake,:

Finally he [the Father Commissioner] reached the flat land, at the edge of the lagoon, where the definitor [member of the governing council in certain religious orders] and another friar, no longer able to withstand the thirst brought on by the sun and tiredness of that day, drank water, that was fresh and very fine, very slowly, from an Indian's sombrero. More about this lagoon will be said further on.

On Saturday January 12 [1585] the Father Commissioner left that little town after the sun rose, and across a grazing land or pasture, climbed some slopes on a very pleasant track, afterwards descending by a worse one, and climbing and descending others as bad as those of the previous afternoon and some even worse, and as the sun was rising high and burning very strongly, neither man nor beast could handle the heat, thirst and tiredness, especially when they descended to the lagoon, where there was no breeze that could aid and refresh them. At last, close to mid-day, the Father Commissioner arrived, very tired, at a small little village called San Bartolomé Tezcueca [Tuxcueca], on a height close to the same lagoon, six leagues from the other where he had slept the night, and so exhausted and weakened by the sun and the route so rugged, that although the Indians took pity on him and offered catfish and other fresh fish, neither he nor anyone could eat, except with a poor appetite and almost by force. That village falls in the bishopric of Xalisco, which is also called the New Kingdom of Galicia and of Guadalajara, in a province that they call Ávalos; it was then visita of a presidencia called Teucuita-tlán [Teocuitatlán]; the Indians of that village, and of others that we saw that day, spoke a corrupt Mexican language, and are under the temporary jurisdiction of Mexico. After the force of the sun had subsided a little, the Father Commissioner left that village, and walking along the shore of the aforementioned lagoon on a good and flat track, reached another little village of the same Indians, bishopric, province and visita, called San Luis [Soyutlán], where the few residents who lived there, received him with great happiness and offered him some fish. He thanked them and continued on. Five leagues later, after passing another two little villages, San Cristóbal and San Pedro [Tesistán], he arrived late at night, not a little tired, at another larger village, called San Martín, of the same Indians, bishopric and province, visita of a friary of ours called Axixique. [Ajijic] There, there were very few necessities, or better said none, because there wasn't anything for the animals to eat, nor for the friars to dine on, nor beds on which to sleep. The Indians did not know anything about the visit of the Father Commissioner, and the guardian of Axixique did not understand, or even imagine that he was going to be there. He was completely unprepared and sent for beds from the village for the provincial [the superintendent of the heads of the religious houses in a province] and his definitors, which were in the friary at that moment. Thus, seeing what poor provisions and shelter they had, nobody dined nor slept, nor even was able to rest, and the others were worried about the Father Commissioner General and the definitor of Mexico, who were the oldest and most needy.

From San Martín, Father Ponce continued northwards only as far as Tlajomulco, before returning to Jiquilpan via Cocula, Zacoalco, Teocuitatlán and Mazamitla. We rejoin him on Wednesday January 30, 1585, as he hastens towards Jiquilpan:

The Father Commissioner went on ahead, and after passing another two or three stream courses and another three leagues, came to the village and friary of Huanimba, called Xiquilpa [Jiquilpan] in Mexican language, where he was very well received, both by the monks, and by the Indians. Half a league before the village, an arbor was made along the route, and from it a bell was hung, which the Indians struck, and they rang it as the Father Commissioner passed, also delighting the fiesta with a dance imitating chichimecas. The mayor of the town and comarca came out to this point with another Spaniard, and accompanied him to Xiquilpa. That place is founded in a plain or valley at the foot of one very high hill and enclosed by others, and thus is tropical land where oranges, cidras, limes and lemons and other tropical fruits grow. A pretty stream flows through it; it is of medium size, of Tarascan and Tzaultec Indians, which is a language in itself, and many of them know the Mexican language. Almost all the visitas of that guardianship are Tarascan, and they all fall in the bishopric of Michoacán. Here close to Xiquilpa are many very good pastures on the shore of the lagoon of Chapala, in which, in the dry season, a very large number of sheep from Mexico and Querétaro and other areas come to graze, similar to Extremadura in Spain. The friary, whose calling is to San Francisco, our Father, was equipped with its cloister, dormitory and church, all small and made of adobe. It has a nice garden in which a wave of water that is taken from the aforementioned stream enters. It is used to water many oranges, cidras, limes and lemons, bananas and avocados, and other trees that are there. Two monks live there; the Father Commissioner visited them and spent that day and the next with them.

The following year, Father Ponce makes another visit to Lake Chapala, this time to the friaries on the northern shore:

On Monday December 1st [1586], the Father Commissioner left that village [Teocuitatlán] at four in the morning, and passing a valley of dry swamps, climbed a slope on a poor track, a league and a half long. After descending a league and a half, he arrived at the shore of the lagoon of Chapala, along which, on a flat track, he went for two leagues, at last arriving at a pretty village called Xocotepec, of the guardianship of Axixique, five leagues from Teucuitatlán. They gave him a very solemn reception there. Many Indians left from three little villages that are located beside the southern shore, called San Pedro, San Martín and Santa María, of the same guardianship, and among them were seven or eight on horseback, who went more than a league ahead of the Father Commissioner. When he reached Xocotepec, all the people came out to greet him, with many dances and creations, with great happiness and devotion. He was offered many eggs and fresh fish from the lagoon of Chapala, much Spanish bread, bananas, sweet potatoes, tomatoes, chile and other fruits, not only by the principals and the village community, but also by private individuals. That village is close to the lake, and about four fathoms from the water the Indians had made a hut of straw, with a long gallery below it, which looked over the lagoon, in which they served food to the Father Commissioner. No Indian in the village, young or old, did not come to see him, and all were bewildered watching him. In one of the dances that they did there, there was an Indian with a guitar, and another danced to the sound of it and found anything that they could hide among those present,... which was certainly a thing to see. To fish in that lagoon, they use some canoes made of canes with a strange quality, in which the water enters and leaves, without them ever sinking, however rough the lake. Two or three Indians can go in each one of these canoes. They brought three of them here, and those who went in them made a fiesta for the Father Commissioner, throwing oranges at many young boys who were swimming next to them, throwing water at each other. The people of this village are very devoted and so sincere that every time the Father Commissioner passed close to them, they would fall to their knees, even though they were told that they need not do so. They have here a little garden in which were some cabbages and another vegetable, to give the friars when they come from Axixique to say mass. The gardener was an old Indian without teeth or molars, who (as they asserted to the Father Commissioner) slept every night in the garden at that time in order to guard the cabbages and onions, and protect them from rats; his bed was the hard earth, on a petate [straw mat] resting beside a wall of the friars' rooms. The Father Commissioner stayed in that town the whole day....

On Tuesday December 2nd the Father Commissioner left that village before daylight and reached, still before sunrise, one league later, another village called San Juan, also a visita of Axixique. At that hour, all the people were together at the entrance to the village, forming a procession with a cross and processional candlesticks, holding lighted white candles in their hands, singing the Te Deum Laudamus in the Mexican language. They asked for the blessing to be sung which the Father Commissioner did for them before carrying on. Another two leagues on, also along the lagoon, he reached, the sun now up, the village and friary of Axixique to say mass, where he was similarly very well received, and the Indians came with offerings of eggs, bananas and fish. That village is of medium size, founded and located on the lagoon. Oranges, cidras, limes and lemons grow there in great abundance; guavas, quinces, pomegranates, bananas, figs and vegetables of every kind also grow there. It is temperate land, more hot than cold. The Indians of the village, and the rest of the guardianship, speak the corrupted Mexican language called Nahuatl. They are in the bishopric of Xalisco in the province of Avalos, and in the jurisdiction of Mexico. Their dress is like that of the Mexicans, except the women, who dress with some petticoats like very wide sacks, which their children also get into, although they were now abandoning that dress and beginning to use huipiles and petticoats like Mexican women. The friary, devoted to San Andrés, is very old, small and made of adobe, with a church, cells and cloister. It has a good orchard with lots of trees and vegetables. Two friars reside in it. The Father Commissioner visited them and stayed with them only that day.

On Wednesday December 3rd, the Father Commissioner left Axixique well after daybreak, and went half a league along the lake to reach a small village of that guardianship called San Antonio. The Indians came in a procession to receive him. He thanked them and carried on. A quarter of a league further, he arrived at another smaller village called San Buenaventura, visita of the friary of Chapala, where he was also well received. He continued on and after another quarter of a league arrived at the village and friary of Chapala where he was received with great solemnity. That place is founded on the shore of the abovementioned lagoon, which takes its name from it, although it is also called Axixique. At the entrance to the village, coming from Axixique, are some hot water springs where a pool has been made in which people bathe. They say it is beneficial for certain illnesses. There are also many very large banana groves. Sweet sugar cane grows, as do grapes, quinces, pomegranates, guavas and every kind of orange. There is so many of all these that the entire village is like an orchard. The Indians make a lot of orange blossom water and from it a lot of money. It is so fertile for oranges, that in the garden of the friary, where there are many of these trees, they took, from a sweet orange tree, a branch that had eleven good, big, mature and yellow oranges, crammed together on top of each other. Being such a very lovely thing, it was given to the Father Commissioner. Some roots that are called xicamas grow there, shaped like, and almost the same color as, round turnips, without any root hairs, so thick that each one weighs at least three pounds. They are sown as seed, like turnips, and make that stump below the ground. It is a very delicious fresh fruit, marvelous medicine for thirst, especially in hot weather and in hot lands. The common xicamas are like medium onions. The village of Chapala is small. The Indians of it, and its visitas, speak the language spoken by those of Axixique.... The friary was a small house, which was still not finished. It had a good garden. It was a presidency in which a single friar resided. ...

Ciudad Real, Antonio de c.1590 *Tratado curioso y docto de las grandezas de la Nueva Espana.*

The 17th century

By the start of the 17th century, military might, at least in this region, had been long replaced and even the spiritual conquest was essentially over. A truly remarkable transformation had occurred in less than a century. The friars convinced civil authorities that Indians should be "congregated" wherever possible into villages and towns to make it easier for them to minister to their needs. Ironically, this only served to hasten the spread of epidemics and public health concerns.

The Franciscan friars had been motivated by a genuine utopian desire to form a new society, in which all individuals were respected. Unfortunately, the Indian population was first relocated, and then decimated. The friars realised that their cherished plans were falling apart. Plans to create a native priesthood were abandoned. Moreover, as the friars gained a strong grip on local communities, the colonial authorities felt the need to reassert their own power.

Some individuals were able to take great advantage of the new opportunities on offer. The moral stance taken by friars was not a restriction for those who gained important civil positions.

The historian Chevalier provides a classic example of burgeoning corruption in his *Land and Society in Colonial Mexico–The Great Hacienda*. Santiago de Vera became President of the Audiencia of New Galicia, taking up his position (in Guadalajara) in the closing years of the 16ᵗʰ century. He soon displayed "flagrant favoritism" towards in-laws and family. By 1602, the city had "only 160 citizens, all but 40 of whom had jobs in the Courts, the Audiencia, the diocese, the cathedral chapter, the municipal government, or the royal treasury". Santiago de Vera had no fewer than 37 relatives and in-laws listed, all living under his roof, in a single building. Between them, they had interests all over New Galicia—in livestock, mining, cattle, mules, money - regardless of official regulations. Part of Santiago de Vera's house was a store selling produce including the orange-blossom extract made at Lake Chapala.

During the 17ᵗʰ century, the frontier of New Spain was gradually pushed ever further northwards by missionaries and settlers. In fact, by 1700, New Spain had become positively international in character, since it also included the Philippines and Spain's Caribbean islands. However, news traveled slowly in 17ᵗʰ century New Spain, so knowledge of significant events such as the riots in Mexico City in 1624 and again in 1692 would have taken a very long time to reach the furthest corners of the Viceroyalty.

The major mineral discoveries at the end of the 16ᵗʰ century were rapidly developed during the 17ᵗʰ. Fortunes were made (and lost) on silver, but mining declined as the century progressed. The decline in mining meant that land became more important as a source of income, and acted as a catalyst in the development of large estates.

As mines were abandoned, or easily accessible deposits worked out, national trade slowed, the merchant fleet was run down, and New Spain's sense of economic isolation began to increase. The largest estates (haciendas) became virtually self-sufficient, with ample crops, flocks, woodland and labor to run their own mills, workshops, and even their own churches. The Church developed and managed its own estates, often very profitably.

During this century, the Chapala area contributed relatively little to the national economy.

By the end of the century, a new mining boom was on the horizon, and economic activity picked up. One major result of the clearance of land for large estates, and then the development of mining and smelting of metallic ores, was deforestation. The landscapes of western Mexico underwent a dramatic transformation as their trees were chopped down to be used for such things as fuel, pit props, wagon wheels and boats.

7

Lake Chapala—as large as an ocean?
c.1600
Bernardo de Balbuena

The earliest known reference to Lake Chapala in a poem must surely be that made by Bernardo de Balbuena in *El Bernardo*, written between 1592 and 1602, published in Madrid in 1624. The poem took a decade to write because of its extraordinary length—some 40,000 *octavo reales* (Royal eighths) in size!

Balbuena was born in Valdepeñas, Spain, in 1562. In 1584, at age 22, he crossed the Atlantic to join his father, who owned properties in New Spain. This was only 63 years after the conquest, but already various cities had been founded and were beginning to prosper.

Balbuena was already a prize-winning poet by the time he was named Chaplain of the Audiencia of Guadalajara in 1592. He later lived for several years in the small isolated village of San Pedro Lagunillas near Compostela, close to Tepic. In 1593, he wrote *Grandeza mexicana*, a poem which appeared in book form in 1604, and was dedicated to Doña Isabel de Tobar y Guzmán, with whom he was in love.

Balbuena returned to Spain in 1606 and was never to set foot again in New Spain, despite having fallen in love with the country and having become a "Mexican" poet. In 1608, he published *Siglo de Oro en las selvas de Erífile*, a pastoral novel. In 1626, he became Bishop of Puerto Rico, dying there the following year.

In El Bernardo, *the author begins by describing France and Spain. By Book XIII, he is describing Asia. Then (Book XV), he overflies Europe. The descriptions of imagined aerial trips are supposedly the best passages of the entire work, with the highlight being Book XVIII which sees the magician Malgesí flying over America, from Patagonia in the south to the northern edge of New Spain.*

Numerous places are mentioned, including the Andes, Brazil and

Chiapas, as well as Zacatecas, Guadalajara and the erupting volcano of Jala, before Chapala gets its moment of fame:

> Come, between the fresh Pánuco and Gualulco
> to Tlaxcala, and the Mexican kingdom,
> to Michoacán, Colima and Acapulco
> the town closest to the southern sea,
> the villages of Quiseo and Tlajomulco,
> and in their environs and flower-filled plain
> the abundant lagoon of Chapala,
> which equals the Ocean in depth and breadth.

Spanish-Mexican philosopher Ramón Xirau describes Balbuena as a "splendid poet who should be remembered and, above all, re-read." However, reading (or re-reading) 40,000 "octavo reales" might well be more than most people can manage.

Balbuena, Bernardo de 1624 *El Bernardo.*

8

A geographic description
1601-1605
Alonso de la Mota y Escobar

The Franciscan priest Alonso de la Mota y Escobar was born in Mexico City on May 18, 1546. After attending university in the city, he held various positions before being appointed Bishop of Guadalajara in 1598. He was the first native-born Mexican to occupy such a high post. In 1607, he became Bishop of Tlaxcala, a position he held until his death on March 16, 1625. Unsubstantiated sources claim that the famous sauce known as *mole poblano* was first concocted in the late 16th or early 17th century by nuns at a convent in Puebla in honor of a Lenten visit by their bishop: Alonso de la Mota y Escobar. What is more certain is that de la Mota founded the College of San Idelfonso for the Jesuits in Puebla, successfully pacified the Indian tribes of the Topica mountains, and converted many Tepehuanes to Christianity.

De la Mota y Escobar clearly used the Geographic Accounts questionnaire sent in 1577 as a basis for a preliminary survey of New Galicia, New Vizcaya and Nuevo León, including the northernmost reaches of his bishopric, the results from which were sent to the Spain in 1601. His superiors asked for a more detailed report, which de la Mota compiled between 1602 and 1605, in which year it was published as Descripción geográfica de los Reinos de Nueva Galicia, Nueva Vizcaya y Nuevo León.

...the number of blackbirds that come is incredible; they are very harmful to the fields of corn and wheat, as they start to seed, because if no-one drives them off, they can destroy a large area of land in an hour, and thus it is no small expense that is incurred to drive away these little birds, which breed in great numbers in the bulrushes and cane thickets of marshes and rivers.

Huge flocks of blackbirds (cowbirds) are still commonly seen in the
Chapala area, either wheeling in fantastic patterns overhead or greedily
chomping on the ground.

The river [Santiago] is navigable by boat and in some parts by ship, but this is impeded by the many waterfalls it has and the large prominent rocks that it has in places. It forms, among others, a noted waterfall [El Salto de Juanacatlán] four leagues from this city, about forty *estados* [about 65 meters or 220 feet] in height, all of strong sheer rock, with the width of a good crossbow shot. The entire river falls over this whole width, similar to when it becomes very swollen; it is a rare, beautiful and wonderful sight....

Fifteen leagues away from here in the area of Jamay and Chiconaguatenco this river makes a lake, lagoon or sea, of the appearance and shape that it is written is made by the Jordan in the vicinity of Tiberias called the Sea of Galilee. From this lake the river leaves with the same strength as it entered. The current running through it is perceived by the eye when the lake is calm, when the flow of the river is clearly seen. This lake is fifteen leagues long from end to end, and must be about seven or eight wide. It is fresh water and exceedingly delicious, for which reason it is drunk in as many villages, and there are many, as there are on its shores. It is very deep so parts can be safely navigated with vessels of good size. [It is] so excessively clean that no weeds grow. In this it resembles the sea, and even in getting angry like her, having storms when it wants, its rolling waves breaking on the shore making a very loud noise.

Among other fish it has some that the Indians call in their Mexican language *amilotes* and the Spanish call *pescado blanco* [white fish]. It is bigger than half a vara. [i.e. about 40 centimeters or 16 inches] Its flesh is whiter than congealed milk. The taste is like such a fine meat, it is not tasty unless aided by condiments. It is exceedingly healthy and given to anyone who is sick; many can be eaten at the one time without fear of harm. I do not remember having eaten fish in Castile that resembles it; only the flounder of Sevilla is similar to it in delicacy. It has no bones except for that of the spine. There is a great quantity of it in season and it deteriorates very quickly. Its delicacy does not allow salting, because it stiffens, and the salt can never be removed even if it is soaked.

This lake is called in this region Chapala, which is the name of a riberine settlement on its shore. The Indians navigate it with canoes and small boats; many drown in the storms that suddenly come up. Its shores are warm and so a large quantity of oranges, citrons and limes, pomegranates and grapes, and many fruits of the earth grow. Admirable beehives for honey are found here, because the bees make them from orange blossoms, of which the honey smells and tastes. It is exceedingly fine and white.

This river does not have any bridge of wood or stone, on account of its great width. Passing across it is in some parts by a boat with thick ropes, in others by small *chalupilla* canoes, in others by rafts resting on drinking gourds that are big pumpkins, guided by two or more Indians who swim alongside the same raft grasping it. It is a very secure passage. Some Indians make their living from these crossings and live on the shores of the river taking care of this work. It ends eighty leagues from here in a village called Centicpac, where it flows very powerfully into the Southern Sea [Pacific Ocean] and there it fulfills its natural destiny, which is to die and end in the sea from which it left....

He then continues on to Guadalajara

Four leagues further [from Cajititlán] is the town of Chapala, of 100 Indian households, Franciscan doctrina, with a warmer climate. Fruits of Castile, of tropical lands, every kind of orange, lime and citron, quince, pomegranate and fig grow. It is a straight route from Guadalajara, and on the shore of the large lagoon that, as was said earlier, they call Chapala.

One league further is the village of Agigic on this same shore, of about fifteen households; doctrina of Franciscans with the same climate as Chapala. The same fruits grow. In the middle of these two villages there is a bath of tepid spring water, which flows hot on the same shore of the lagoon. The water is healthy and is where those sick with chills and pains bathe.

Four leagues further is the village of Jocotepec; of sixty Indian households, situated on the shore of this lagoon, with a somewhat cooler climate; a doctrina of Franciscans. On its borders are ranches of Spaniards for cattle and farming; it is fifteen leagues from Guadalajara in a straight line.

Mota y Escobar, Alonso de la. 1605 *Descripción geográfica de los Reinos de Nueva Galicia, Nueva Vizcaya y Nuevo León.*

9

Fishing and farming
1621
Domingo Lázaro de Arregui

Lázaro de Arregui's *Descripción de la Nueva Galicia* has been characterized by distinguished historian José María Muriá as marking "the beginning of the historical geography of Nueva Galicia."

The work is a significant contribution to the social and economic history of many areas west of Mexico City. It was written in 1621 (the date of 24 December 1621 appears in the original text, which resides in Madrid), but remained unpublished until 1946.

Domingo Lázaro de Arregui was a very important chronicler of the 17th century, but relatively little is known about his life, though Carmen Castañeda was able to work up an interesting profile of the cleric, based on documents pertaining to his estate.

She describes a knowledgeable priest who was lustful in his youth, a cloak-and-dagger character, who had two illegitimate offspring by a respected young lady. Lázaro de Arregui died on February 4, 1636.

On the subject of population numbers in the region, Lázaro de Arregui considered that, "There is so much uninhabited space in these realms that I doubt whether Europe's entire population could fill them; not only do they have no known boundaries, but all is empty."

Perhaps the most noteworthy novelty in Lázaro de Arregui's work comes when he writes about how the roots and bases of the leaves of certain agave plants are roasted and eaten, and "by pressing these parts, thus roasted, they extract a must from which they distill a wine clearer than water and stronger than rum." This is the earliest known historical reference to the making and consumption of tequila.

Elsewhere, Lázaro de Arregui remarked on the linguistic diversity of New Galicia, claiming that 72 distinct languages were spoken in the region. He also visited San Pedro Lagunillas where Balbuena had lived a decade or so earlier.

Lázaro de Arregui makes several brief references to Chapala, as well as an extended description. Among the former are the phrases, "large lakes such as Chapala", "hot springs", and that "the Río Grande enters the lake". This lengthier description of the lake comes at a time when the number of livestock being pastured on the lake shore is starting to fall.

The Indians of this jurisdiction [Poncitlán] are almost all occupied in fishing in the lake and river, and take very good fish to the city on Fridays to sell and to distribute, more on account of the concern of the governing officials than of the work and desire of the Indians; their laziness is so great that if the authorities do not order them still to sow a little corn for their sustenance, they will not sow it, leaving their sustenance to that which their own land produces, such as herbs, roots and fruits. And this must be understood of all the Indians that work, carry, provide or help in any place or hacienda, because if the governments were not to foresee this, their interest or any other natural virtue would not help in any way.

What this jurisdiction most fattens then are sheep, which come to pasture in great herds, as soon as the rains pass, from Querétaro and Michoacán, and they are in this jurisdiction which has lots of land and appropriate grazing until it wants to rain again by the end of May. And, by now, the ranchers in this jurisdiction have bought many ranches that have no other purpose all year except seasonal grazing, and from which a great advantage is taken of the land, although the livestock is not shorn here.

Lake Chapala is the most notable thing in this jurisdiction for its size; it has more than 30 leagues of perimeter with hardly a rush or a cane in any of it, except on the edge. It has not more than two small islands in the middle, and has a movement that resembles the undertow of the sea; it is all very suitable for anchoring and the water very good to drink. It has a lot of fish, and the best is what they call white [blanco]; and it is to be greatly marveled at that in these same lagoons catfish are caught; those that are taken from a part of the lake towards a village called Parcocoran [Pajacuarán?] in New Spain are very good, and held in great esteem; very rough catfish, of less taste and not so good, are caught in the same lake in other parts; those that are caught in the river, even close to the lake, are the worst, and those further downstream are better.

On the shore of the same lagoon in the village of Chapala, which is in the jurisdiction of the province of Avalos, six or seven leagues from Guadalajara, there are some warm water baths, where they have made a hut and washing place, which are very good for slight humors and better for bathing in terms of comfort because the water is very tepid, so much so that it does not cause a sweat or problem being in it all day.

Lázaro de Arregui, Domingo. 1621 *Descripción de la Nueva Galicia.*

10

San Francisco de Tizapán
1690
Fr. Nicolás Antonio de Ornelas Mendoza y Valdivia

Relatively little is known about the life and interests of Ornelas Mendoza y Valdivia. He was born in Jalostotitlán, a town in the Los Altos area of what is now Jalisco, to a creole couple in 1662. In 1719, he petitioned the church to serve as chronicler of the province. He compiled his history of the area between 1719 and 1722, and died only a few years later. His account, conserved unpublished in ecclesiastical archives for more than two centuries, was finally prepared for publication in 1934 by Fray Luis de Nuestra Señora del Refugio de Palacio, a monk then residing in the monastery of Zapopan, Jalisco.

The work includes a relatively detailed second-hand account of the early history of the Chapala area and the baptism of the Coca Indian chief, but does not include any description of the lake or the villages on its northern shore. The following short extract refers to the town known today as Tizapán el Alto on the southern shore of the lake.

There are ten leagues of hills between the doctrina [Indian community converted to Christianity but lacking a parish; similar to a curacy] of Teocuitatlán and the village of Tizapán, which is a visita [small chapel] and doctrina of it: the motive for requesting a priest from the same settlers of Teocuitatlán: they took him, and those that are necessary for the administration have lived there since then. This village is close to Lake Chapala, and, in addition, the river called "of the passion" flows close by; they call it that because, in the middle of some rocky crags that box in the river, paintings of all the insignia of the passion of Christ our Lord can be divined, very clear and very well made; but with such conditions of height, both below them as much as above them, that we can only see them, never touch them.

Ornelas Mendoza y Valdivia, Fr. Nicolás Antonio de, 1719-1722 *Crónica de la provincia de Santiago de Xalisco.*

The 18th century

As we enter the 18th century, it is worth remembering, as historian Felipe Fernández-Armesto has pointed out, that European writers of the time such as Georges-Louis Buffon and Cornelius De Pauw still "derided America (including New Spain and South America) as a degenerate and degenerating place, which produced only stunted species, inferior people—effete men, insensitive women—and regressive civilizations." It is, according to Fernández-Armesto, during this century when the European view "of the scale and variety of the Americas gradually grew and began to shadow reality."

Much more knowledge of New Spain was acquired, and disseminated, during the 18th century. Highlights included the discovery of Palenque in 1773 and the unearthing of the Aztec calendar stone in 1790. Nationwide, this was a century of scientific expeditions, pioneering explorations and rapid city growth.

The Lake Chapala region was a kind of border or frontier zone. The boundary between the provinces of Michoacán and Jalisco passed right through the middle of it. It was perceived more as a barrier or hurdle to communications than as an opportunity.

Across the region, the disparities between rich and poor were growing as some landowners, practicing large-scale commercial agriculture, gained control of more and more arable land, often at the expense of that available to smaller-scale peasant farmers. This was a time when large country mansions were built, while most of the rural population lived in rustic huts.

Chapala's relationships with other places changed significantly as the century progressed. Early on, Chapala had close economic and administrative ties to the province of Ávalos (Sayula). In 1786, the province of Ávalos was subsumed into the Intendency of Guadalajara. The links between Chapala and Guadalajara became much more important as the century wore on.

Indian horticulture, which had employed irrigation even before the conquest, grew in importance, with a particularly significant role supplying fresh fruit and vegetables to Guadalajara. The area available varied seasonally, especially on the fertile lakeshore, responding to changing lake levels.

The Chapala area haciendas, including Huejotitán, Cedros, Potrerillos and Atequiza, rose rapidly in value during the 18th century. Having previously been considered of only marginal importance, they now received substantial investments in buildings, dams, irrigation and fencing. Influenced by the proximity to Guadalajara, there was a gradual but marked shift by the century's end from a farming system based only on cattle production to a mixed farming system, combining both grain and cattle.

The hacienda of San Andrés del Monte near Ocotlán (part-way to Jamay) was owned (but leased out) throughout the 18ᵗʰ century by the Augustinian friary of Guadalajara. During the last decades of the century, it usually had around 1000 cattle, 250 horses and 800 sheep. However, by 1819, (several years into the struggle for Independence), its animal population had fallen precipitously to fewer than 200 cattle, 50 horses and it no longer had any sheep. This hacienda was later owned by the Castellanos family. (chapter 27)

Throughout the 18ᵗʰ century, population pressure on the available land was perceived as a serious problem in the Lake Chapala area. Compounding the pressure was the fact that the amount of land available for cultivation varied from season to season, and from year to year, in response to the level of the lake. Prime garden or vegetable-growing land in spring became a swamp following the summer rains, and if the lake rose more than usual, might remain underwater the following year.

Economic historian Eric Van Young examined several specific examples of land disputes during the 18ᵗʰ century. At the western end of the lake, by mid-century, population pressure in Jocotepec had caused one group of residents to leave and start a new settlement. A few kilometers east of Chapala, Santa Cruz de la Soledad claimed that the adjacent hacienda, San Nicolás de la Labor, was farming land that it did not rightfully own. The argument centered on whether Santa Cruz was only a barrio of Chapala (entitled to less than one square kilometer of land) or was actually a village in its own right, in which case it was entitled to about 17.5 square kilometers. In 1806, the latter was proven and the hacienda had to return a quantity of land.

Another serious land dispute arose in Ajijic. Van Young describes how Ajijic, in 1797, disputed control of wooded pastureland with its neighboring villages on either side—San Juan Cosalá and San Antonio Tlayacapan—as well as with a local Spanish landowner. Ajijic claimed that its neighbors had encroached upon its land, and that this, coupled with its own population growth, had resulted in people being forced to leave the village. Fortunately, a compromise was readily agreed, and Ajijic had its land restored.

By the late 18ᵗʰ century, New Spain was one of richest parts of the world. Its territory (prior to Mexican Independence) included most of the modern U.S. states of Texas, New Mexico, Arizona, California, Utah and Colorado.

Even so, at a national level, Lake Chapala was still being largely ignored. For example, in 1791, The Royal Scientific Expedition to New Spain (1787-1803) deliberately ignored the lake, opting instead to explore volcanic areas in Michoacán and Colima en route to Guadalajara.

11

The south-eastern marshlands
1746
Joseph Antonio de Villa-Señor y Sanchez

Joseph (José) Antonio Villa-Señor y Sanchez, born in San Luis Potosí in 1703, is one of the earliest Mexican geographers. He studied at the College of San Idelfonso in Mexico City, and was later employed, in the collection of taxes, becoming comptroller of revenue from mercury (a chemical essential to the refining of silver ores). He was subsequently appointed cosmographer of New Spain.

In this capacity in 1742, he was commissioned by the Viceroy, Pedro de Cebrián y Agustín, Count of Fuenclara, to write a descriptive history and geography to comply with a royal edict from King Philip V of Spain. The extracts included here come from this work, *Teatro Mexicano; Descripción general de los Reinos y Provincias de la Nueva España* (1746).

Villa-Señor y Sanchez wrote several other books, including *Observación del Cometa, que apareció en el hemisferio de México en Febrero y Marzo* (Mexico, 1742) and drew several maps, including one of the Jesuit province of New Spain, from Honduras to California (1754).

He died in 1759. More than 200 years later, the planners of Ciudad Satélite, an urban development in the northern part of Mexico City, named a street in the Circuito Geógrafos area after him.

While the accuracy of some of Villa-Señor's population figures has been questioned, his descriptions help to paint a wonderful picture of what New Spain was like in the middle of the 18th century. For instance, he describes the city of Guadalajara as having eight plazas; fourteen churches, monasteries and convents; two colleges and a university; two hospitals and a dozen government buildings or public facilities, making it a fine, surprisingly spacious and prosperous city.

Villa-Señor y Sanchez provides us with our earliest description of the marshy areas at the south-east corner of the lake, which at that time had several small islands. This is the area that was deliberately drained in the early years of the 20th century. The former islands are now visible only as small hills protruding above flat, intensively cultivated farmland:

The position of the settlement of La Palma, located in a pleasant and spacious valley, of warm and humid climate, is a little over three leagues from the Capital [Zamora], adjacent, to the east is the Hill of Canoes, and, to the west and north, the Chapala Sea, whose margins are a distance of half a league from the settlement, and from where its households, 24 families of Spaniards, mestizos and mulattos and thirteen of Indians, obtain abundant fish.

Four leagues away from the seat [Zamora], towards the west, on the shore of the said sea, is the village of Coxumatlán [Cojumatlán], backed by a towering hill, covered with fruit trees and other worthy trees, inhabited by 17 families of Indians, who work in fishing and farming. Close to the Lake is another hill of similar size and frondescence, and from its foot, towards the north, at a distance of three leagues, is San Pedro [now San Pedro Caro, or Venustiano Carranza], whose climate is more humid than warm, and which has 22 families of Indians. On a small island in the said Lake is a hill which only the Divine Omnipotence could put in such a spot, and so attractive; on its summit was founded the village of Puxaqueran [now known as Pueblo Viejo, the original location of Pajacuarán]. Surrounded by water, canoes are needed in order to enter and leave it. Its climate is cold.... It is inhabited by thirty families of Indians, who have their church and hospital, administered by a Vicar appointed by the Curacy of the capital; and they have no other work than fishing, because although they cultivate some fruits and vegetables on their small farms, these are very few, as are their corn plots.

After the briefest of references to "the large Chapala marshes", he goes on to describe another settlement:

The small little island of Comuato [Cumuatillo on modern maps], in the same Lake [Chapala] is an Administration of the same Capital [Zamora], nine leagues away. Its location is in a warm and humid climate. It is encircled by thick reeds and bulrushes, canoes being used for comings and goings in the rainy season, because in the dry season it becomes terra firma, where, as well as on its plains, many herds of cattle have seasonal grazing, and up to twenty families of Spaniards live in the settlement. Within eight leagues, are four cattle haciendas, which sow some fields of corn. They are inhabited by thirty-two Spanish, eight mestizo and fourteen mulatto families.

Villa-Señor y Sanchez, Joseph Antonio de. 1746-8 *Theatro Americano, descripción general de los reynos y provincias de la Nueva España y sus juridicciones.*

12

Early censuses
1768 and 1791-1793: Antonio Manuel Velázquez de Lara and José Menéndez Valdés

*I*n 1768, the parish of Chapala extended eastwards from the pier in
Chapala to Tlachichilco. West of the pier was the jurisdiction of Ajijic. The
parish priest, Antonio Manuel Velázquez de Lara, responded to a petition
from Diego Rivas y Velasco, the "Bishop of Guadalajara, the New Kingdom
of Galicia and of León, Provinces of Nayarit, Coahuila, California and Texas"
for an accurate head count of the people in the parish:*

Chapala has 57 households of Indians that speak the Mexican language,
and maintain themselves by fishing in the Lagoon, and by tending some
crop land as well as some fruit trees. There are also 17 households of
"intellect" ... in total 350 inhabitants.

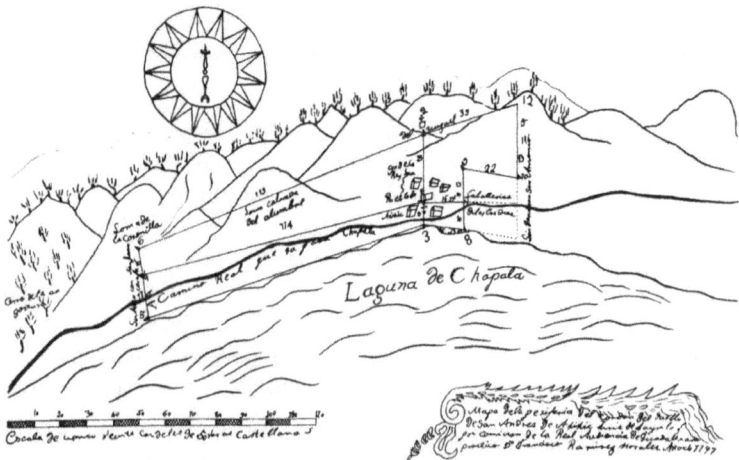

Francisco Ramirez Morales A.'s Map of Ajijic, 1797

Social status in colonial times

Social status in colonial society was almost exclusively determined by one's place of birth, skin color and parentage. Those born in Spain, known as *peninsulares* or (derisively) *gachupines*, were at the top of the ladder. Anyone born in New Spain, but of Spanish parents, was a creole (*criolla*). This was (financially speaking) an upwardly mobile class, and many creoles amassed vast fortunes. This was especially true for those who chose wisely in marriage. Anyone with a mixture of Spanish (or creole) and Indian blood was a mestizo. A mulatto was of mixed European and African descent. Those of more mixed parentage than mestizos or mulattos were collectively known as *castes*. On the bottom rung were pure-blooded Indians and imported African slaves. A complex vocabulary developed since even being able to claim 1/32nd Spanish blood was a cut above being a pure-blooded native Indian.

In addition, there were 28 households in Santa Cruz. Further east 28 people, including the servants, lived on the estate (rancho) belonging to the Ibarras, a Spanish family. Still further east, San Juan Bautista was home to a further 40 households (140 people). Heading north, three haciendas, Yxtlahuacán, Buenavista and Cedros, were home to 269, 154 and 124 persons respectively. The remaining smaller settlements in the parish added a further 120 persons.

Towards the close of the 18th century, the Spanish Crown wanted an up-to-date census of its subjects in New Spain. The Viceroy, Count Revillagigedo II, was ordered to draw up three census lists: the tributary population (Indians and mulattoes); eligible men (subject to military service); and the total population, divided into ethnic and occupational categories.

Spanish-born José Menéndez Valdés was appointed Visitor by the Viceroy and given responsibility for compiling the third list. He worked on it between 1791 and 1793. The location of the original manuscripts on which the figures are based, if they still exist, is unknown, but summary results have been published several times. The most reliable presentation is considered to be that by Ramón Maria Serrera.

Presenting the results of the Revillagigedo Census, Menéndez Valdés wrote that:

Jocotepec, where the clergy collect rents of 3,000 pesos, is inhabited by 587 Spaniards, 1,184 Indians and 3,739 castes [see box], who are occupied in the growing of corn, wheat, garbanzo (chick peas) and other seeds. Some Indians fish in Lake Chapala.

Ajijic has 35 Spaniards, 921 Indians, 23 mulattos and 39 castes.

Chapala, where the clergy collect rents of 1,300 pesos, has 123 Spaniards, 451 Indians, 37 mulattos and 671 castes.

San Juan Cosalá has 743 Indians, many of whom are fishermen. They catch delicious whitefish, catfish, boquinete, charal and sardine (of bad flavor).

Tizapán el Alto, where the rents amount to 1,500 pesos, has 511 Spaniards, 133 Indians, 519 mulattos and 426 castes; Tuxcueca has 145 Spaniards, 143 Indians and 63 castes.

Velázquez de Lara, Antonio Manuel. 1768 *Unpublished census and map from Chapala parish records* and Menéndez Valdés, José. 1980 *Descripción y censo general de la Intendencia de Guadalajara, 1789-1793*

Emergency aid from Chapala towns

Mid-century difficulties were compounded by the epidemic (of *matlazáhuatl*, thought by some scholars to be typhus), which hit the Indian population of the villages bordering Lake Chapala particularly hard in 1737-1738, and a harvest failure in 1749-50. A two-year drought in 1784-1785 led to regional famines, and a sharp increase in death rates, in 1785-1786. The growing city of Guadalajara (and other cities) had to cope with both serious food shortages and a rising tide of desperately hungry immigrants. Supplies of grain were commandeered from towns all round the lake, as well as further afield, as emergency relief; in November 1785, La Barca was ordered to release some of its maize stocks to help stave off the imminent catastrophe. Food prices rose dramatically. The price of *frijoles*, for example, increased 500% within 12 months.

13

A rift in the tableland?
1803
Alexander von Humboldt

It is impossible to do justice in these few lines to the brilliance of Friedrich Heinrich Alexander von Humboldt, aptly described by Charles Darwin as 'the greatest scientific traveller who ever lived'.

He was born in Berlin, Prussia, in 1769 to a very well-connected family and studied political economy before turning to science at the University of Göttingen in 1789. One of his friends there, George Forster, had been scientific illustrator on Captain James Cook's second voyage. This friendship undoubtedly reinforced Humboldt's determination to undertake his own long distance travels. Humboldt systematically prepared himself for a life as a scientific explorer, first studying commerce and foreign languages at Hamburg, then geology and mining at Freiberg, followed by anatomy at Jena, as well as astronomy and the use of scientific instruments.

He spent five years in the New World, from 1799 to 1804, and more than twenty years back in Europe writing and publishing his results. The crowning glory of Humboldt's career was his five volume *Cosmos*. Begun at age 76, this masterpiece proposed conceptual generalizations based on his observations made decades earlier.

Humboldt's work was the foundation for the subsequent development of physical geography and meteorology. Developing the concept of isotherms allowed climatic comparisons to be made. He recognized that altitudinal differences in climate echoed latitudinal differences. His essay on the geography of plants related the distribution of plant forms to varying physical conditions. Finding that volcanoes fell naturally into linear groups, Humboldt argued that these presumably corresponded with vast subterranean fissures. In addition, he demonstrated the igneous origin of volcanic rocks for the first time.

Humboldt died, at the age of 89, on May 6, 1859. His travels, experiments, and knowledge transformed western science in the 19th century. Humanist, naturalist, botanist, geographer, geologist: Humboldt was all of these, and more.

Humboldt arrived in Acapulco, Mexico, on March 22, 1803, and set sail from Veracruz for the United States on March 7, 1804. In the intervening months, he measured, recorded, observed and wrote about anything and everything, with remarkable industry and accuracy. He climbed mountains, burned his boots on active volcanoes, descended into mines, recorded geographical coordinates, and collected specimens and antiquities. He also drew a large number of maps, drawings and sketches.

Humboldt's Political Essay on the Kingdom of New Spain *was the first systematic scientific description of the New World. It appeared in 1811, and marked the birth of modern geography in Mexico. His figures and ideas were used and quoted by writers for many many years. Humboldt's work awakened considerable European interest in the Americas and caused many later artists to travel to Mexico to draw and paint.*

While Humboldt recognized that the limitations stemming from insufficient water supplies placed considerable pressure on lakes in much of Mexico, he made a favorable comparison between Lake Chapala and a certain European lake:

The lakes with which Mexico abounds, and which for the most part appear annually on the decline, are merely the remains of immense basins of water, which appear to have formerly existed on the high and extensive plains of the Cordillera. I shall merely mention in this physical view the great lake of Chapala, in New Galicia, of nearly 160 square leagues, double the size of the lake of Constance; the lakes of the valley of Mexico, which includes a fourth part of its surface; the lake of Patzcuaro, in the intendancy of Valladolid, one of the most picturesque situations which I know in either continent; and the lakes of Mextitlan and Parras in New Biscay.

Prior to the advent of highways and railroads, water transport was considered a key element in development. In considering this region's potential for waterways, Humboldt wrote:

The intendancy of Guadalaxara is crossed from east to west by the River Santiago, a considerable river which communicates with the lake of Chapala, and which one day (when civilization shall have augmented in these countries) will become interesting for interior navigation from Salamanca and Zelaya to the port of San Blas.

While apparently not present in Black's translation, a note in the Spanish version Ensayo Político sobre la Nueva España, *cited in de Alba (1954), reveals Humboldt's ideas about a possible connection behind the formation of Baja California, Banderas Bay (Puerto Vallarta) and Lake Chapala:*

If one goes east from the Banderas Bay into the interior of the continent, one finds Chapala Lake and the important depression of Sayula, which constitutes a true lake in the rainy season, and which comes to confirm the idea of a sinking in this region. If the axis of Lake Chapala is extended, it will meet Banderas Bay, suggesting, in my concept, the general direction of this sinking, which must be considered in consequence like a ditch or open crack in the table-land, very similar to the tectonic ditches of Africa, now lakes, like Victoria Nyanza, etc., which form the sources of the Nile.

Humboldt, Alexander von. 1811 *Political essay on the kingdom of New Spain.*

Mexican War of Independence

The beginning of Mexico's War of Independence (1810-21) was Father Miguel Hidalgo's call for action in his parish of Dolores (now Dolores Hidalgo) in Guanajuato, delivered early in the morning of September 16, 1810. Eleven years of unrest preceded formal Independence from Spain in 1821. September 16 each year is Independence Day, a Mexican national holiday.

The motives and timing of the Independence movement have been intensively debated by historians, but several factors seem to have played an important role. The degree of Spanish control over activities in New Spain was irreparably damaged when Napoleon Bonaparte occupied most of Spain, and placed his brother Joseph on the Spanish throne in 1808. Hidalgo's initial rallying cry (*El Grito*) was more an expression of discontent with Joseph Bonaparte and the actions of Spaniards in Mexico than it was a call for Independence. Leading creoles, including Hidalgo, were very dissatisfied with Spanish-born administrators. A harvest failure in central Mexico in 1809-1810 may have played a minor role, serving to decrease people's sense of security, and increase their mobility.

The initial military impetus of the improvised insurgent army was repelled at the Battle of Calderón, near Guadalajara. Hidalgo and several of the other leaders were later executed. But the unrest continued, on a regional level, with isolated campaigns in different parts of the country, punctuated by periods when discontent smoldered just beneath the surface. More than 400 priests took up arms during the war.

One of the most extraordinary events in the War of Independence was the occupation of Mezcala Island in the middle of Lake Chapala by a determined band of insurgents who successfully held off all attempts by the organized Royalist army to dislodge them for four years, between 1812 and 1816. An honorable surrender was finally agreed, and the surviving insurgents were allowed to return to their lakeshore villages without further reprisals.

14

The first detailed map of Lake Chapala
1816-1817
José María Narváez

Captain George Vancouver is usually credited with discovering the site of the city in Canada that now bears his name, but actually José María Narváez y Gervete was the first European to sail those waters a full year earlier in 1791. History has largely overlooked Narváez, who probed northwards "as an uncelebrated 23-year-old pilot in command of a small sloop, the Santa Saturnina." (McDowell)

Born in 1768, probably in Cadiz, Narváez entered the Spanish Naval Academy in April 1782 at the tender age of 14, and soon saw his first combat. In 1784, he sailed west, visiting various places in the Caribbean, as well as New Spain.

In February 1788, he was assigned to the naval station in the busy Pacific coast port of San Blas. For the next seven years, he explored the coast to the north, including the Strait of Georgia, which today separates Vancouver Island from the city of Vancouver. He also sailed to Manila, in the Philippines, Macao and Japan.

On October 23, 1796, he married María Leonarda Aleja Maldonado in her hometown of Tepic. The couple raised six sons and a daughter. One of his great-great-great grandsons became President of Mexico: José López de Portillo, who held office from 1976 to 1982.

After 1797, Narváez mapped several sections of the west coast. He also surveyed the route for a new road from San Blas to Tepic. But in the early stages of the War of Independence (November 1810), he found himself unable to prevent San Blas from falling to the insurgents. His superiors tried him for failing to defend the port, but Narváez successfully argued that the true cause had been a lack of firepower, since his men had only 110 rifles and shotguns at their disposal.

Over the winter of 1813-1814, Narváez set sail across the Pacific once more to take Spain's new constitution to Manila. On his return, in 1816, he was summoned to Lake Chapala to map the lake. Later, he would produce a truly fine map of the entire province of Jalisco, a version of which, with updated boundaries, became the first official state map of Jalisco in 1842.

Following Independence (1821), Narváez remained in Guadalajara with his family. This long-overlooked sailor and cartographer went on to draw many more maps, before his death in the city on August 4, 1840, at the age of 72.

Narváez's map, based on surveys carried out in 1816 and 1817, is the first detailed map of the lake. It became the basis, with only minor modifications, for the later maps in many publications.

The map was commissioned by General de la Cruz, who needed all the help he could get in order to try and dislodge the group of determined insurgents who had installed themselves on the island of Mezcala and were refusing to surrender. Narváez, and the Spanish Navy, arrived to help. Narváez was still working on his map of the lake when the Royalist troops and the rebels agreed their honorable truce in November 1816.

The map is described in detail in the introduction (thought to be by Victoriano Roa) to the Spanish translation of the paper by Galeotti (1833):

Soundings of the lagoon in various places, in the months of July and August, which is when the water rises to its maximum height, give varied depths. At the western end, close to Jocotepec, it is from 2.5 to 3.5 fathoms (each one of six Spanish feet) [4.17 to 5.85 meters], and three leagues further into the lake, in the direction of Chapala island, are found depths of 4 to 5.5 fathoms. In the middle part of the lake, there is always 6.5 fathoms [10.85 meters] of depth, which diminishes gradually towards the eastern end, until it is reduced to 1.5, near the mouth of the river Tololotlan or Santiago. On the northern and southern shores, the depth does not exceed 2.5 to 3 fathoms, but the soundings increase towards the center of the lake. Only in the place called Punta de San Miguel and its environs is there a rapid descent from the shore to 5 fathoms. The same depth is found around the islands of Mescala and Chapala; but it is necessary to say that in the months of April and May the waters drop 5 feet 3 inches, and because of this, a large section of its shores is reduced to a swamp, and the Cumureato marshland becomes completely dry, leaving some short channels navigable only by canoes.

It is very natural that the floor of this immense lake should rise with the passage of time, on account of the quantity of sand that is brought annually by the rivers and torrents that flow into it, as can be seen close to the mouth of the Tololotlan, where in 1816, there was only 1.5 fathoms of depth, and it is to be expected that since the water can not abandon its bed, it will extend further, eventually causing the islands of today to disappear, with other new ones appearing.

Narváez, José María. 1817 *Plano del lago de Chapala.*

15

A post-Independence statistical account
1821-1822
Victoriano Roa

Victoriano Roa was a politician and writer, of whom relatively little is known. It is likely that he was a native of Jalisco, given that the surname is common there. He held various state government posts in the period immediately following Independence, and it was at the behest of the state government that he wrote his *Estadística del Estado Libre de Jalisco (Statistics of the Free State of Jalisco)*.

After being turned down for the post of Secretary to the state Congress in 1830, he moved to Mexico City as director of the Banco de Avío, founded in 1830 to promote the development of the wool, cotton and silk industries. This marks the beginning of modern industrial development in Mexico. The Banco de Avío, founded by Lucas Alemán (Foreign Relations Secretary in one of Bustamante's governments), is recognized as the main precursor of Mexico's commercial banks. The bank was closed by presidential decree of Antonio López de Santa Anna in 1842.

By 1836, Roa was in charge of *El Mosaico Mexicano*, a journal in which several important articles relating to Lake Chapala were subsequently published, including one of his own on Mezcala (see chapter 20) and that by Henri Galeotti (chapter 21).

Roa died in Mexico City sometime in the middle of the 19th century.

The details, provided by Roa in his Estadística del Estado Libre de Jalisco, for Chapala, the "Third District" (Tercer Departamento), which stretched from Jocotepec in the west to Poncitlán and Cuitzeo in the east, cover most places on the northern shore. Very few details are provided for places on the south shore.

In chronological terms, this was the first statistical account for a very long time.

The gathering of statistics

A renewed emphasis was placed in the 19th century on the gathering of reliable statistics. Officials of the state of Jalisco made several attempts to gather relevant information, primarily in order to better monitor the state's development. These efforts began with Victoriano Roa (1825) and were continued by Manuel López Cotilla (1843), Longinus Banda (1873) and Mariano Bárcena (1888). These statistical reports may not be as fun to read as the travel accounts, but are a veritable gold mine of useful information.

Cultivation of the fields

The cultivated lands in this district generally comprise 800 *fanegas* of corn, 255 loads of wheat, and 150 of beans and chick-peas (garbanzos). The first yields 100 *fanegas* for one [equivalent to about 1300 kilograms per hectare, see glossary for definition of *fanega*], and sometimes even 150, but this is very rare; the wheat from 10 to 25; and the beans and chickpeas from 10 to 20. In several villages of this region, some fruit trees are also cultivated.

Water

In part of the area of this district is the large lake called Chapala, or sometimes the *Mar Chapálico* [Chapala Sea], whose area is usually 160 square fanegas. In its interior is a small island, called Mezcala, which served as an invincible fortress for the old patriots, and afterwards was converted into a prison for the convicts sentenced by the courts of Guadalajara. The Grande river, which will flow into the same lake of Chapala flows by the edge of Poncitlán. In the village of Chapala are several fresh water springs and their currents also end in the lake. There is another in Ixtlahuacán, whose water is sufficient to water the orchards; there are some in the Jocotepec area though not very abundant, and in the Huejotitán hacienda is a very noteworthy dam, because, with only the seasonal rains that it receives, it is sufficient for watering all the area sown in wheat and even for turning the mill. In Atotonilco el Bajo is another dam, whose water is taken from the Grande river, and used to water the fields sown by the village and those of the Atequiza hacienda.

Quality of the hills

In this district none is more notable for its height than that of Atotonilco, which is situated south of the main village; it is covered with acacias, mesquites and *palo dulce*. [Arizona kidneywood] In other areas, some small hills are found, planted with brambles and other shrubs.

Churches

Each of the villages comprising this district has its respective church, in regular condition, and in the Atequiza hacienda is a chapel prepared for services.

Industry

The majority of the inhabitants are dedicated to agriculture, others to the weaving of ordinary lengths of wool and cotton, and some to the cultivation of the orchards and fishing in the rivers and the lake. This produces an abundance of the fish known as whitefish, catfish, sardines, bocudos, *popocha* [*Algansea popoche*, endemic] and *charales* [*Chirostoma* spp., also endemics], which results in a profitable trade for the villages found on its shores.

Livestock

Cattle and pigs, although not in abundance; horses, only on the haciendas.

The population of the Third District consisted of 4 925 married men, 4 927 married women. 3 062 single males of all ages, 3 632 single females and 7 clergymen, making subtotals of 7 994 males and 8 559 females, for a total population of 16 553.

Roa, Victoriano 1825 *Estadística del Estado Libre de Jalisco.*

Post-Independence

Immediately following Independence in 1821, Mexico still suffered from internal rivalries and faced a number of major unresolved issues. Disparities between rich and poor were vast. The Treasury was empty. Many hacienda workers had been forced into debt by hacienda owners and the credit system used in the hacienda stores (*tiendas de raya*). Some mine owners had become fabulously wealthy, resulting in the so-called "silver nobility". Titles were bought, and luxurious homes (and churches) built.

In Europe, the realization was dawning that the Americas offered incredible prospects for economic expansion. There was a veritable investment fever as the U.K. and other nations scrambled for the most valuable pieces of the economic pie.

As the political situation in Mexico stabilized, European visitors, encouraged by the positive spin of Humboldt, arrived to explore the best options. Sir Henry Ward, for instance, the British consul, was particularly interested in identifying the best mining prospects.

From a social perspective, as historian Alfredo Avila has pointed out, English and U.S. post-Independence visitors had very different ideas, compared with travelers from continental European nations such as France, Germany and Italy. Whereas the latter group of travelers shared some cultural background with some aspects of Mexican life and culture, thought processes and political systems, the English-speaking travelers, in general, found things very different, and had many problems understanding Mexico.

This makes the sympathetic account written by George Francis Lyon all the more remarkable. Lyon saw the Indians as an agreeable group, and did not believe they were being extinguished. Most Anglo visitors at this time paid scant attention to the Indian population, who "simply did not feature in national plans" (Avila, in Ferrer Muñoz, 2002) It also helps to explain the more sociological perspective of J-C Beltrami's fascinating account.

16

Mezcala Island—scene of rebellion
1824
Giacomo Costantino Beltrami

An "incurable romantic and inveterate roamer" (Barker 1969), Giacomo Costantino Beltrami (usually J-C Beltrami in English sources) was an Italian judge, traveler and explorer, who visited western and northern Mexico in 1824. Beltrami was born into a well-to-do family in Bergamo, Italy, in 1779. He embarked on a career in the Napoleonic courts, and quickly became a magistrate, moving in exalted social circles where, in 1809, he met Giulia Spada de'Medici. Their close friendship was cut short by her tragic death eleven years later.

In 1816, after the Battle of Waterloo, and Napoleon's final defeat, the Papal state took a hard line on possible independence movements. Beltrami, suspected of being a member of the secret political society of Carbonari, was accused of treason. Only the influence of his powerful friends, including Giulia Spada de'Medici, prevented him from being formally brought to trial.

In 1821, Beltrami, heartbroken following the sudden death of Guilia, left Italy for a prolonged, self-imposed exile.

After a whirlwind tour of Europe, including France, Germany and England, Beltrami crossed the Atlantic to Philadelphia. Driven by his desire to explore the wildest portion of North America, and to see "as many of the noble Indians as possible" (Hill 1867), Beltrami set off on a trek towards New Orleans. At some point en route, he became obsessed with finding the source of the Mississippi river.

On August 28, 1823, he found a lake which was the northern source of the Mississippi river. He named it Lake Giulia (anglicized to Lake Julia), after his departed friend. This is Beltrami's defining moment as an explorer, but his written report, *La Decouverte des Sources du Mississippi et de la Riviere Sanglante*, was dismissed by critics as fantasy, and labeled marginally heretical by the Catholic church.

Definitive recognition came much later, in 1866, when the Minnesota state legislature established Beltrami County.

He visited Mexico from 1824 until 1826, when he returned, via Haiti, to Europe, where, in 1830, he published *Le Mexique*. The governments of Austria and Italy were still antagonistic towards Beltrami and immediately censored the book. However, the Angelo Mai library in Bergamo, Italy, was permitted to retain the copies he donated to it. The Pope continued to deny permission for *Le Mexique* to be published, until after Beltrami's death in 1855.

During his lifetime, Beltrami was honored by many of the learned institutions of the day, ranging from the Medical-Botanical Society of London, to the Paris Geographical Society, the Ateneo di Bergamo and the Geological Society of France.

Besides exploring the source of the Mississippi, he had found new species of plants and had also discovered one of the earliest known Nahuatl texts, the so called *Evangelarium epistolarium et lectionarium Aztecarum*. This codex, written on Agave leaf papyrus, relates the stories of the evangelists and apostles translated into Nahuatl. It was created in Mexico under the guidance of Father Sahagún in 1529 and is one of the earliest known examples of written Nahuatl. Beltrami considered it possibly a more significant find than even the headwaters of the Mississippi.

In April, 1824, Beltrami left New Orleans for the Mexican port of Tampico. During the next several months, he traveled to San Luis Potosí, Zacatecas, Aguascalientes, Real de Catorce, Arandas, Lake Chapala, Ameca, Tequila, Guadalajara, León and Guanajuato, collecting a wide range of botanical and geological specimens.

The two volumes of Le Mexique *are written as a series of letters addressed to a friend, Countess Compagnoni. This may well be why some sources mistakenly refer to Beltrami as a Count.*

The Angelo Mai library's description of Le Mexique *is short, but to the point: "an oft overlooked work which records not only his travels but also countless details regarding the political and social mores of that country during some very turbulent years."*

Beltrami's work is best read as a socio-political report, rather than a straight factual account of geography and natural history. Among many interesting facets of his description of the Chapala area is his account of interviewing Padre Marcos Castellanos in August, 1824, only three years after Mexico's independence was officially recognized by Spain. Castellanos had been one of the leaders of the group of independence fighters based on Mezcala Island from 1812-1816.

Mescala rises in the middle of this earthly paradise. It is a village of pure, indigenous Indians who, during the last revolution, showed the utmost courage, discipline and resolve.

After the defeat of Hidalgo, near Guadalaxara, the Indians fighting under his banner disbanded but were not appeased. With his harassment and atrocious cruelty, General Cruz caused them to become only sour and irritated rather than submissive. On top of this, he also arbitrarily renewed forced labor and other oppressive measures that had been afflicted on the Indians by the Spanish Government from the time of the Conquest until they rebelled against the suppression of the Jesuits.

The Indians from Mescala, influenced by the priest named Castellanos, rebelled with others from neighboring areas. Believing they were too exposed in their own villages to the ire of the Spaniards, they sought refuge on the island of Mescala, situated 4 or 5 *milles* from the coast. They attacked it, took it over, and fortified it as best they could. The priest Castellanos was the only Creole and was at their head: as lieutenant, he had Santa Ana, a fearless Indian who obeyed him blindly. This alliance gave them the strength they had been missing, and prevented anarchy, which everywhere else confused and weakened the Patriots. For five years they resisted, succeeding in repelling repeated attacks, while enduring on this sterile rock all kinds of privations and sufferings with a determination equaled by their courage. They only surrendered when peace was offered in 1818, [actually 1816] on condition that Santa Ana remain as governor of the island. It was at Santa Ana's own house that I stopped in Mescala: I breakfasted in the shade of a Zapote, a majestic tree from the same family, I think, as the platanus montanus, which protects his humble abode from the rays of the sun and from the fury of storms.

In the evening I arrived at a place called, during the revolution, el campo, an entrenched camp, where the Royalists had their supply depot and from where they prepared and directed their operations against the island of Mescala. Now the place is called the Commissary: here is the reason why.

This island has become a penitentiary where those condemned to hard labor, expiate their sentences. A company of infantry, relieved every month from Guadalaxara, forms the resident garrison. This establishment needs an administration that is on top of daily events and that supplies all needs from the mainland. Therefore the Commissary of the Campo is in charge. He is, simultaneously, commissary of land and sea, because a flotilla, composed of two or three feluccas is used for transportation and for surveillance. He is a Spaniard and insisted that I be his guest....

The island of Chapala has therefore, as I said previously, become a penitentiary, where the convicts of the province of Guadalajara expiate their sentences. They are less harshly treated than in the penitentiaries of our World, the dictator of civilization. Those long and heavy chains, whose mournful and cruel sound distress the ear and soul of humanity in our streets and on our squares, only ensure more mutinies. These prisoners walk around without obstacles, breathing the air freely, in some periphery of the island where the waters are the only ramparts and the distance to the mainland the only difficulty to overcome. Some of them try it, but they rarely avoid death.

It is here that the lake is the widest. The island is not in the middle; it is 4 or 5 *milles* from Mescala and 14 or 15 *milles* from the opposite bank. The garrison lives in a narrow fortress that dominates the central part of the island; this is where the priest Castellanos and Santa Ana fought against the Royalists for five years. The island produces only a little grass, sprouting here and there on shallow earth covering the volcanic blocks. It is surprising that the champions of Independence were able to hold out for so long receiving no other help, food, or ammunition than that which passed through the encircling blockade, so tightly held by the enemy. It is an event of which the details, exploits and heroic episodes deserve to be remembered for posterity and yet are barely known. As for myself, I already said too much for a letter—I will end by worshiping the goddess who made, for a short time, a Paphos out of this penitentiary: the wife of the captain in command here for this month, a pretty Jalapeña, a superb example of the pretty faces with which the town of Jalapa has the reputation of supplying Mexico. Her amiability only added to her beauty. She showed plenty of honesty to this poor trinket salesman, and the poor trinket salesman begged her to accept a small trinket to remind her of a European's gratefulness....

On August 15th, I left for Chapala which is 15 *milles* from the Campo, following the lake's truly enchanting shores. Chapala is an important village. Except for a few mestizos, all its inhabitants are Indians and call themselves pure-blooded, in retaliation for the distinction of degradation to which the Spaniards condemned them, returning contempt for contempt. Facing Chapala is another small island, totally deserted and of no importance.

On the 16th, I lunched in the village of Axixis, about 10 *milles* from Chapala, with the famous priest Castellanos who is the curate there. He is a venerable 80-year-old man. He was seventy five, he said, when he stopped fighting. But he added:

"I still feel enough vigor to fight if the Europeans ever return to assault our land and our rights. I led a life of tribulation and I hope that God will prepare me a resting place in the heart of Eternity. To honor and defend the most beautiful work of his hand, work he designed in his own image and likeness, and which some barbarians came to hunt and tyrannized like animals, such was the task he imposed on me. In Europe, for three centuries, you saw, with a dry eye and a cold heart, the horrors committed in America against humanity, so cruelly sacrificed to politics and greed. We had to help ourselves, to fight against this terrible oppression. We have awakened from this degradation. May my fellow countrymen listen to me: until the last breath of my soul on this earth I will preach that we have to watch like lynxes and fight like lions to assert our independence. If we had known better how to unite our efforts and our hearts, this independence would have been assured a long time ago! Brutalized, we had too many anarchic passions to overcome; but we will change as they become clearer to us. I hope to die with the consolation of seeing that these passions are decreasing more and more, and that my homeland is advancing gloriously with its rebirth."

The priest Castellanos appeared to me greater than a Las Casas. I may be exaggerating; but if you think about it: isn't Castellanos, at one and the same time, the protector, apostle and defender of the Indians and all other American castes? He risked his life and is still ready to risk it; alone with his Indians, contained within Popilius' circle. Without means or hope, he was able to stand firm against threats and promises at a time when other patriots, with thousands of resources, and on a vast field of operations, prostrated themselves when offered amnesty, the common Circe of tyrants, and used as an instrument of perfidy and treason.

Castellanos was, in my eyes, more man then priest: I was not able to help myself from observing to him that, in this world, following the commandments of God and the order of Providence, every man must stand at his post with the priest at his altar. This might be, he answered me, in a country in the normal course of events, but when everything has fallen into chaos, blackness, despotism and extravagance, each one of us has to do his best to fill the voids left when the incompetence and blindness of others has allowed the homeland to disintegrate. God is capable of glorifying himself, when he calls his ministers to meet more pressing needs than those of the visible church. "I have been, everywhere", he added, "priest and soldier, like so many priests of antiquity, like all the catholic and protestant pontiffs, like all the Theocrats." Do you remember, Countess, in my letters from London, the Quaker who confounded me with San Augustine's answer, "I love him (God), and serve him as you like." I saw that father Castellanos knew much more than me; I dropped the question in respect for his venerable age. He allowed me to embrace him, deigned to accept a small token from me and gave me one of his own, a collection of strange fruits that adorned the front of his small library. He told me that I was a *bueno muchacho* (a good kid) and gave me his blessing. I had never received one with so much devotion since the ones my wonderful father gave me in his last hour; he gave me them with such tenderness that he reminded me of the ones given by the good patriarch Jacob to his dear Benjamin, when he saw him off to Egypt. But do not conclude that I pretend to be a Benjamin even less a *muchacho*. Castellanos is a Creole.

Oxotopec, ten *milles* from Axixis, sits on an elevated piece of land, almost in the central part of the western extremity of the lake and dominates the entire area. It is the largest village of all those around the lake. It has nothing worth noting except for the pretty niece of the curate, and its rich land which begins behind the village and unfolds into a charming countryside in the background before disappearing in the hills rising gently towards the interior.

Beltrami, J. C. 1830. *Le Mexique.*

Reporting the story of Mezcala Island

The dramatic events on Mezcala Island from 1812-1816, during the early years of the War of Independence, are a truly remarkable chapter in the history of Lake Chapala. At the time, events on Mezcala perhaps seemed to have only local or regional significance; with the hindsight afforded by history, they assume truly national importance. It is entirely fitting that attention should be refocused on the island of Mezcala as Mexico prepares to celebrate in 2010 the bicentenary of the start of her struggle for Independence.

The first two published accounts of events on Mezcala island appeared in 1828. They are the English-language travel accounts by George Francis Lyon, based on a visit in 1826, and Henry George Ward, who visited in 1827.

An account based on an earlier visit, by J-C Beltrami, who visited the area in 1824, and met two of the insurgent leaders— José Santa-Ana (José Santana) in Mezcala, and Padre Marcos Castellanos, in Ajijic— was published in French in 1830.

An unsigned article in The Episcopal Watchman, based on a visit in 1831 provides an excellent description of the island.

The earliest published and detailed account in Spanish appears to be that by Victoriano Roa, published in 1836.

A brief description of the penal settlement of Mezcala is offered by Manuel López Cotilla in 1843.

Later in the century, several other writers and historians continued to publicize the insurgents' struggle.

The first monograph by a modern historian is that by Manuel J. Aguirre: *Mezcala, la Isla Indómita*. Guadalajara: Editorial El Estudiante. 1968. Alvaro Ochoa's excellent *Los insurgentes de Mezcala—estudio preliminar, selección documental y notas* (El Colegio de Michoacán) 1985, has five short chapters, and the full text of 47 key documents concerning the history of Mezcala island.

"The Island of Mezcala–Lake Chapala's National Monument" is chapter 2 of Tony Burton's *Western Mexico - A Traveller's Treasury*. (Guadalajara: Editorial Agata, 1st edition 1993) and the translated later edition, *El Occidente de México - un tesoro para el viajero* (Canada: Sombrero Books, 2003).

Christon I. Archer contributed "Rebellion in the Rebellion of New Spain: The Indian Insurgents of Mezcala Island on Lake Chapala Front, 1812–1816", as Chapter 5 of *Native Resistance and the Pax Colonial in New Spain* (ed by Susan Schroeder); University of Nebraska Press. 1998.

Salvador Navarro Sánchez tells the story of the island informally in *La Isla de Mezcala, la gesta olvidada*. Guadalajara, Jalisco: Editorial Agata. 109 pp. 1999.

17

A visit to Mezcala Island
1826
George Francis Lyon

Captain George Francis Lyon was born in Chichester, England, in 1795. He joined the Royal Navy in 1809 and sailed to North Africa. In 1818, he was a member of a group exploring central Africa. *Narrative of Travels in Northern Africa* (1821) was published shortly after his return home.

In 1821, he joined an expedition led by Captain William E. Parry searching for the Northwest Passage. In command of the HMS Hecla, he spent two winters in the Arctic region but was unable to advance beyond the Fury and Hecla Strait before sailing home in 1823. The trip is described in *The Private Journal of Captain G. F. Lyon* (1824), which includes some of the earliest detailed accounts (with illustrations) of the "habits and dispositions of a people entirely separated from the rest of the world": the Inuit. Lyon was astonished at their resilience and marveled at how they could survive such harsh conditions. The story of his next trip to the Arctic, also looking for the Northwest Passage, became *A Brief Narrative of an Unsuccessful Attempt to reach Repulse Bay, through Sir Thomas Rowe's Welcome* (1825).

On September 5, 1825, he married Lucy Louisa Fitzgerald. She died only a year later in September 1826, while Lyon was in Mexico.

Lyon had arrived in Mexico on March 10, 1826, on a commission to supervise the English mining companies working at Real del Monte (Hidalgo) and Bolaños (Jalisco), as well as to inspect mineral deposits abandoned by the Spaniards. This period, immediately after Independence (1821), was one of intense English mining activity and investment.

Captain G. F. Lyon died at sea in October 1932, while on his way home to Europe from Buenos Aires.

Lyon spent several months in central and northern Mexico, and visited Lake Chapala from September 11-13, 1826, on his way from Guadalajara to Zamora and Morelia. He was the first native English speaker to write about the lake. Fortunately for us, the author and some of his notes from this trip survived a shipwreck at Holyhead (Anglesey) on his return to Europe.

While Lyon was favorably impressed with newly Independent Mexico (and with the local ice-cream), he was often alarmed by the negligence in the application of justice by the authorities. Lyon regarded them as partly responsible for the proliferation of highway robberies, and for the high number of deaths and injuries resulting from assaults. Lyon was particularly interested in the people, describing their varied occupations in some detail.

In the extract, Lyon laments his lack of ability to write a romantic novel about the heroic struggle that had just ended on Mezcala Island. One speculative possibility is that this one-liner supplied Charles Embree with the idea he so ably developed more than seventy years later in A Dream of a Throne.

At two leagues to our left flowed the Rio Grande from the eastward, at the foot of a fine range of hills; and we here and there crossed small tributary streamlets, in which I observed a small species of crane, egrets, and two varieties of ducks. We arrived at length, after a ride of twelve leagues, on the highly cultivated lands of the Hacienda of Atequiza, at the Casa Grande, where a letter of introduction procured me a very kind reception from Don Pedro de Olasagarra, and his son Don Manuel, who had been educated in England. These gentlemen showed me their garden, —rich in the fruits of their country; dairy, cheese rooms, and large granaries, and I passed a most agreeable evening in their society. The Hacienda, which has the advantage of being traversed by the Rio Grande, is now one of the richest in the immediate neighborhood of Guadalaxara, although it had suffered severely by fire and pillage in, the war with the Indians of Chapala.

Sept. 11.— Don Pedro having very obligingly furnished me with a guide, I set out early for the Lake of Chapala, sending my people and cargoes by a shorter route to Poncitlán, which is about six leagues ESE of the Hacienda. Heavy rain which had fallen during the night had quite flooded the country, and made our road very unpleasant, till on passing a low mountain we saw beneath us the beautiful Lake with its great expanse of water, and two small but celebrated islands. Descending the partially cultivated side of the mountain, we arrived at the Campo de Tlachichilco, erected by the Spaniards, and situated on the northern bank at about three leagues SE of the Hacienda of Atequiza. It is perhaps but little known out of Mexico, that the Lake Chapala was the scene of one of the longest and bloodiest revolutionary struggles between a strong Spanish force stationed at the "Campo," and the Indians on the small isle of Mescal. In consequence of some wrongs which had been inflicted on them, these poor people fled with their families from the villages of Mescala, San Miguel, San Pedro, Chican, Tlachichilco, and other places, all situated along the borders of the Lake. Under the command of a much respected priest, the Cura of Xacomatlan (named Don Marcos Castellanos), they maintained with wonderful bravery and perseverance a war of five years' continuance, during which they never once suffered themselves to be surprised, and underwent, most patiently, extreme hardships and privations. Opposed to them the Spaniards collected a force of a thousand men, including soldiers and seamen; and fourteen large launches with a schooner were with great labor and difficulty conveyed in frame, and with their guns, from the port of San Blas by the Barrancas of Mochitiltec. Three of the boats carried long 24 pounder guns; two had 8 pounders, and two 6 pounders, while each of the others had large swivels, and the schooner mounted six guns. Yet with all this force incessantly besieging and attacking the little island, these brave Indians held out from the year 1812, —keeping themselves constantly supplied with provisions by the activity of their small canoes, which nightly eluded the cordon of guard boats,, and in the most extraordinary manner kept up a constant communication with the shores of the lake: nor would the offers of terms from the enemy, or their own great sufferings, induce them to yield until 1817, when all resources from the main land had failed. It was then that the remaining handful of gallant men, amounting as it is said to two hundred out of above two thousand in number, consented to surrender on the promise of life and liberty, —articles which the Spaniards kept more faithfully than had been their custom in the revolutionary war. At this time the Spanish force was commanded in chief by a Capitan de Navio, and in second by a Teniente de Navio; yet the canoes captured one launch with fifty men, by the Indians splashing water over the arms of the Spaniards during the battle; sunk another; and in various attacks with muskets and their slings killed great numbers of their assailants.

I had brought an order from Guadalaxara for a boat to carry me to the Indian Isle; and the eight men who rowed me having all been engaged in the war, under the Spanish flag, recounted to me such anecdotes of the bravery, activity, endurance and devotedness of these people, that I never more regretted my deficiency as a writer to embody so romantic a history in the form of a novel. One of the most daring exploits took place at a time when the island was closely invested night and day by the cordon of Spanish guard boats; yet the canoes passed unseen between them, and a body of Indians landed and marched to the Hacienda of Atequiza. They burnt and plundered it, and carrying off a store of corn and provisions of which they were in great want, returned safely and unobserved through the same impediments to their little retreat. They frequently landed and destroyed the outposts of the Spaniards at the Campo, and by their constant surprises kept them in continual alarm. Even the women fought with as much determined bravery as the men, and were scarcely less feared by their besiegers; instances sometimes occurring in which these devoted creatures rushed on the bayonets of those who had slain their husbands, for the wild satisfaction of killing with their daggers the soldiers who had fired the fatal shot.

Until the "Grito" (war cry) ran through their country, the Chapala Indians had ever been esteemed the most mild and quiet of the agricultural villagers, and their countenances bespeak a peculiar placidity of temper: but a sense of wrongs called forth a latent spirit which struck terror into the disciplined troops of their oppressors, and placed their name conspicuously on the list of the liberators of their country. At the beginning of the contest, an incident occurred which is worthy of the brightest age of the Romans. Unarmed, ignorant of war, suffering from want of food and shelter, surrounded by their wives and children, Cruz (the Spanish commander) sent to them a proclamation, exhorting obedience to the king of Spain. The commissioner read it in a loud voice to the Indians, (who listened to him most attentively,) concluding with energy, and saying that if they did not submit, *blood would flow in abundance!* Having finished reading, he inquired of the Indians, 'How reply you to this?' when they, as if inspired by the same spirit and speaking with one voice, replied simultaneously, *Let the blood flow!*"

The Island of Mescal is a small rocky place, little more than half a mile in length and a quarter in width, of an irregular form, and having a small narrow isthmus running from its northern end. It could be ascended with ease in any direction. The island is about four miles from Tlachichilco, and sixteen from the opposite southern shore of the lake, which extends from it SW. by W. about thirty miles, and in the opposite quarter fifty more, hemmed in on all sides by steep ridges of mountains, which to the east are but dimly seen in the distance.

Off Mescal is a smaller islet, of about eight or ten acres, on which the Indians also for a time maintained themselves, until the straitness of their siege obliged them to join their companions on the larger one. I looked in vain on the little rock for traces of Indian habitations, and learnt that throughout the contest the warriors had not even huts, but sheltered themselves and their wretched families from the burning sun or overwhelming tropical rains, beneath boughs, blankets, or mats, brought from the main land. In all their misery, they sowed maize every year on one or two small ridges; but the produce, although cultivated with the greatest care, and held sacred by the famished women and children who saw it growing within their reach, did not answer an hundredth part of their necessity. Not a bush or tree was left standing, and the want of fuel was latterly as severely felt as that of food. One solitary building alone remains, to record at once the poverty and piety of the Indian patriots. It is a very small unornamented chapel, of about twelve feet square, which was respected by the Spaniards after their hard earned Conquest, and stands as an affecting monument to the memory of those who fell, and whose graves, as I was informed, were dug round the sacred edifice.

The Spaniards on becoming masters of Mescal, erected two large fortresses, which, although strong from their situation, are never likely to be of any other use than as depots for convicts; to which I hear that they are about to be appropriated. Great sums have been expended on these works; but before they were completely finished, the country had changed masters. There were no guns in the principal fortress, which is now in the custody of one man; but within its walls were piled large heaps of stones, which he informed me were ammunition for the slings, which the Indians use with great dexterity.

While at Tlachichilco, which has a ruined little shrub-covered fort, a few huts, and some sheds over the Spanish launches, now falling rapidly, into decay, I shot some very handsome gray marmots, of the size of Guinea-pigs, and having very bushy tails. They live in the stone walls round the maize fields, and commit great havoc amongst the young green crops.

The lake is said to be of a pretty equal depth, six to seven fathoms; and one of the seamen of the schooner informed me that there are but two small shoals in it, and that the anchoring ground is excellent in every part. It produces the delicate "White Fish" (Pescado Blanco), the Boquinéte, Bagre, and some few other kinds. The mangroves on the banks are the resort of numerous birds of the crane and heron tribes. The beautiful white egrets abound, and ducks, grebes, shags, (a small species of tern), with a variety of beach birds, can from their tameness be procured with ease.

Lyon goes on to describe La Barca and the hot springs and geysers of Ystlan (Ixtlán) in similar detail.

Lyon, G. F. 1828 *Journal of a residence and tour in the Republic of Mexico in the year 1826.*

18

From Tlachichilco to La Barca; hunting water-fowl
1827: Sir Henry George Ward

Sir Henry George Ward's *Mexico in 1827,* with illustrations by his wife, was an early appraisal of the fledgling Mexican Republic, published on his return to the U.K.

Ward was born in the U.K. in 1797. He entered the diplomatic service in 1816, and first visited Mexico in 1823, as a member of a British government commission assessing the desirability of establishing trading relations following Independence.

Ward married Emily Elizabeth Swinburne in 1824. His wife accompanied him on his return to Mexico in 1825 after he was appointed the first British Chargé d'Affaires. He took up his post shortly before Joel Poinsett was appointed as first U.S. minister to Mexico in 1825.

Ward was anti-Spanish and anti-American. Besides promoting British influence in Mexico, his main goal, apparently, was to prevent the U.S. from territorial expansion at the expense of Mexico. Ward considered that the incorporation of Texas to the Anglo-American states was inevitable unless the Mexican government could stem the wave of U.S. immigrants. How times have changed!

While both Ward and Poinsett were acting for their respective countries, the former acted as a moderate balance to the interventionist politics of the latter (for whom, incidentally, the plant poinsettia was named).

Ward promoted the signing of a U.K.-Mexico treaty of friendship, trade and migration, but the U.K. lost influence in Mexico despite his best efforts. Ward's concern that U.S. control over Texas ports would put them only three days away by boat from Tampico and Veracruz, Mexico's main trading port, became reality later in the 19th century.

Meanwhile, Poinsett's efforts to purchase Texas and his meddling in Mexican politics had antagonized the government of Vicente Guerrero to the point where his recall was demanded in 1829.

After Ward's return from Mexico, and publication of *Mexico in 1827,* he entered the British parliament, and was appointed Secretary to the Admiralty in 1846. Following press criticism over his financial affairs, and some ill-judged invest-ments, he was appointed High Commissioner to the Ionian islands (1849) and governor of Ceylon (1855-1860). He died of cholera on August 2, 1860.

At the time Ward was writing, the Mexican government was relatively unstable, with frequent changes of leaders and some inconsistency in policies. Ward summed up the political situation that he encountered as one in which, after 13 years of civil war, the form of government had still not been determined, with great differences of opinion existing with respect to the desired degree of central authority. He found it difficult to conceive of any country less prepared than Mexico for the "transition from despotism to democracy".

Ward is especially interested in the potential for trade and Mexico's economic prospects. His book is replete with descriptions of trade, mining, economic aspects and topography, and Ward appears to take particular pleasure in pointing out factual errors in Humboldt's Political Essay on the Kingdom of New Spain, *which Ward says have "since been copied by everybody".*

After several days in Guadalajara, Ward left the city on January 7, 1827, traveling towards Mexico City by way of Atequiza, Lake Chapala, Ocotlán and La Barca. The traveling group, on horseback, included Ward, his wife, two Mexican servants, "the girls", Mr. Martin (the French consul in Mexico) and Mr. Carrington. The party's baggage required 16 mules.

We breakfasted at the village of Puente Grande, a magnificent bridge with twenty-six arches, thrown over the River Lerma, or Rio Grande de Santiago, six leagues from Guadalajara, and four from Zapotlan. The breadth of the river at this point is very considerable, and the volume of water in the rainy season great; but during six months of the year the greater part of the bed is dry; and from this uncertain supply, as well as from the masses of rock brought down by the waters during the periodical rains, I should conceive that any attempt to render the Rio Grande navigable would be attended with much difficulty. Many, however, regard it as the future medium of communication between the Bajio and the Pacific, and look forward confidently to the time when Mexican flour, exported by this channel, will replace that of Chile in the markets of Lima and Guayaquil. Without deciding on the practicality or impracticality of this plan, it is only necessary to say, that Mexico must be in a very different state from that in which it now is, before the execution can be attempted. The work must be the work of a highly prosperous and populous country, and not of one in which the elements of prosperity are only beginning to develop themselves. It, therefore, certainly does not belong to the period embraced in my present work, although, in 1927, its advantages may perhaps be descanted upon by some future Mexican historian.

The party sets out from Tlachichilco the following day (January 8):

We embarked on board one of these gun-boats, which is still in good preservation at the camp, after breakfasting with the wife of the Commandant (La Señora Rodriguez) upon the Pescado Blanco, for which Chapala is celebrated. This fish is found in most parts of the Table-land, but it does not attain so large a size in the lakes about the Capital, from whence, upon great occasions, it is sent express to Mexico, slightly sprinkled with salt, or preserved in snow. I was glad to be able to furnish Señora Rodriguez in return, with a quantity of the water-fowl, which abound upon the edges of the lake, but are seldom tasted by the natives, as they have no guns that will kill a duck at fifty yards from the shore.

We sent our horses to San Pedro, an Indian village three leagues from Tlachichilco, and proceeded there ourselves by water, stretching half across the lake, in order to get a better view of Mescala, where we regretted not having time to land. San Pedro is situated upon the steep ridge which separates Chapala from the Valley of Ocotlan, through which the Rio Grande pursues its course. The view of the lake from the height called La Coronilla, is almost equal to that of the Lake of Geneva from the mountains above Vevay. Its vast extent, its form, the bold outline of the surrounding mountains, and the clear blue of the sky above, render it a very striking scene, and one to which few pencils could do justice.

From San Pedro to the banks of the Rio Grande, at the point where it reissues from the Lake of Chapala, which it enters near La Barca, we calculated the distance to be about five leagues; the two first mountainous, the three last over a level plain, which we crossed at a rapid passo. Even at this pace we could hardly keep our guide (an Indian runner, from San Pedro) in sight. He continued at a very fast trot over every sort of ground, now disappearing in a barranca, and now half seen, in the obscurity of the evening, fifty yards before our horses' heads, until we reached the ferry, to which he had promised to conduct us. Ocotlan is situated upon the Southern bank of the river, a broad and rapid stream. We found the passage not unattended with danger; for, as we had but one servant with us, Mrs. Ward, Mr. Martin, and I, were seated in a punt just large enough to contain us, guided by a man with a pole not sufficiently long to reach the bottom in the deepest parts. We each held a horse by a lasso, while the saddles and bridles were piled up between us; the servant remained upon the bank to force the animals to enter the water, which, as it was dark and cold, they did with great reluctance; and when they got into the middle, not discovering the opposite bank, they began to swim in different directions, and very nearly upset the boat. More than half an hour elapsed before we were all landed; and Mr. Carrington, who had gone on in the morning to superintend the passage of the baggage mules and the coach, told us it had taken nearly four hours to accomplish it....

We rejoined our party at the Hacienda of San Andres, three miles from the river, where Mr. Carrington had got a lodging for us, there being no inn in Ocotlan; and on the following morning, (Jan 9,) we proceeded to La Barca, where we arrived at an early hour, the distance being only eight leagues.

La Barca is the head of a "Canton", containing four "departamentos," with 96,178 inhabitants. The town is uninteresting, and only worthy of remark as being the last place visited by us in Jalisco, which is divided there by the Rio Grande from the neighbouring States of Guanajuato and Valladolid. [Michoacán] Our road lay through the last of these, and we consequently sent our carriage and mules over in the evening of our arrival. During this process, which occupied four hours, I went to shoot in the great Cienega, or marsh, which commences a little to the Westward of La Barca, and extends in a line with the river almost as far as the Lake of Chapala. I found there a prodigious variety of every species of water-fowl, – wild ducks, geese, swans, bitterns, and herons, some of enormous size, with many others, the notes and plumage of which were equally new to me. I tried in vain to get within shot of the larger kind, for my progress was interrupted, at almost every step, by deep canals, or impassable swamps. At last, however, by the advice of an Indian guide, I embarked upon a large bundle of rushes, which, though soon water-logged, still supported my weight very tolerably, for a considerable distance, while he accompanied me upon another equally primitive conveyance. By this means I contrived to shoot several ducks and a couple of wild geese; but when I wished to return with my booty, I found the attempt by no means easy. A strong current was setting towards the lake, and every attempt to propel our rush rafts in a contrary direction had the effect of immersing them still more deeply in the water; until at last, wet up to my middle, and with every prospect of sinking still lower from the quantity of water that my rushes had imbibed, I was forced to land, and to take a round of nearly two leagues, in order to avoid the marsh, and reach La Barca, where I did not arrive until a very late hour.

Ward, Henry George. 1828 *Mexico In 1827.*

19

Visiting the prisoners on
Presidio (Mezcala) Island
1831: Anon

By an unknown writer, presumed to be American, this article from the Episcopal Watchman describes an excursion to the lake in 1831. It is almost certainly the earliest American account of the lake.

Frequently having heard of the Lake of Chapala, distant about 16 leagues from Guadalajara, I determined upon visiting it, and accordingly set out, in company with an American gentleman, on the 26th of February.... We mounted our horses at 12 o'clock, passed through the city, crossed the Paseo, and through the suburbs, composed of low houses of unburned bricks. We found it extremely warm, though before arriving at the town of San Pedro [Tlaquepaque], distant one league, a cool, pleasant breeze sprung up. The road was *covered* with market people, some going, others returning; besides several small droves of jackasses, walking slowly along, and driven by Indians from the Lake, carrying fish to the city.— the fish are white, about foot long, have few bones, and are of a delicious sweetness....

We now travelled on a stony and hilly road, and through an uncultivated country, about half way to the Lake; we ascended a low but steep stony hill, which the guide told us had been the scene of an action between the Indians of the Lake and a party of the Spanish troops. The former fought with slings, and bows and arrows, and having the advantage of position, succeeded in dispersing the Spaniards. We had rode nearly 3 leagues, but as yet had gained a view of the Lake, until rising the brow of an intervening hill, this magnificent sheet of water burst suddenly upon our sight, glistening in the beams of a bright morning sun;

"And thus an airy point I won,
Where, gleaming with the rising sun,

> One burnished sheet of living gold,
> Chapala lay; beneath me roll'd,
> In all her length, far winding lay,
> With promontory, creek, and bay,
> And islands, that empurpled bright,
> Floated amid the livelier light;
> And mountains, that like giants stand,
> To sentinel enchanted land."

The view, while we were slowly descending to the shore, was one well calculated to please an admirer of Nature, combining the beautiful with the grand. The waters were scarcely ruffled by the mild breeze which played upon its surface, and in no way impeded the progress of a boat which was rapidly receding from the shore, towards an island in the midst of the Lake; whilst the appearance of several small villages, and cultivated patches upon the banks—the Lake embosomed in hills, over which, though far to the southward, majestically rose the snowy peak of the Volcano of Colima—all presented such a variety of beautiful scenery that the eye turned from one object to another, with equal wonder and pleasure.

At 11 A. M. we arrived at a village, called the Campo de Clachechilto [Tlachichilco], composed of some 20 huts, several of them built under the shade of a wide-spreading tree. There is also a very decent house, belonging to the Governor of the Presidio, (or of the Island, where state prisoners are kept,) and where we took up our quarters. We found it placed between two long low houses, formerly used as barracks, and in front of a chapel falling to ruins. The whole is surrounded by a high wall of loose stones, and each corner defended by bastions, now only garrisoned by a number of grey squirrels, who unmolestedly play about it....

On the 28th, we embarked in a Falva, for the Island, distant 2 ½ leagues from the shore. We were accompanied by 3 or 4 wives of the prisoners, who had obtained permission to visit their husbands. It was perfectly calm, and the boat passed rapidly through the quiet Lake, propelled by 8 or 10 oars. Chapala is said to be 38 leagues long, and from 5 to 7 wide. There are 21 towns, or villages upon its shores, besides several large farms, or haciendas. Cultivation is however confined to a short distance from the Lake, as the hills approach very near, and in places commence rising from the shore. It has from 4 to 7 fathoms of water, except near the shore, where there are many rocks. The fish taken here are of the perch kind; and the Indians of the villages carry on considerable trade in this article, particularly during Lent and upon Fridays, supplying Zamora, Guadalajara, Zayula, and all the towns around the Lake with fresh fish. I found it, however, very difficult to obtain any, even upon the borders of the Lake, for the Government allow but a certain number of fishing canoes, (fearing that they might aid in carrying off prisoners from the Island,) and was obliged to send to the villages of Mescala and Chapala, distant 3 or 4 leagues, and even then I obtained but three. It unfortunately happened to be Monday, and their custom is to catch fish on Thursday, so as to carry them to market by Friday, when the church prohibits meat. The water of the Lake is fresh, and entirely free from the saltish taste observable in the Lake of Zayula. At 10 A.M. we arrived at the Island; the boat was brought along-side of a stone wharf—the word passed that two gentlemen had come to visit the Island; we were then permitted to land, having provided ourselves in the city, with an order from the Vice Governor, to the Castellan or Governor. We were very politely received by a well dressed young man, of prepossessing manners, who, I supposed to be concerned in the establishment; I was, however, much deceived, for I afterwards learned, he was a prisoner, confined for having committed two murders. As they are all obliged to work, this young man was acting as secretary. [Monday Feb 28]

The Island is high, and the ascent up which we were conducted was very steep and fatiguing, being cut in a zigzag form, paved and walled in the same manner as the Barranca of Beltran. Reaching the top, we were received by the commander of the troops, and the Alcayde, or magistrate of the prisoners, (the Governor being absent) who invited us into the *Casa fuerte,* or strong house. This is a large square building, built round a yard—having thick walls, and surrounded by a deep and wide flosse, over which a draw-bridge leads into the gate. This house is occupied by the Governor, and the different officers employed in the establishment, —the soldiers, of which there are generally about 70, beside a part of the prisoners, who conduct themselves well, or whose time is about expiring. There are now about 250. Some are employed in weaving cotton cloths and Rebozos, others in tanning leather and making shoes—while those unable to work in any trade are employed in bringing water from the Lake, or grinding corn for Tortillas. This is done by placing the corn upon a flat stone made for the purpose, and then passing a round one backwards and forwards. Most of them are Molettos of the country, three or four Spaniards, and some South Americans; among the latter, I was shown two Limenian Negroes, who I recognized as slaves of a gentleman of that place. I inquired of one of them the nature of his crime. He told me he had given a man eight sabre cuts, of which he accidentally died, and consequently had been unjustly confined! The greater part are confined for robberies, others for murder; and to judge from their dark countenances, upon which a sullen discontented defiance was expressed, they seemed a most fit band of desperados. At night they are confined in a long low house, into which the door alone allows fresh air to enter, and are strictly guarded. Many, however, have escaped by means of canoes from shore, others by swimming a distance of 6 miles, the nearest point. I was told of two who attempted the latter mode. They managed to remain concealed in a retired part of the Island, at the hour for shutting up the prisoners, and at night commenced their perilous undertaking. They retired very quietly from the Island, unobserved by the guards, and finally exerting themselves, one reached the shore in safety; but seeing his companion almost exhausted, and imploring assistance, which he was too fatigued to render, he called upon the Indians of the town at which he had come ashore, to save the life of his companion; which being done, they were both immediately secured and returned to the Island.— This was a very generous act on the part of the one who had reached the shore, as he might have escaped.

The Island is small and very rocky. To form a small garden near the shore, it has been necessary to collect earth from other parts. Towards the southern extremity, a gallery of stone, remarkable for strength and security, was commenced by Cruz, the former Intendant of Jalisco, but remains in an unfinished state. In the same situation is a chapel. At present there is not a resident priest, but one had come from a neighboring town to receive the confessions of a dying man. The climate is healthy; but three persons had died for the last ten months, out of 320 who reside here.

Anon. 1832 *From an Unpublished Journal.*

20

Mezcala Island: picturesque place of pain
1836
Victoriano Roa

This piece appears to be the earliest published Spanish-language description of Mezcala Island. As we have seen, several accounts had already been published in English. (A biographical note on Roa appears in chapter 15)

There are some places in the world that, even though they seem insignificant today, achieved, in another time, just fame for having been the scene of great historic events. Among these celebrated places we must include the island of Mescala, an arid and stony crag located in the interior of the Chapala Sea, where a band of brave Mexicans resisted for a long time a persistent blockade by a multitude of vessels of war, brought together and directed by the Spanish general José de la Cruz.

...

The isle of Mescala is about a quarter of a league [about one kilometer] long and a little over 500 *varas* [420 meters] across: its shape is irregular, the rugged ground covered with thorny plants, and its shores are defended by large crags, so that it is only accessible from its wharf, where there is a regular anchorage for boats of shallow draft: everywhere else the island extends with gentle slopes beneath the water and can only be approached by canoes or flat-bottomed boats. The highest part of this mountain could be 30 *varas* [25 meters] above the level of the lagoon and on this prominence a rectangular building has been constructed, of sound architecture, without exterior windows, known as the *casa fuerte* [stronghold]. Its patio is spacious, it is surrounded by dwellings, and on the four corners of its roof are an equal number of sentry boxes for look-outs. The spectacle that the lake offers from this height is overly picturesque, at the same time as magnificent: to the west are the fertile shores of Tlachichilco, graced by fruit trees, under whose foliage can be seen, as in a picture, the huts and cattle, which, struck by the rays of the sun, stand out against the somber background of the mountains. To the east, north and south, a vast horizon is discovered, or an expanse of crystalline water, lightly stirred by the wind that by dividing it into waves, presents a face sparkling with all the colors of the rainbow. When the sun disappears behind the high hills, when its light is no longer reflected from the objects, then the great lake of Chapala seems like an immense and stormy sea: its waves rise, crash, break, and with a frightening noise, end by dashing themselves against the crags of the island: all that vital liquid seems to conspire to undermine its foundations and to bury the fortress beneath its waves. What grandiose thoughts, what sublime ideas could not be inspired by the majestic spectacle of Nature in that isolated, solitary place, when the weak light of the moon shines, with its sad reflections, on the vast plain of Chapala! The thinking man, the philosopher, the poet, exalted by the sweetest melancholy, would find magnificent and terrible pictures there to consider and describe.

Today, however, the isle of Mescala is nothing more than a place destined to suffering, a place of pain and weeping: it is the jail of the Department where criminals go to serve their sentences for a certain number of years. Free for their jobs during the course of the day, but shackled by night and enclosed in an unhealthy galley, they watch their sad days slip away on a narrow crag, devoid of all vegetation. The sweat of these men has been, for some time, the exclusive right of certain contractors who, obliged to give them poor and little food, have taken advantage of their work for every kind of task, under the inspection of a Spaniard and watched over by a detachment of troops paid for by the public treasury. More than two hundred unhappy men, that are usually held in the gaol, have been (and we do not know if they still are) devoted to increasing the wealth of a private individual, with no other advantage for society than that resulting from having those dangerous beings secure. But who can doubt that the country could have made better use of the forced labor of those men? The government could have established a factory for paper, or for thread, or cotton cloth, using water power, which would be raised, in a permanent fashion, by means of an ingenious pump, like that at Chaillot [a steam pumping plant that supplied water to Paris]. The products of this industry would be sufficient to procure, for those unfortunates, a more comfortable existence and a more useful role for themselves.

Roa, Victoriano. c.1836 *La Isla de Mescala en el Departamento de Jalisco.*

21

The natural history of Lake Chapala
1837
Henri Guillaume Galeotti

Henri Guillaume Galeotti was born on September 10, 1814, in Paris. In early childhood, he moved, with his Milanese father, to Belgium.

He was a student of natural history at the Establissement Géographique de Brussels, founded in 1830 by Philippe Vandermaelen, a very famous Flemish cartographer. Galeotti's paper on the geology of the province of Brabant won the gold medal in Science in the 1835 awards of the Belgian Royal Academy of Science and Fine Arts. Since the young Galeotti had already left for Mexico, on a trip sponsored by the Vandermaelen brothers, the prize was received by his father.

Galeotti arrived in Mexico in December 1835; it turned out to be a visit which lasted several years. Galeotti was primarily a botanist, and one of considerable note. He was responsible for the first scientific descriptions of scores of plants, including a wide variety of cacti, for which he had a particularly fondness. During his time in Mexico, Galeotti amassed an extensive collection of Mexican flora.

On his return to Europe, Galeotti decided to set up his own business, collecting Mexican cacti and importing them to Europe. He apparently revisited Mexico briefly in the winter of 1840-1841. Regrettably, tumultuous events in Europe caused the cactus venture to fail by 1849, leaving Galeotti in dire straights. Galeotti had been granted Belgian citizenship in 1843, and for several years, had corresponded regularly with Adolphe Quetelet, a noted mathematician of the time, who was permanent secretary of the Royal Academy. Even Quetelet was unable to help convince the authorities to sponsor Galeotti's dream of continuing his work with cacti.

Galeotti was reduced to selling some of his prize specimens, and even parts of his massive collection of more than 8,000 pressed plants from Mexico. One of his more expensive cacti had a price of 500 francs, equivalent at the time to a laborer's salary for an entire year. In 1853, Galeotti was appointed director of the Brussels Botanical Gardens, though his salary was equivalent to that of a head gardener. As director, Galeotti organized the publication of the Gardens' first magazine. He continued to hold this post until his death in 1858.

It is unclear what prompted Galeotti to prepare his excellent article devoted to the geology and natural history of Lake Chapala. The article, written in French and based on a visit to Chapala in February-March 1837, was mailed to Brussels, Belgium, in August 1837. It was first published in 1839, with a Spanish translation (undated) appearing in Mexico, in the magazine El Mosaico Mexicano, shortly afterwards. It was the first detailed scientific account of the lake.

An immense quantity of water bordered to the north and south by some scarped mountains, located 14 leagues south of Guadalajara, the capital of the Department of Jalisco (formerly the province of New Galicia), and 130 leagues west of Mexico City, is known by the name Lake Chapala, derived from the name of the old village of Chapala, situated on the western shore of the lake. Excavating in the environs of the village, old Indian burial ditches, skeletons, idols, earthenware vases called cantaros, and monetary tokens of obsidian or reddish clay etc. are found....

We have observed in the lake the phenomenon of occasional waves (seiches) which are in the habit of lasting plenty of time, with one part of the water remaining calm next to the rough part. This occurs, usually, at about five in the afternoon. We noted several of these singular effects, on February 27 and 28, and in March of 1837: the weather was calm and the temperature between 18 and 22 degrees Centigrade. The phenomenon is visible on the southern shore and in Tlachichilco and Chapala. The flood water rises from one to four feet (from 33 centimeters to 1.33 meters).

We also observed on the lake the phenomenon of the "mirage" of water, this is when one part of it reflects the objects and remains calm next to another which is rough. It is seen with more frequency close to the island of Chapala, at mid-day with the weather serene and the Sun high. These two phenomena—the water movement and the mirage—are without doubt, correlated.

From time to time, very strong whirlwinds or cloudbursts agitate the lake, snatching fish from their hideouts, and hurling them onto the nearby mountains. Some have been found on quite a high mountain near Ixtlahuacan, two leagues from the lake.

This phenomenon, which causes great damage to the inhabitants of the shores, occurs usually in March, April and May, before the rainy season. It is during the same season when the waters reveal the idols and cups of the ancient Indians. The inhabitants believe that an old city was buried by a sudden flood, and at some distance from Chapala, several trunks of *Sabino* [Bald cypresses] (*Taxodium distichum* of Richard), partially covered by water, can still be found.

A multitude of aquatic birds which feed on the insects of the lake inhabit its shores and the shores of the islands. There are two species of gulls (*Larus*), one cormorant (*Carbo*) which gives off a strong smell; they move slowly and stand in isolation on the rocks, or swim in groups of six or seven individuals, diving in order to eat the fish easily: water fowl (*Fulica*) which always collect in great numbers, and eat, from preference, the weeds the lake provides: herons (*Ardea*) of various species, including the egret walking alone along the shore, showing their white feathers and aiming their long pointed beak from time to time at the fish that are within reach, and other grey storks (They include the *Ardea herodias*, which is a large species, brownish and black in color) and water sheep or pelicans (*Pelecanus*) which live on the island of Chapala, and fly in flocks of 50 or 60 individuals, at about five in the afternoon, to search for food on the shores, where some little fish called *javai* are abundant. The pelicans are very fierce and plump, and have white feathers with a yellowish green tint at the tips of their wings. Similarly, there are diving ducks (*Colymbus*) which hide in the water at the slightest noise: others called *alcaldes*, brown and small, that are not very common in the environs of the island of Chapala, royal plovers (*Charadrius*) and of a beautiful white color with red, curved beak; rose-colored spoonbills (*Platalea*), of the island of Chapala, where they are very rare, since I believe they emigrate from tropical areas in the months of June and July: night-herons (*Árdea nycticorax*) that have on their heads three or four fine feathers, long and flexible: there are many on the island of Chapala: green kingfishers (*Alcedo*) and a multitude of ducks and herons that vary enormously in color, size and species. (We have sent to Mr. Vandermaelen's geographical establishment in Brussels, an almost complete collection of these birds. It was difficult to make it, even though they are abundant in the lagoon.)

There is a great diversity of fish in the waters of the lake. The whitefish and the *bagoc* are very well-liked for the table. A great quantity of fish is caught in Easter week. The inhabitants of the vicinity subsist on little else apart from the product of this fishing, for which they prepare by building reed shacks on the shores of the lagoon, and lighting large bonfires between 6 and 7 in the evening to attract the fish. Some small tortoises (*Testudo*) are frequently seen, warming themselves in the sun on top of rocks; but they hide at the slightest noise. Near Lake Chapala are found small crabs, two to three centimeters, with clearly unequal pincers and some molluscs such as *Unios* (we have not managed to collect even one in good condition), *Planorbis* and *Lymnaea*, which are not found whole, which we attribute to the force with which they are washed up.

In the part where these animals live, the lake has depths from 60 centimeters to 20 meters. Off the shores of the island of Chapala the depth is one meter 33 centimeters, at a short distance 3 meters, and it is claimed that further away it is up to 18 meters.

In the vicinity of the lake many animals are abundant, such as wolves (*Cani lupus*), rabbits, hares (*Lepus*), foxes (*Cani*) that the natives call coyotes: pumas (*Felis puma*): brown and red squirrels (*Scicirus*), and skunks (*Viverra*) which give off an unsupportable stench. In the not very thick woods are beautiful *coas* (*Trogon*), misanthropic birds: very loud and agile blue jays (*Corvus*), which perch on the elevated trees, moving their long tails, and also brown-colored birds (*Cuculus cayanus*). On the sides of the hills are owls and burrowing owls (*Strix*) which live in hollows they make in the ground: clouds of robins (*Turdus*) and green and violet grackles; sparrows (*Fringilla*) with thick blue beaks; pheasants (*Fatianus*) etc. Snakes and insects are very rare, and sometimes some dragonflies are obtained.

The vegetation is unremarkable. In the porphyritic mountains of Tlachichilco and Mescala, there are some cirius (*Carambouillos*), *Echeverrias* and *Sedum*; large cypresses in the Tizapan mountain range: *Erythrinas* with pink flowers adorn the tracks: *Sebanias*, *Mimosas* (*Acacias*), *Verbena*, *Stachys*, *Salvia*, *Plantago*, *Plumbago*, *Phaseolus*, *Dolichos*, *Cineraria*, *Steevia*, *Tagetes*, *Erigeron*, etc., some *Tillandsia* in the mimosas and large oaks, and the *Bletia grandiflora* in the vicinity of Ajijic. In Chapala there are streets of white and pink *Plumieras*, which the Indians have named Cacaloxochil. This place is protected from northerly winds by a conical hill, so it enjoys a climate similar to that of the tropics. Sugar-cane (*Saccharum officinarum*), papaya (*Carica papaya*), zapotes (*Achras sapota*) and bananas (*Musa*) all grow well.

There is a sublime view of the lagoon from the summit of the mountains located north of the hacienda of La Labor. To one side is revealed an immense spread of water with its islands and rock-covered shores, white villages, fishermen's huts, the prison building, haciendas, fertile shores covered in maize and chickpea fields, large herds of cattle grazing on the plains, streams shaded by willows and *Cinerarias* and the snow-capped summit of Colima volcano, which stands out from the mountain range to the SSW. Canoes formed from tree trunks fly over the smooth or lightly rippled surface of the lagoon in which a blue sky is reflected. The sombre mountains of Tizapan in the SSE and SE belong to the Department of Michoacán. The ends of the lagoon are hidden by the haze. In the other direction, the rich and fertile plains of Ixtlahuacan and Atequiza, together form a combination that enchants the naturalist and landscape artist who leaves the arid valleys of Guadalajara to enter this chain of mountains, from where the views extend towards an ever-cheerful horizon.

A very detailed account of the geology and fossils of the area follows. Later, Galeotti concludes with some thoughts about the many lakes in the region:

The multitude of lakes which now occupy parts of these immense plains, located from one branch of the mountain range to the other, are proof of the former existence of water. The eruptions and emissions of lavas deepened large valleys, forming receptacles where the water accumulated, which afterwards retreated for similar causes, and because of the destruction of the natural dikes.

We have dedicated ourselves so far as possible to examine the diverse chains of mountains in Mexico, ascertaining the connection the rocks of which they are made have between them, and mainly the upheavals, the agglomeration of mixtures and the diverse phenomena that there have been, which are the concern of geognostics. The study of the immense area of this vast country is very difficult. We believe that no geographic map of Mexico exists which shows the irregularities or undulations of the earth which, perturbed in every sense by volcanic action, has been raised to a great height by quite recent phenomena.

Galeotti, H. G. 1839 *Coup d'oeil sur la Laguna de Chapala au Mexique, avec notes géognostiques.*

22

Villages, farms and floods
1843
Manuel López Cotilla

Manuel López Cotilla (1800-1861) was born in Guadalajara. His father, a Spaniard, was a captain in the Royalist army, and hated the insurgents who were fighting for an independent Mexico; he died in 1816.

At age 18, López Cotilla contracted tuberculosis, following which he led a reclusive life for many years, dedicating himself to drawing and studying mathematics.

When he entered public life, he became a popular politician and successful educator. He occupied various posts on the city council and in the state government following Independence and was instrumental in reforming primary education. He founded several schools, including the first night school dedicated to adult education.

López Cotilla was also responsible for producing noteworthy textbooks, including a handbook of practical geometry for schools.

In 1851 he made a formal proposal for the creation of a teacher training college. This proposal was not carried out until long after his death.

He retired in 1855 on the grounds of ill-health and died on October 27, 1861. His remains now repose in the Rotunda of Illustrious Jalisciences in downtown Guadalajara, overlooked by a fine commemorative statue.

Manuel López Cotilla's statistical account provides no details about the lake itself, but does include short descriptions, all following a set pattern, of each of the main villages on its shores. By this time, administrative reorganization has resulted in most of the northern shore of Lake Chapala falling in the Third Division—Tlajomulco—of the District of Jalisco. Apart from Tlajomulco itself, which boasted 3,066 inhabitants, the most important village in the district was Jocotepec, as the figures reveal.

Jocotepec, a village located at the western end of Lake Chapala, is the seat of the curacy and receives payments. It has a justice of the peace, a municipal school and 2,742 inhabitants dedicated to farming, fishing and manufacturing. Its municipal fund produced in 1840 the sum of 456 pesos and 3 reales. It is 16 leagues from Guadalajara and 8½ leagues SSE of Tlajomulco.

San Pedro Tesistán, also situated on the shore of the same lake and with a population of 712 inhabitants dedicated to the same activities, has a justice of the peace and belongs to the parish of Jocotepec. It is 19 leagues from the seat of the District...

San Cristóbal Zapotitlán, similarly situated on the shore of lake Chapala and belonging to the parish of Jocotepec, has a population of 735 inhabitants mainly working in farming, fishing and making mats (petates or esteras). It is 12 leagues SE, ¼ S. of Tlajomulco and 20 from Guadalajara.

San Luis Soyatlán is also situated on the shore of Lake Chapala and belongs to the parish of Jocotepec. Its population is 1,066 inhabitants, whose main work is like the other villages; it has a justice of the peace, and is 22 leagues from the capital and 14 SE of Tlajomulco.

San Juan Cosalá, situated like the previous villages, has 667 inhabitants dedicated to farming, fishing and the manufacture of equipales, which are low round seats, with or without high backs, and very commonly used in the country. Its climate is warm compared to its neighbors; it has a justice of the peace and belongs ecclesiastically to the parish of Jocotepec. It is 14 leagues from the capital of the District and 9 SE, ¼ S from Tlajomulco.

San Andrés Ajijic, with 954 inhabitants dedicated to the same jobs as the previous village and whose location and climate it shares, belongs to the curacy of Jocotepec and has a justice of the peace. Its distance from Guadalajara is 15 leagues and from Tlajomulco 11 SE, ¼ E leaning towards the SE.

San Antonio Tlayacapan is in similar circumstances to the previous village, except for the occupation of its inhabitants, who number 423, and their dedication to only farming and fishing. It is 14 leagues from the District capital and 12 SE, ¼ E from Tlajomulco.

Chapala is the village that gives its name to the extensive lake that bathes the shores. It is the seat of a curacy, sub-office for payments, has a justice of the peace and 1,029 inhabitants employed mainly in fishing, farming and the cultivation of orchards. It is 14½ leagues from Guadalajara and 12½ ESE of Tlajomulco. Its municipal fund produced in 1840 the sum of 46 pesos 1 real.

Santa Cruz de la Soledad belongs to the parish of Chapala, whose situation and work it also has. It has a justice of the peace and 379 inhabitants. Its distance from the District capital is 13½ leagues...

In this District (La Barca) there is an abundance of regular and thermal water. The various rivers that water it generally flow into Lake Chapala and their currents flow from north to south, being considerably greater in the rainy season. The main ones are the River Grande and the River Zula, both navigable in canoes, in which they are crossed in that season, since only in winter are the rivers fordable at some points. In the period when they rise the water leaves the channel in both rivers, and extends over a great distance. In the year of 1814 the first overflowed by a league on the shore which belongs to Michoacán, facing the city of La Barca, and in that of 1837, it extended a little less.

A footnote added later gives more recent information:

In a report which the prefect of the District of La Barca has just given to the Government of the Department about the flooding experienced in the immediate environs of La Barca from the beginning of September this year, it shows that, in the judgement of several residents, it has been more severe than that of 1814, reputed to be one of the largest. Calculating the losses that have been caused, it says that on the shores of the River Grande, where lands belong to various people, they can be adjudged to be 6 to 8 thousand fanegas of corn. In the hacienda of San José de los Moras, which unites its seed-planting with that of Cumuato of the Department of Michoacán, the loss is estimated at 30 to 40 thousand fanegas, without counting the fact that the land can not be occupied until two years have passed and assuming that the rains in those years are not abundant. It says that the same situation is found in the *ciénega* [blind valley] of Cumuato, where 25 to 30,000 head of cattle, horses, etc. graze annually, the majority of which will probably perish, since they must feel the effects of the change of summer pastures, as well as not having any in the intermediary places. In the island of Maltaraña, where land is so fertile that it generally produces 200 for 1, the loss is considered to be 4 to 5 thousand fanegas of corn, 8 to 10 thousand rows of sugar-cane and also 8 to 10 thousand pesos because the chapel, houses, huts and mill have been ruined, the island remaining under the water. In the village of Jamay, the loss of corn was valued at 2,000 fanegas and the large-scale sowing of cantaloup and water melon that the residents do annually is believed to be very difficult. It indicates other misfortunes experienced in the part that belongs to the Department of Michoacán. All are attributed to the flow of the River Grande, River Zamora and others into Lake Chapala, which does not have sufficient drainage for the water to leave in years of abundance, so that the water then extends 2 and 3 leagues in those places. It concludes by showing the necessity that exists of facilitating the drainage of the lake, expanding the channel of the River Grande in its exit close to Cuitzeo, and destroying a stone dam that has formed in the vicinity of the villages of Poncitlán and Atotonilco el Bajo.

There are no minerals known in this District, but its land is useful for the cultivation of corn, beans, wheat, barley, chick peas, potatoes, sugar cane, and *camote*; fruit trees that do not demand a cold temperature grow well, and orchards, cantaloupes and water melons are cultivated on the sides of the rivers with equal success. The temperature shares in the differences between places. On the shores of the River Grande, on the coasts of Lake Chapala and even 10 or 12 leagues inland, summers are quite hot, the mercury rising in Réaumur's thermometer to 24°. *[René Antoine Ferchault de Réaumur (1683–1757) invented a temperature scale in 1730, still used in some parts of France. On the Réaumur scale, freezing is at 0°, and the boiling point is at 80° as opposed to 100° Celsius, or 212° Fahrenheit.]* The breeze from the south, which comes daily in that season, brings cooler temperatures from three o'clock in the afternoon onwards. In the rainy season, so much mud is formed in those plots that they are impassable at some points, and in winter the mercury does not go lower than 10°. The temperature of the higher part or Los Altos is much colder, as also is that of the mountainous part.

López Cotilla, Manuel. 1843 *Noticias Geográficas y Estadísticas del Departamento de Jalisco.*

23

Earthquake!
1847
J. Antonio Ximénez

J. *Antonio Ximénez was the Mayor of Ocotlán at the time of the October 2, 1847 earthquake. The following day, he wrote to advise the State Governor:*

Yesterday, Saturday the 2nd [of October 1847] at seven thirty in the morning a strong earthquake, which lasted more than five minutes, was felt in this town. It did not, however, cause any damage. The repetition, happening between nine and ten o'clock on the same morning, was terrible. In an instant, some of the town's buildings were knocked down, and the others were completely destroyed or in imminent danger of collapse.

As of yesterday, 46 persons of both sexes, and of various ages, had been found dead, and it is not possible now to know with certainty the number of injured and wounded who miraculously escaped the destruction. It was not only the town that suffered this misfortune. The same thing occurred in all the other places in the municipality. There was terror and fright everywhere, especially when rocks broke away from the hill and the wild animals were terrified.

This morning, your Excellency, 24 hours after the unfortunate events, the perfect image of Our Lord Jesus Christ on the Cross was seen between west and north, formed between two clouds and lasting for half an hour: in which time more than 1,500 people who were in the plaza fell to their knees, performing acts of contrition and crying to the Lord to show mercy...

From the ruins of Ocotlán, October 3, 1847.
J. Antonio Ximénez

Ximénez, J. Antonio. 1847 *Letter to the State Governor.*

24

Lake Chapala—prospects for the future
1857
Mathieu de Fossey

At the time Fossey (1805-1870) moved to Mexico, most Europeans had only a scanty knowledge of the New World. Emigrating there not only allowed individuals like Fossey to escape from Europe, it also offered them the chance to help develop what was then perceived as being a "backward" part of the world, likely to be held back by its sizable indigenous population.

From a Mexican point of view, large swathes of its territory, such as Texas, Arizona, New Mexico and the Californias in the north, as well as the strategically important Isthmus of Tehuantepec in the south, were almost uninhabited. Immigration could help settle these areas, improving national security. By 1831, even some of the Spaniards exiled by Vicente Guerrero in 1827 and 1829 were beginning to return, now that Anastasio Bustamente had become president.

Fossey, politically disillusioned following the end of the reign of King Charles X in 1830, responded positively to an intriguing pamphlet he read publicizing the challenges and opportunities for French settlers in the Isthmus of Tehuantepec, Mexico. He arrived in Mexico on February 13, 1831 as a member of a large group of French colonists intent on making a new life for themselves.

When the settlement (at Coatzacoalcos) failed, partly because of its organizers' unrealistic promises and claims, Fossey moved to Veracruz and later to Mexico City. Some settlers did succeed in establishing French communities in Nautla (between Veracruz and Tuxpan) and in San Rafael Jicaltepec; others returned to France.

The failure did not alter Fossey's view that European, especially French, settlers were essential for Mexico's political stability and for its economic and cultural development. Fossey maintained that Mexico was unable to govern itself adequately and would benefit from a political alliance with France to offset the potential dangers attached to its relationship with a U.S. seeking to expand. His beliefs were no doubt only strengthened by witnessing the U.S. invasion of Mexico in 1847. To some extent, his proposed closer ties to France became a reality after Porfirio Díaz consolidated power towards the end of the 19th century.

Fossey lived for periods of time in several Mexican cities, including Mexico City, Oaxaca, Guanajuato and Colima, which gave him a sound basis for *Le Mexique*, a book describing the entire country. Fossey returned to France in 1866 and died there in 1870.

Informative and factual, Le Mexique *was used by European diplomats and prospective settlers as a reference work. This short extract describes the lake, as Fossey made his way to Guanajuato.*

The fresh water lake of Chapala is about 20 leagues in length, by six to eight in width. It is no longer criss-crossed, as at the time of the conquest, by the boats of the Indians who captured fish there to take once a week to the markets of Guadalajara and the small towns nearby. The catfish there has an insipid taste; but the whitefish, eaten in *matelote* [a kind of fish chowder] is a delicious meal.

A little to the west, rising from the heart of the water, is the small island of Mezcala, where a jail for criminals has been established. In 1810, a few hundred Indians took refuge there, and became openly hostile toward the Spanish power. There were many confrontations on the lake between them and the king's soldiers; but being more agile than them in handling the oars and controlling the canoes, they had much better luck than their adversaries and, if my memory does not fail me, only surrendered much later, under advantageous conditions.

When industry, the younger sister of agriculture, takes off in Mexico, Guadalajara will be called upon to become the center for business from north to south and from west to east. Then the population of Jalisco and neighboring states will multiply rapidly. Lake Chapala, dead so to speak in the hands of the people at present, will receive, from those who think and act at the same time, a life that will convert the poor villages built on its shores into flourishing cities.

At the start of the 21st century, it looks as if Fossey's prescient words may finally be coming true, even though it is not yet clear how, given local conditions, such large settlements can become environmentally sustainable.

Fossey, Mathieu de 1857 *Le Mexique.*

25

The lake's potential value as a trading route 1854-1863
Longinus Banda

Longinus Banda (1821-1898) was an engineer, and is described on the book-jacket of the 1982 edition as a man of great culture, a specialist in the mathematical sciences.

He was born on May 15, 1821 of a Mexican father and Filipino mother. By 1842 he had qualified as an agricultural surveyor and was living in Guadalajara. In 1843 he taught mathematics in the College of San Juan. In 1847, during the American Intervention, Banda was a Deputy in the Congress of the Union. He was appointed Mayor of Guadalajara in 1863. Three years later, he was giving classes in natural history at the Boys High School in the city, and mathematics classes at the Catholic High School. Later he taught geography in several schools. He retired in 1896 and died in May 1898.

In his Statistics of Jalisco: compiled from the best official figures and *information supplied by suitable individuals in the years of 1854 to 1863, Longinus Banda attempts to bring order to all the readily available statistics he can find about the region, often noting discrepancies found in earlier accounts, as exemplified by widely contrasting figures for the true area of Lake Chapala.*

According to Banda, Narváez had calculated an area for the lake of 63 square leagues for his 1840 map of the Departamento de Jalisco. Calculations by Domingo Torres y García, using the original map, gave a figure of 75.88 square leagues. A few years later, Pedro García Conde used the Carta General de la República Mexicana (1849) to arrive at 95.93 square leagues. Similar discrepancies are noted for the area of Jalisco and other significant figures.

He makes it clear that almost all his figures are taken from other sources and official documents, some of which have been lost when archives were destroyed in the "revolutions".

The book, published in 1873, includes a map of the state of Jalisco made from that published by the Geography and Statistics Society in 1867.

He includes some relatively lengthy discussion of the potential of various rivers for navigation, which was of far greater significance in pre-railroad days than it is today. Elsewhere, he notes, with interest, that the "best road surface"—MacAdam—had been used on the Guadalajara–Mochitiltic road.

Banda concludes by prioritizing the tasks that should be undertaken in order to improve the information available to administrators. The first priority is to make a topographic map of the state to acquire a "complete knowledge of the geological formations, rivers, lakes and mountains; ascertaining the true usefulness that they offer for internal navigation, and the possibility of using their water for the benefit of agriculture and machines." The second priority is a population census of the entire state, and the third is to carry out property valuations.

The grandiose idea of making this [Lerma] river navigable does not seem to us to be possible in all of its parts, because of the enormous difficulties presented by its channel and the steep barranca that marks its course from the Juanacatlán waterfall, or rather from the Puente Grande waterfalls, until north of Tepic. What we do believe to be very possible is the usefulness of its waters, and those of Lake Chapala, both for secondary canals which inland commerce has needed, as well as for the stimulation and development of the agricultural and manufacturing industries.

Certainly, this idea was not unknown to some illustrious Jaliscienses, since in 1826 the opening of a canal began which would carry water from Lake Chapala to the outskirts of Guadalajara, and in 1833, the State Governor [Pedro Tamés] ordered studies to be made to assess the possibility of such a project which had not been realized and had been forgotten on account of our continued revolutions.

If a work of this sort was to be begun, and if others that we calculate would not be too costly were to be added, a short and active navigation would be established from Guadalajara to Zamora, which would give an incalculable boost to the agricultural industry of Jalisco and Michoacán, as well to the trade of foreign items that are currently brought with such burdens and difficulties from San Blas or Manzanillo to Morelia and other interior towns. And if we did not want to achieve such beneficial results, at least we could manage to open irrigation canals for a good system, to promote the exploitation of the beautiful and rich haciendas in the Toluquilla, Atejamac and Santa Ana valleys.

Jalisco also has several lakes worthy of mention, as much for their size as for the usefulness which they could be for agriculture, industry and commerce.

The most important of all is the beautiful and picturesque Lake Cha-pala, which covers an area of 95.93 square leagues, giving it the reputation of being the largest of those that exist in Mexico. Its shores, scattered, so to speak, with villages and haciendas, form the most enchanting spectacle when the panorama is viewed from the summits of Mt. García, south-west of the lake....

The grandiose idea of taking water from Chapala to the edge of Guadalajara is not impossible, nor only a dream as claimed by people who perhaps lack the necessary knowledge to judge; but in order to carry it out, erudite officials, who desire the nation's material improvement, are needed as well as substantial funds. The former have not been lacking in Jalisco, but the latter, unfortunately, have never been available to any of our governments.

The services that Lake Chapala would offer inland navigation can scarcely be calculated. It is not adventurous to say that, using only dredges and some short canals, trade could be extended from close to Zamora to Jocotepec, or from this point to Juanacatlán and to La Piedad....

The lagoons of Zacoalco, San Marcos, Atoyac and Sayula, are, to our way of thinking, parts of an old lake, because being located only very short distances apart, on land of about the same height, they tend to join together in the seasons of heavy rains. But even if is not believed that these lagoons have been joined, their existence may be attributed to filtrations from Lake Chapala, from which they are separated by only a small range of hills. This could have been formed by one of the earth's upheavals, subsequent to the existence of the said lakes, which produced the uplift which separates them today from the large lake of Chapala, after giving them a lower level....

Lake Chapala, as we have already said, could be navigable by smaller vessels almost throughout its extent. The circumstance of being commu-nicated with the Lerma, Cuitzeo, Zamora and Tizapan rivers, could result in an active trade of seeds, woods, and other items of the agricultural and manufacturing industries, between the various villages that are situated on their shores, as well as with the fertile and productive district of Zamora.

The advantage of having some small islands has made it useful for establishing a presidio [jail] which our government has never been con-cerned to use properly. In some periods of time, it has become a burden rather than a benefit; to the extent that in one of them the destruction was ordered of the buildings that had been established through steadfast ef-forts and sacrifices.

The large area of the lake and the constant winds are similar to the sea. Some colleges could have vessels on it in which young mariners

Plans to improve navigation

The potential for waterborne trade from Salamance and Celaya (on the River Lerma) to the port of San Blas (at the mouth of the River Santiago), via Lake Chapala, had been recognized at the start of the 19th century by Humboldt.

Prior to the advent of the railways close to the end of the century, various schemes were hatched to improve navigation in the Lerma-Chapala-Santiago system. In 1833, the then governor of Jalisco, Pedro Tamés, wanted to bring water from the River Santiago at Poncitlán, via a canal, to Guadalajara for a mill. This would have made much of the river navigable, as Humboldt had proposed. The engineer who looked at the proposal, Samuel Trant, used a modified version of the map of Narváez (1816), to sell the scheme, but a change of government took Tamés out of office shortly afterwards, and the plan was shelved. In 1842, Mariano Otero proposed a similar route for a canal but, once again, the proposal did not prosper.

On December 26, 1865, the papers to form the Compañia de Navegación y Comercio del Lago de Chapala y Río Grande (Company for Navigation and Commerce on Lake Chapala and the River Santiago) were filed in Mexico City. The company's stated aims were to purchase boats, canalize the river to make it navigable, and build warehouses and other infrastructure for commerce. Promotional brochures included a detailed map showing the anticipated commercial sphere of influence of the project. The plans were never fulfilled, perhaps because prospective French investors pulled out when Maximilian was deposed.

In 1871, engineer Juan B. Matute published a pamphlet outlining plans for a 50-kilometer-long canal for navigation from Yurécuaro via Lake Chapala to Juanacatlán. The project had an estimated cost of $83,783 pesos. The state governor of the time, Ignacio Vallarta, approved it, and even suggested adding a railway from Juanacatlán to Guadalajara, but the plans were never carried out.

Even in 1888, the year the railway finally reached Guadalajara, Mariano Bárcena still argued for the possible advantages of constructing a canal in improving commerce. But the days of canals were over; the age of the railways was upon us.

learning sailing and piloting could have practical training, perhaps with incontestable advantages, whether on the small island of the presidio or in one of the villages situated on the shores of Chapala. In this way, the state of Jalisco would have mariners with which to supply Mexican vessels, and, with time, there would be a truly national navy and merchant navy.

Banda, Longinus. 1873 *Statistics of Jalisco*

26

Overnighting in haciendas
1864-1865
William Henry Bullock Hall

Barrister and seasoned traveler William Henry Bullock Hall (1837-1904) was born in Essex, England, and educated at Balliol College, Oxford, where he was a pupil of the legendary Benjamin Jowett.

It is unclear what motivated Hall to visit Mexico during the time of Maximilian, though his route, which began in Veracruz and took in Mexico City, Tepic, San Blas, Guadalajara, Querétaro and Tampico suggests that he had business interests, perhaps connected to the textile trade. In San Blas, for instance, he spent time at Casa Barron y Forbes, the Anglo-American import-export firm founded by Eustace Barron (then British Consul in Tepic) and Alexander Forbes (the American consul).

Hall loved the game of cricket (he represented Oxford University on three occasions: in 1857, 1858 and 1860) and alongside many other fascinating insights into the life of British expatriates in *Across Mexico in 1864-5*, there is a noteworthy description of a cricket match played in Mexico City.

Hall, who wrote several other books, died in San Rafael, France, on April 21, 1904.

Hall's route from Zamora to Guaracha hacienda, and then via Buenavista to La Barca and Ocotlán skirted the edge of the sometimes marshy wasteland at the eastern end of Lake Chapala.

Armed with letters of introduction, Hall visited many of the wealthy hacienda owners, including the Castellanos brothers and General Velarde, the "golden ass". He was singularly unimpressed by the latter's limp handshake and failure to offer him either a cigarette or cup of coffee.

Compared with earlier travelers, Hall was less convinced about the potential navigability of the River Santiago, due to both its steep gradient and its limited depth near the ocean.

Hall's travels were not only sometimes inconvenienced by the vagaries of stage-coach travel, but also by the vagaries of war, since this was the time when Maximilian was desperately trying to gain control of a fractured country. Hall recognized the huge gulf between the very poor and the very rich, but found both classes equally hospitable.

On his return to Guadalajara from San Blas, he found that he "had not even the requisite coppers left, to pay the toll demanded of all travelers on entering the city. In my anxiety not to be worth robbing,... [by] traveling with a light purse, I had quite overreached myself, and was reduced to living on dry bread during the latter part of the journey."

The party sets off, after spending the night at the hacienda of Estanzuela:

Next morning, soon after sunrise, we were again on the road, bound for the *hacienda* of Buena Vista—the seat of General Velarde, the most notorious personage in those parts. With the exception of the hot springs of Ixtla—a number of natural fountains, from which the boiling mineral water spouts up several feet into the air, and which would make the fortune of the place, were they anywhere but in Mexico—I observed nothing worthy of note until, after a three hours' ride, we came in sight of Buena Vista.

From the moment we entered upon the territory of General Velarde, which is a kind of border land between the states of Jalisco and Michoachan, I was struck with the neatness with which everything was kept. The fences, gates, farm buildings, etc., would have done credit to any civilized country in Europe.

Like Dumnorix in Caesar's Commentaries, General Velarde maintains a regiment of soldiers at his own cost, and I must do him the justice to admit that his men present a more soldier-like appearance than the regular troops.

Having foreseen that a letter of introduction to this provincial potentate would be useful to me, I endeavoured, before I left the capital, to furnish myself with credentials of some sort. My efforts, however, all proved fruitless, for most of my influential acquaintances in Mexico were engaged in lawsuits with this eccentric personage, who is commonly known by the *soubriquet* of "el burro de oro" (the golden ass). In Zamora, however, thinking that any kind of introduction would be better than none, I had obtained a letter from the storekeeper, in whose house we were lodged. This letter was artfully couched in the most obsequious terms, and intended to flatter the vanity of the "golden ass."

On riding up to the main entrance of the *hacienda*, I learned that General Velarde, who had lately been appointed by the Emperor, whose cause he had espoused, Prefect of the neighbouring town of La Barca, was at that time residing at his town house.

In his absence, the major domo received me so insolently, that I rode off to try if more hospitality was to be met with elsewhere. My next attempt however was even more unsuccessful, for, on entering a neighbouring house, I found it untenanted, except by a little child, which was prowling about by its bedside with its face covered by black plague spots. Not encouraged by this spectacle, I beat a hasty retreat, and retraced my steps to the *hacienda*, determined this time to force an entrance at any price.

However, as I passed through the iron gateway leading into the court yard, I encountered no opposition of any kind, and proceeded to establish myself quietly in the comedor—the walls of which were decorated with tawdry paintings of fruit and flowers.

Anticipating that I should find nothing to eat, I had purchased some *pan dolce* at the *tienda*, and being already provided with tea and teapot —my inseparable traveling companions—I only stood in need of boiling water.

But how to obtain boiling water in such inhospitable precincts? I would at any rate try, so I sallied forth from the *comedor*, and proceeded to make a thorough investigation of the premises.

Outside I found myself in a court yard, the walls of which were covered with glaring frescos in the worst possible taste and style, representing mythological subjects. Into this court yard most of the rooms opened, on the principle of a Roman or Pompeian villa, which the architect had evidently aimed at reproducing. Nor was the attempt by any means unsuccessful, for the whole house was characterized by an air of solidity and elegance, unsurpassed by any with which I had yet met in town or country in Mexico. Indeed, but for the vile and profuse daubing on the walls, one could have imagined that one was wandering in some luxurious villa at Pompeii or Herculaneum.

In one of the recesses of the building, I discovered, over her earthenware pots, the old woman, upon whom you are sure to stumble, sooner or later, in Mexican houses, if you only persevere. As good luck would have it, this old crone was in the act of trying to blow into a sufficient glow to boil a jug of water, the bits of charcoal which, laid in a square receptacle sunk in the face of a solid brick counter, do the duty of a fire all over Mexico. From this old lady I obtained not only boiling water, but a couple of poached eggs, so that I fared sumptuously.

At noon I took my departure for La Barca, and in about an hour found myself standing on the banks of the Rio Grande de Lerma, waiting for the ferry to cross into the town, round the base of which the river sweeps. After considerable delay, the passage was safely effected, our horses swimming over, while we crossed in the ferry.

Immediately overhanging the river, on the opposite or Jalisco bank, stands the town house of his Excellency General Velarde—a substantial well-built residence, which would be reckoned a sumptuous dwelling anywhere. About the entrance were buzzing, like bees at the entrance of a hive, some of those soldiers, whom the general keeps at his own expense. Demanding admission, I was at once shown into the presence of the potentate, who was taking his after dinner cup of coffee in his office.

Reclining at full length on an elongated arm chair, fitted with a rest for the feet, lay a flabby white faced giant, dressed in a pair of bright red trousers, black jacket and waistcoat, and wearing a short highly polished jet black wig, carefully plastered down over his forehead—reminding

El Burro de Oro—"The Golden Ass"

José Francisco Velarde (1820-1867) owned the haciendas of Buenavista, Cumuato and San José, the town-house of La Moreña in La Barca, and a city residence in Guadalajara. He owned an area equivalent to a small state in its own right.

Velarde's misguided political ambitions and ostentatious love of wealth led one outspoken chronicler to call him "as rich as he was ignorant"..."a golden ass"! This epithet sums him up better than most. Velarde's houses boasted a wealth of imported items—furniture and perfumes among them—and he habitually wore coats with gold buttons and carried a gold walking stick. He maintained a harem of assorted locals, mixed-race women and black former slaves.

In the 1860s, Velarde paid 50,000 dollars for the dubious privilege of forming his own private army to support the French Intervention in Mexico and Emperor Maximilian. When Maximilian arrived in Mexico in 1864, with his wife Carlotta, he is supposed to have asked immediately, "And who is the rancher prince?", referring to none other than donkey-brain Velarde. It is possible that the two men actually met, and it is likely that Velarde's sumptuous decoration of La Moreña with European-style murals, was part of his preparations for receiving Maximilian in his country-seat one day.

Unfortunately for both men, Maximilian was captured and executed in Querétaro in 1867. Velarde, in turn, was captured in Zamora. Despite offering his firing squad over one million dollars if they missed, he was executed on June 14, 1867.

His extensive land-holdings, instead of passing to his wife Nicolasa and their three children, were confiscated by the government.

one irresistibly of a gigantic knave of spades. The great oval face wore an inane, self satisfied expression, and was as innocent of hair as a woman's. The skin was perfectly white, and it was very evident that the general had been particularly careful of his complexion.

The conversation of the man—at any rate, that of it to which he treated me—was much of a piece with his appearance, and he had not even the civility to offer me a cigarette or cup of coffee. The office, in which our interview took place, was a most unpretending apartment, opening on to the street. What interested me most about the premises were some excellent maps of the various states into which the country was formerly divided—a division, which has since given place to departments on the French model, in order to facilitate centralization.

On my rising to take leave, the general was condescending enough to hold out a white flabby hand for me to shake, and I retain to this hour the sensation of inert clamminess, which it imparted to mine.

Leaving La Barca at about 2 P.M. I made for Ocotlan—a small town situated between two arms of the Rio Grande, a little below the point where that river issues from the great lake of Chapala. Unfortunately, owing to a misunderstanding, we had taken the inland road, which only afforded here and there an unsatisfactory glimpse of the great lake, which is said, with very little truth I suspect, to rival the Swiss lakes in beauty.

We had expected to reach Ocotlan, especially by the short cut we had taken, before sunset, but our short cut turned out a very long one, for an hour after nightfall we found ourselves still wandering about in the darkness, uncertain which way to turn. Antonio was quite at fault, and I of course utterly dependent upon him. Fortunately, however, in this extremity we stumbled upon some natives, who put us on the right road, and after a somewhat perilous ride over very uneven ground, we at length espied the lights of Ocotlan, and effected a safe passage across the long narrow bridge, looking fearfully down upon the black mysterious river. Crossing bridges in a country like Mexico, in the pitch dark, is an amusement exciting enough in its way, for you never feel sure that the bridge will not leave off in the middle, and you may reckon with tolerable certainty on finding more than one yawning gap.

Just outside the little town of Ocotlan, stands the huge establishment of the brothers Castellanos, the wealthiest people in the place, for whom I carried a letter of introduction. Riding into the spacious court-yard, I left Antonio in charge of the horses; and went in search of the brothers, and soon discovered one of them serving his customers in the *tienda*. This gentleman received me with great politeness, and had a room prepared for me at once,

After a somewhat restless night, during which my slumbers were much disturbed by the movements of a dog which had been accidentally shut into my room, I rose an hour before dawn to be in time for the diligence, which passed that way *en route* for Guadalajara. For I had arranged overnight with Don Pedro—one of the brothers Castellanos—to accompany him in the diligence to Guadalajara, while his servants were to lead my horse, along with several which their masters were sending to their own house in Guadalajara. In accordance with this arrangement, I had dismissed the faithful Antonio, with whose services I could now fairly dispense.

Soon after 6 A.M. a light covered van, drawn by six jingling mules, rolled up to the door, where Don Pedro and I stood awaiting its arrival. As the vehicle was quite empty, I supposed that we were destined to have the interior all to ourselves, until a lady, who turned out to be Don Pedro's sister, appeared upon the scene, and seated herself on the back seat.

Inasmuch as you can hardly travel in a Mexican diligence for five minutes together without coming into violent contact with some portion of your neighbour's person, the conversation begins of itself with apologies for these involuntary concussions. When you have given your neighbours several good digs in the ribs, and in return received their heads several times in your stomach, you seem already to know a good deal about your fellow travelers, and conversation is thus rendered comparatively easy.

Hall, William Henry Bullock. 1866 *Across Mexico in 1864-5.*

27

Request to drain part of the lake
1867
Ignacio E. Castellanos

The Castellanos family was one of wealthiest land-owning families on the north side of the lake, and probably the richest family in Ocotlán. Their estates included much of the shore between Ocotlán and Jamay, an area known as the Ribera Castellanos in the latter part of the 19th century. To the east, José Francisco Velarde, "the Golden Ass", had amassed a similarly large estate prior to his execution in 1867.

Ignacio Castellanos inherited the family property on the death of his father, Pedro Castellanos, sometime in the middle of the 19th century. The family seat, complete with stables, was a mansion located opposite the old parish cemetery, extending to the bank of the River Santiago. From there, Castellanos managed the affairs of several haciendas, including that of San Andrés, which was fortuitously little damaged in the massive 1847 earthquake.

Castellanos added a huge *mirador*, almost as high as the church tower, atop the family home, from where a spectacular view could be enjoyed, encompassing parts of his extensive land holdings, the River Zula, and the "Castellanos" bridge, used by everyone entering and leaving Ocotlán from the east.

After Castellanos married Esther Tapia Ruíz (see chapter 29) from the neighboring state of Michoacán, the couple divided their time between their country home in Ocotlán and a city residence in Guadalajara.

Following Mexico's independence, life in the Lake Chapala region had been relatively unaffected by major demographic or political crises. The cholera epidemic of 1833 took its toll, but appears to have hit the city of Guadalajara much harder than the lakeshore villages. Village life continued through the uneasy period when Mexico was disputing its northern territory with the U.S.. Even the Pastry War against France

*in 1838 and the U.S. invasion of Mexico (1846-1848) had no obvious or
immediate repercussions in the Chapala region.*

*As Mexico's economy grew, so did serious suggestions that perhaps
the lake could play a larger part in regional and national life. In 1842, for
instance, Mariano Otero proposed not only a canal to allow navigation
between Chapala and Guadalajara, but also the draining of part of the lake
for agriculture. The plan came to nothing, but was only the first of several
similar proposals made during the next seventy years.*

*In a letter to the Development Ministry dated August 27, 1867, Ignacio
Castellanos states his case for being allowed to drain a large part of the
lake:*

I, Ignacio E. Castellanos, resident of Ocotlán, in the state of Jalisco,
do, with all due respect, declare to the municipality of Ixtlán, in the department of Zamora in the state of Michoacán, that I, together with my
co-inheritors, possess a country estate called "Cumuato", which is adjacent
to the great lake of Chapala, as are some other properties of mine called
the Islands of the Mouth of the River, Magdalena and Cajetillas. The Lerma River which gathers various tributaries in its course and which rises
powerfully in the rainy season has its mouth in the property, and spreads
over a considerable area within the valley limits.

Very rare is the year when the lands on the shores of Lake Chapala
repay the hard work of the farmer who fights unceasingly to prevent
the flooding of the river and the rising of the lake which almost always
devours his efforts.

Immense are the expenses demanded by the construction of barricades
and parapets, which, with few exceptions, yield to the power of that
element, which, everywhere, brings life to the fields, and which, in the
valleys adjoining the lake, consumes great fortunes annually, depriving
the nation of very large profits.

Up to now, the methods that have been tried to harvest large fields and
abundant pasture lands have proved useless. The experts who have been
consulted believe, with good reason, that until the main river is drained,
an ample and efficient channel opened for the same river, and the mass of
rock at the Poncitlán waterfall is destroyed, all these efforts over a length
of at least eight leagues, we will remain victims of the floods which in
past years have carried away our crops, destroyed the houses and caused
large losses of livestock.

The importance of this project is that it would bring immense benefits,
not only to the Department of Zamora and to the Canton of La Barca,
but to the entire Republic, which is interested in developing agriculture,
encouraging an increase in this activity which has always protected peoples

and governments. As this project requires a very large expenditure, it cannot be done by one owner alone in benefit of the surrounding owners and villages. It needs all those interested to cooperate to overcome the common peril and it needs, moreover, that the person who undertakes such an important enterprise with his own funds gets from it compensation for his expense and efforts, given that in attempting such an important measure he saves other people's property and does the country a service.

The idea of this great project of known public worth is not a new one; actually, my late father, Mr. Pedro Castellanos, studied it with success and recommended it to his children, for the future of their farms, and the improvement of the country's agriculture....

For these reasons, I ask the Ministry, by means of this petition, to consider granting the following:

First. Exclusive privileges to drain Lake Chapala, by dredging the Santiago River, opening an ample and efficient channel, and destroying the mass of rock at the Poncitlán waterfall.

Second. That my costs and labor be compensated for by the new land left dry on the shores of Lake Chapala.

Third. That the beneficiaries of this work be obliged to pay me, in accord with the judgement of experts, that part of the expense that proportionately corresponds to them according to the benefits received.

Fourth. That I am given a reasonable time period in which to complete the work, whether this is done by me personally or by an association which serves my interests and circumstances.

The Ministry accepted the request for consideration but, prior to making a decision, the various government departments involved sought the opinions of the communities on the shores of Lake Chapala.

Castellanos, Ignacio.1867 *Request to drain part of the lake.*

28

The opposition of local villagers
1868
Anonymous villagers

The response by Chapala, Ajijic and San Antonio Tlayacapan was to reject it:

1. Because a consequence of the draining would be that the waters would retreat to a great distance from the actual shores and deprive the shoreline villages from using them

2. Because fishing, the main activity of these villages, would collapse completely, causing their ruin

3. Because they would be deprived of the benefit of the irrigation they do using the water of the lake

4. Because the benefit, if there was any, of drainage would be for Mr. Castellanos and not for the majority.

The reply from Tuzcueca (1,500 inhabitants at the time) was longer and more detailed:

Cognizant of what was expressed on November 18 last [1867], this issue, which for certain insuperable motives to the contrary, could not naturally be resolved; **we that know our village**, as well as the others around the circumference of the great Lake Chapala, its civic and natural standing, its condition, the gains, or disadvantages, that could result if this planned work is carried out, when we see the benefits bestowed by Nature that these villages enjoy; we say that in relation to the petition being considered, **We cannot agree** that a concession be given for the draining of Lake Chapala, on account of the fact that all the villages around it depend on it, as much for cultivating their vegetable gardens, as for the activity of fishing, from which not only poor families derive a living; it even provides for exclusive trading in the market of the capital of the State every Friday in the year, and on fish days, as well as for that taken to Aguascalientes, Zacatecas, San Luis Potosi, etc.

The natural vegetation that surrounds it, its vegetable gardens of various kinds of fruits and vegetables, its crystalline waters, like the sand on some of its shores, its diverse types of fish, varied birds, and everything it possesses, display a grandness, beauty, elegance and loveliness to the eye of the spectator, like an attractive, exceedingly delightful place of recreation...

The draining (of the Lake) would evidently cause terrible damage, aridity and ruin to the settlements on its circumference.

And, from Jamay, came a document stating that the people were opposed to the proposal because of:

1. The dry season plantings of vegetable gardens that are done on the shore of the said lake,

2. The fishing for large fish by dragnet where the river enters and leaves the said lake, which is a water right belonging to the native people

3. A reedbed that exists at the entrance of the river in the East, from where all the natives get abundant supplies of what they need for roofing their houses, and bulrushes for making petates [rush mats], the manufacture of which supports most of the poor families, and likewise supplies the capital, Guadalajara, and all the villages within its jurisdiction; the fishing for big fish, catfish, whitefish, popocha and charal, supplies Guadalajara, Zacatecas, Toluca and part of Mexico, including the minor settlements in its center; the same occurs with the delicate cantaloupe, watermelons, cucumbers and green chiles which are grown in the rains from this municipality to the city of La Barca: draining the lake would leave these activities producing no result, and the land which today is fertile would become sterile: moreover the traffic of canoes and boats that bring to this town the supplies most needed by its inhabitants should also be taken into account; in addition to this, the islands that Mr. Castellanos claims as his property, with the name of Río Magdalena, belong to the indigenous community of this village; the reason for this gentleman possessing them is because, as a powerful wealthy man, he has waged war, and the unfortunate indigenous race has not been heard by any tribunal. It will justify its ownership by the documents that will

be shown to the President to receive the verdict that he, in his highest consideration, considers convenient and just, in order to end the discord between the two parties.

Given the extent of public opposition, Castellanos's request was subsequently rejected. This was the earliest formal proposal for draining a large part of the lake, but certainly not the last. Official permission was granted for an enormous area to be drained in 1906-8, with far-reaching economic and environmental impacts. Several other serious proposals have been made since that time to drain still more of the lake.

Anon.1868 *Colección de Acuerdos, Ordenes y Decretos sobre Tierras, Casas y Solares de los Indígenas, Bienes de Comunidades y Fundos Legales de los Pueblos del Estado de Jalisco.*

29

The romantic shores of Lake Chapala
1869
Esther Tapia de Castellanos

Esther Tapia de Castellanos (1842-1897), born in Morelia, Michoacán, became the wife of Ignacio Castellanos and wrote what is believed to be the first poem of any substance specifically about the lake.

Tapia de Castellanos and her husband had homes in both Guadalajara and Ocotlán (see chapter 27). Her very long Lake Chapala poem, inspired by her husband's absence on business, was entitled, *A orillas del lago de Chapala* (On the shores of Lake Chapala), and was finished on January 22, 1869. Shortly afterwards, the poem was sent by Mr. Vaca, a family friend from Zamora, to *Siglo XIX* in Mexico City. It is not known whether it was accepted at the time for publication but, a century later, both the poem and an accompanying letter were published in the January 1969 issue of *La Civilización*.

The letter describes Mrs. Tapia de Castellanos as living in Ocotlán, a "village located between two powerful rivers and comprised of a small number of homes". The hacienda occupied by Mr. Castellanos and his wife, has "a mirador on top, from where the view dominates Lake Chapala, home of aquatic birds and humble boats," and the cultivated fields of the San Andrés hacienda. Their section of the lake shoreline is often referred to as Ribera Castellanos in guide books dating from the latter years of the 19th century.

Tapia de Castellanos wrote several volumes of poetry, including *Flores silvestres* (Wild flowers), published in 1871, *Cánticos de los niños* (Songs of the children), and *Obras poéticas* (Poetic works), as well as several plays. In 1886, she was one of the co-founders of *La República Literaria,* a magazine of science, art and literature, published in Guadalajara, which rapidly became one of the best known publications in the country. The other co-founders were José López Portillo y Rojas and Manuel Álvarez del Castillo, one of whose relatives founded the *El Informador* daily in Guadalajara.

In the following fragments of A orillas del lago de Chapala, *Tapia de Castellanos describes the scenery, flora and fauna from a very romantic, idyllic point of view.*

On a tranquil afternoon
The sun advances to the west
leaving, as it departs, the clouds
tinted with gold and mother-of-pearl.
Its last rays gild
the clear water of the lake,
which seems, when it moves,
to be flecked with diamonds.
The light, sonorous waves
are teased into gentle undulations
making a tender murmur
that is only understood by the soul.

...

The willow bends its branches
As the warm waves kiss
and a perfumed breeze
jealously removes them.

Tapia de Castellanos, Esther. 1869 *A orillas del lago de Chapala.*

30

The journal of an English lady
1872
Rose Georgina Kingsley

Rose Georgina Kingsley (1845-1925) was the oldest child of the Rev. Charles Kingsley, the celebrated English clergyman and novelist, who contributed the prologue to her book *South by west or winter in the Rocky Mountains and spring in Mexico.*

Rose Kingsley had crossed the Atlantic to Colorado Springs in November 1871 to join her brother, Maurice, who was assistant treasurer of the company developing Colorado Springs. Even by 1872, there were less than 800 residents, so both Kingsleys were pioneer settlers. The founder of Colorado Springs, General William Jackson Palmer, a railway entrepreneur, also owned a newspaper *Out West* which published several columns and sketches by Rose Kingsley.

The Denver and Rio Grande train had been operating for only a week when Rose Kingsley boarded it en route to Colorado Springs. She quickly felt at home and rapidly made friends in the ever-changing community that she grew to love. She taught in the local school, begun by Palmer's wife, Queen, for a short while, but did not enjoy the experience. Little did she realize at that time that she would, in 1884, and with the help of Dr. Joseph Wood, later Headmaster of Harrow, found The Kingsley School, in Leamington Spa, England.

Rose Kingsley went on to write many more books, including *A History of French Art, 1100-1899* (1899) and *Roses and Rose Growing* (1908).

When General Palmer decided in 1872 to examine possible routes for a railway linking Texas to Manzanillo, Rose Kingsley was invited to join his wife Queen and General William Rosencrans on the trip. The group landed in Manzanillo and then headed inland to Colima, Guadalajara, Guanajuato, Querétaro and Mexico City.

In chapter XVII of South by west or winter in the Rocky Mountains and spring in Mexico, *Kingsley describes the route from Guadalajara past the northern shore of Lake Chapala on the way to Mexico City. Following a common convention of the time, she uses only initials to identify important people; several of the individuals referred to have been identified by historians. For instance, "Mrs. P." is Mrs Queen Palmer, and Mr. C. is Mr. Duncan Cameron.*

Kingsley's account of this route serves as an introduction to set the scene for so many other travelers, who would follow this exact same route from Guadalajara to Chapala in years to come. It is 1872...

April 13.— Guadalajara to Ocotlan.

At 6.15 A.M. we left hospitable Guadalajara, carrying away none but the pleasantest reminiscences of our stay of six days.

Pablo, a pleasant young fellow, who had been our *cochero* in Guadalajara, came with us as *mozo*, and was in a state of supreme delight at being armed with a Henry rifle and revolver. Mr. M. also came with us as far as La Barca.

The usual route from Guadalajara to the capital is by La Venta, Lagos, Leon, and Guanaguato; but for two reasons we chose the more southern route, past Lake Chapala and up the Rio Lerma. First, because the engineer's party from the north (of whom we had heard nothing as yet, which made us very anxious) must pass along that route, and so be able to give a report on it. Secondly, because we were told the Chapala route was shorter and better, if there can be anything "better" in one Mexican road than another. Certainly, after the first few miles it was bad enough—rough and stony, and in the softer places there were clouds of dust.

At San Pedro [Tlaquepaque] we stopped and got three men as escort, and at 9.30 came to San Antonio, a hacienda where we changed mules, and had breakfast in a hut by the roadside. The women in the hut, which was only made of sticks and thatch, gave us eggs, frijoles, tortillas, and *carne seca*, in *chilli colorado* sauce, which for hotness almost beat the *mole de guajalote* at Atenquique. But besides these native viands we got capital chocolate, made from some cakes we had brought with us. So, on the whole, we fared well.

At 12.15 we came to the summit of a small pass (4850 feet), and there before us lay a splendid valley, rich with golden wheat-fields, with a fine river flowing through it on our left to the north-west; and we knew we had struck the great central valley of Mexico, commonly known as the Valley of the Lerma.

This valley is one of the richest portions of the Republic. Its length, between Guadalajara and Queretaro, is about 230 miles, and its greatest width (between Leon and the mountains of Michoacán), 60 miles. About one-tenth of the available land in it is under cultivation. Wheat, maize, and beans grow freely without irrigation, yielding good crops year after year without the slightest pains being taken to improve the soil. With irrigation and better farming two crops might be obtained; and when a market for the produce, and easy means of transportation are supplied, this tract will become one of the most important wheat-growing districts of the world. The amount of wheat which could be raised in this valley alone has been variously estimated from 500,000 to 1,000,000 tons yearly, equal to or surpassing the whole yearly yield of California.

The river rises in the Lago de Lerma, near Toluca, outside the western rise of the Valley of Mexico; and from its source, till it flows into the eastern side of Lake Chapala at La Barca, is known as the Rio Lerma. It passes out of the northern side of Chapala at Ocotlan, and from thence to San Blas, where it falls into the Pacific, is called the Rio Grande de Santiago. North of Chapala the Santiago flows through a very deep cañon; and there are also two fine falls on it—one a horse-shoe fall; and another about twenty miles from Guadalajara, of which I saw a photograph, which the Guadalajarans consider only second to Niagara.

The valley, as we jolted along it, seemed one vast corn-field. High mountains lay on the north, and our road ran along a southern ridge which divided the valley from Lake Chapala. There was very little timber on the mountains, and in what little there was many fires were burning, for everything is as dry as tinder.

At 4.30 P.M. we left the hills; crossing a bridge over a branch of the Santiago, where the Indian women were filling their water-jars and swimming about in the water like a shoal of fish; and reached Ocotlan, a large hacienda two miles from Lake Chapala. [Ribera Castellanos]

We stopped here, intending only to get a relay and go on the last stage to La Barca: but Mrs. P. was ill, so we decided upon staying there for the night. The owner in Guadalajara had given our party letters to his Administrador, so we were most kindly received, and rooms instantly prepared for us. The hacienda was the prettiest we had seen. The center of the patio was filled with a garden of the loveliest flowers and shrubs imaginable; roses, carnations, plumbago, oleanders, oranges, and bananas growing together in wild luxuriance; and on one side was a high tower, with shaky steps and shakier ladders leading to the top, up which I followed the rest, after seeing to our invalid, and was rewarded by a glorious view.

North and west were the mountains, with the forest fires flickering up and down their slopes. South we got a glimpse of the lake, beyond a rich flat with various branches of the river winding down round the little town.

East stretched away a valley through endless hills. A thunderstorm was raging over the mountains of Michoacán, on the further side of the lake. The sun was setting behind the mountains we had passed, in a perfect glory of crimson and gold; and over our heads, so close we stretched our hands to catch them, flew flocks of black rice-birds, thousands upon thousands, in a ceaseless stream, to the eastward....

The Administrador came in to supper, and gave us the latest *"nove-dades,"* which here means robber stories. The Pronunciados have been giving him a good deal of trouble lately. About two weeks ago they came down on the hacienda, made a levy of thirty dollars; and as he did not pay fast enough, they carried off his corn and sold it....

After supper came a delicious lazy lounge in the corridor while the gentlemen smoked, with the air full of the scent of roses and orange-blossom, and then I went off to my room in intense heavy heat, and tried to sleep on a bed which almost rivalled those at San Marcos for hardness.

April 14.—Ocotlan, 4875 feet, to Piedad, 5400 feet.

At 6.15 A.M. we started, with the Administrador and four of his men, well armed and mounted, as escort. In about two miles, after crossing various bridges, we struck the lake (its level is 4850), and drove eastward along its shore for nearly two hours. Here it is between twenty and thirty miles wide, and on the further side the mountains of Michoacán rise in grand rugged masses to a considerable height. Between the water and the road runs a narrow stony strip, which the Indians have irrigated thoroughly, and where they raise fine crops of chilli, tomatoes, sweet potatoes, and cucumbers.

At 7.30 we passed Tamein, [Jamay] a town of 3000 inhabitants, who get their living chiefly by fishing and gardening; raising, besides cattle, corn and wheat.

Soon after this we turned away from the lake, which here makes a southerly bend; cut off a corner of some miles; and reached La Barca, on the Rio Lerma, just above where it flows into the lake, at 9.30.

It was market-day, and the Plaza was densely crowded with a noisy mass of buyers and sellers. We stayed there for breakfast. The food was very good at a dirty little *Fonda* (restaurant) close to the stage-office; all the walls of which were decorated with little bits of Guadalajara pottery, hung in patterns round some larger bowl or plate. We heard here of a most fortunate escape we had had the night before. When we stopped at Ocotlan, a courier from a house of business in Guadalajara, who had ridden beside us all day, went on, thinking we had only halted to change mules. A few miles on he fell into an ambush of robbers, who robbed him; beat him within an inch of his life; and asked where the stage was. He declared it was but three or four miles behind. "Well," they said, "we will keep you here; and if it doesn't come we will kill you." In the night, however, he got to his horse, and managed to escape to La Barca; where some of our party heard his story....

We walked down to the river through the Plaza, laying in on our way a good store of splendid water-melons, and crossed in one of the dug-outs to the further bank, where the stage was in readiness. The river level was 4900 feet, a rise of fifty feet from Ocotlan.

Mr. M. left us here, to our great regret, to return to Colima; going back across the lake by a little steamer belonging to Mr. C., an enterprising American, who runs it once a week from Chapala, at the western end, to La Barca. Just across the lake at this point is La Palma or Tequiqui, a place to which great part of the goods for the Western States are brought by a mule route from the city of Mexico *via* Morelia.

Bidding farewell to Mr. M. we started from the river bank at 12.30, and in half an hour reached the Hacienda de Buena Vista, where we stopped for an escort. This hacienda stands on a little rise above the river; and the *casa* is really a very fine building, with deep portales, fresco-painted walls, and a high and picturesque bell-tower rising at one end. It occupies one side of the Plaza, which is in the center of a town of 5000 inhabitants, all belonging to the estate.

This is the same hacienda, belonging to General Velarde, where W. H. Bullock Hall stayed a few years earlier. The frescos ("glaring frescos in the worst possible taste and style" in the words of Bullock) are still there.

Kingsley, Rose Georgina. 1874 *South by west or winter in the Rocky Mountains and spring in Mexico.*

31

A fanciful sketch of Lake Chapala
1867-1877
Felix Leopold Oswald

Felix Leopold Oswald (1845-1906) was born in Belgium and became a physician before turning his attention to natural history. He traveled extensively, all over the globe, and was a prolific writer. *Summerland Sketches* seems to have been Oswald's first full-length work. Many, if not all of the chapters, were first published in *Lippincott's Magazine*. Shortly after *Summerland Sketches* was published, Oswald moved to Polk County, Tennessee.

Summerland Sketches *purports to tell the story of explorations over a period of eight years. In the introduction, the author writes that:*

This collection of *Summerland Sketches* is therefore neither a record of a pilgrimage to the shrines and cathedrals of Spanish America, nor a bid for the patronage of Southwestern land-agencies, but rather a guide-book to one of the few remaining regions of earth that may give us an idea of the tree-land eastward in Eden which the Creator intended for the abode of mankind. In the terrace-lands of Western Colima and Oaxaca, near the head-waters of the Río Lerma and the mountain lakes of Jalisco, and in the lonely highlands of Vera Paz, we may yet see forests that have never been desecrated by an axe, and free fellow-creatures which have not yet learned to flee from man as from a fiend.

Let us make the best of that last chance, for the time may be near when princes and sages shall envy those who have managed to get a glimpse of Paradise before the gates are closed forever.

Garold Cole, in his descriptive bibliography of American travelers to Mexico, wrote that "because Oswald was a doctor and naturalist, his observations on the healthfulness of the region and on the flora and fauna should be authoritative."

Unfortunately, Oswald's descriptions, especially those in the chapter entitled "The Lake-Region of Jalisco", appear to be a pastiche of half-remembered, or invented experiences. I take the liberty of including some brief extracts from Summerland Sketches *here if only to show those familiar with the region today just how fanciful Oswald's accounts are. However, it should be remembered that at the time they were written, they were well received by an American public willing to devour almost anything, real or imaginary, about its southern neighbor.*

Men in general are unacquainted with the fairest regions of their world. I am almost sure that there are towns of ten thousand inhabitants in the United States, and much larger cities in Western Europe, where it would be impossible to find one man who ever in his life heard even the name of Lake Chapala, while every other village schoolmaster in Europe and North America could write a treatise on Lake Leman or Loch Lomond.... Yet this fair *lacus incognitus* is ten times as large as all the lakes of Northern Italy taken together, and forty times larger than the entire canton of Geneva,—contains different islands whose surface area exceeds that of the Isle of Wight, and one island with *two secondary lakes* as big as Loch Lomond and Loch Katrine!

......

The shores of Lake Chapala had not borrowed their enchantment from the distance of the view. Sturdy hemlocks and bignonia trees crowd the impertinent underbrush out of the way, forming natural avenues along the beach, which slopes so gradually that the water line is almost everywhere accessible. The water is steel blue and wonderfully transparent, in spite of the algae and pond weeds that weave their tangled tendrils wherever the bottom is a little less obdurate. From the racks of an open wagon we could see the mountain forests of the opposite shore glittering with a moist and tremulous light and a thousand hues,—all possible shades, variations, and combinations of green and blue, darkened here and there by the gloom of a mountain gorge or the floating shadow of a cloud. But on the eastern shore the sierra presents a mural front to the lake, and discharges its drainage in the form of dripping springs and cascades, tiny rivulets mostly, except at the northeastern extremity of a triangular bay, where the falls of the Rio Blanco come down with a thunder that can be heard and felt for leagues around. A mile below the falls a few jagged rocks rise from the water, forming the southern outposts of the motley archipelago of cliffs and islands that extends along the eastern shore for at least sixty English miles. A meadow of pond reeds near one of the mid lake islands seemed to be a rendezvous for all possible kinds of waterfowl. Moor hens, surf ducks, flamingoes, a long legged bird that looked like a stork, but might be a species of white heron, coots, and black divers, arrived and departed from and in all directions; and a little apart from the rest a flock of *gansas*, or swamp geese, disported themselves in the open water.

LAKE CHAPALA.

This illustration of Lake Chapala (from page 84 of Summerland Sketches) *would do justice to many an Alpine lake, but bears no resemblance whatsoever to the real lake then or now.*

Oswald, Felix Leopold. 1880 *Summerland Sketches.*

32

The first English-language guide book
1886
Alfred Ronald Conkling

Appletons' Guide to Mexico, including a chapter on Guatemala and an English-Mexican vocabulary; with a railway map and illustrations, though it lacked an index, was a general travel guide, with particular reference to railways. It was published in 1886, shortly before the completion of the Mexican Central Railway, and was one of the earliest guides to attempt a nationwide coverage. Tourists were advised to "carry soap and matches", and encouraged to visit in the rainy season: "if the tourist wishes to avoid the clouds of dust that rise on the great plateau of Mexico, he should travel in the rainy season. i.e. June to September."

The guide was penned by Alfred Ronald Conkling (1850-1917), the grandson of Alfred Conkling (1789-1874), a lawyer, writer, U.S. Congressman, and Minister to Mexico (1852-1853). The younger Conkling, a lawyer, geologist and author, was a graduate of Sheffield Scientific School at Yale.

Appletons' Guide to Mexico *was greatly praised as meeting a "long-felt want", with one contemporary reviewer congratulating the author for being so "heroically self-sacrificing... in finding out the truth about the discomforts of the poor hotels and poorer fare".*

The entry on Chapala is regrettably brief:

An excursion may be made to the Lake of *Chapala*, about 40 miles distant. This lake is the largest in Mexico, having an area of 415 square miles. There are several islands in it, on one of which ruins have been found. A small American steamboat makes a tour round the lake daily. The depth of Lake Chapala has not yet been ascertained.

Conkling, Alfred Ronald. 1886 *Appletons' Guide to Mexico.*

33

The marshes and wildlife of the eastern lakeshore
1886: Ernst von Hesse-Wartegg

Ernst von Hesse Wartegg was born in Vienna, Austria, on February 21, 1854, and died in Triebschen, Switzerland, in 1918. He began traveling at age 20, and quickly became fascinated by new places and experiences. His enthusiastic accounts of unlikely locations were very well known in Europe by the end of the 19th century.

His travel accounts include books about Venezuela (1887), Mexico (1890), Korea (1894), Tunisia (1895), China and Japan (1897), Siam (now Thailand) (1899), India (1906), the United States (1908) and the Balkans (1917). In addition, he had written works about insects, wood-working and the possible construction of a tunnel linking England to France.

Today, he is probably most remembered for his early account of *Travels on the Lower Mississippi, 1879 1880: A Memoir*, but his work on Mexico, "Mexico, its land and people", was actually more popular during his lifetime. In his introduction, the author writes, "May this book not only complete the knowledge of today's Mexico but also become a guide for travelers in the most beautiful and most interesting country of the New World." Hesse-Wartegg was opposed to language barriers and had a healthy distrust of the expansionist policies of colonial powers.

Hesse-Wartegg's book was based on two trips to Mexico, the first in 1884 and the second in 1886. He set out to describe the whole realm of the Aztecs from the Rio Grande to the Yucatan, and gave credit to the Americans for making this possible, through the development of railroads, which were considerably faster, and safer, than horseback. He claims to have been among the first passengers on some stretches of the railway system, and to have come to know "old" Mexico before the "shiny Yankeegloss" changed it for ever.

Writing at a time when chronicling the difficulties of travel still played an important role in most travel accounts, Hesse-Wartegg was more interested in writing about his interactions with local people than about describing the landscapes of the regions he was traveling through. Even so, this extract offers a vivid description of Lake Chapala, as he encountered it in 1886, while traveling from Uruapan to Guadalajara, by horse and stagecoach (diligence).

It was a pleasure to find tolerable lodging [in Zamora] after the exertions of the last days, so that the next morning we felt invigorated enough to continue our ride to La Barca, situated close to Lake Chapala. Now, we could have used the diligence from Morelia, but, as we had our horses, we decided to enter the state of Jalisco as genuine caballeros in the local manner. Zamora was already behind us when the clock of the big church on the plaza struck four hours, for we faced a long day's journey. Instead of following the long northward Guadalajara route to reach La Barca by land, we took the less comfortable westward route toward the town of Jiquilpan, on Lake Chapala, and planned to travel the balance of the route to La Barca by boat, across the lake. In Zamora, the people had shaken their heads when they heard of our plan. Why take a detour of six or seven leagues and then go by boat, when you have your own horses available? The good Zamoranos found it difficult to understand that one might travel for any other reason than on urgent business; however, when we told them that we wished to see and to describe Lake Chapala, we grew in their estimation and a respectable looking man who seemed to be enjoying a position of great authority even gave us a letter of recommendation to the "authorities" of Jiquilpan. We were assured that we would not have to worry about robbers since the Indios in this area were good-natured and hospitable. Nevertheless, we took more provisions along than previously; it appeared that with our plans we might be heading for an adventure.

During the first four hours we travelled across an unusually fertile, richly cultivated plain that was closed in by wooded heights to the north hiding the lakebed of Chapala from us on the other side of the slope. The road led us across the mountains and around noon, since we did not see any hacienda or rancho anywhere, we simply rested and took our lunch in the shade of a mighty spruce tree. [there is no genuine spruce in this region; this was most likely a fir] When we had reached the crest of the mountain pass about three in the afternoon we spotted, in the distance, the broad, blue surface of the lake and saw an extensive green plain spread out before us; the plain is possibly a former lake bottom. We proceeded rapidly downwards and had reached Jiquilpan around five in the afternoon, much sooner than we had expected. Foreigners in Jiquilpan!

All of the residents streamed into the small town when we, the Caucasian horsemen, rode through the village to the plaza and dismounted in front of the only fonda of Jiquilpan. We were very tired. The "authorities" to whom our letter was directed, consisted of a dignified old man who advised us against continuing to La Barca the same day because the distance was approximately six leagues and that we would be surprised by nightfall. In addition, it would take at least two hours to negotiate the terms of the crossing with the boatman. Incidentally, Jiquilpan is shown on the map as being located on the shore of the lake, but it is actually a league off shore. We were bone-tired and quite happy to accept the old man's advice, and decided to stay overnight in Jiquilpan.

It was Sunday which was celebrated by a cockfight on the plaza which we attended in the company of the "authorities". Fortunately, the owner of the boat whom the alcalde was going to recommend to us was also among the spectators. Soon, the negotiations were completed. We agreed that he would take us, at a price of six pesos, to La Barca, or actually to the landing spot located about half a league away from La Barca. La Barca is not on the lakeshore, but on the Rio Lerma, east of it. The horses were to be taken by a servant around the eastern shore to La Barca where we would find them. A few minutes after we had closed the deal with the boatman at the arena of the cockfight, he returned and asked us to advance half the fee for transporting us. When we refused, he told us that he had just lost all of his money in a bet and would be unable to ferry us unless we prepaid; he needed to make some purchases before the crossing. Now we refused even more strongly to give him a single *real*, fearing that he might now also lose our money owing to an unfortunate bet.

We were already in bed, when there was a knock at the door. The boatman wanted to know if our arrangements were still on and told us that he would be expecting us at the lakeshore at 4 a.m. the next morning. We let him know that we expected him to pick us up. We did not want to burn our bridges, i.e send the horses away to La Barca and possibly find ourselves stranded at Jiquilpan. He came at 5.30 instead of 4 a.m. and then it took two more hours before we found ourselves in a small open sailboat, manned by two Indian boatmen, which took us across the beautiful wide lake. We were able to see only a fairly small part of the lake because the rocky peninsula, La Palma, juts out several kilometers into the lake west of Jiquilpan on the southern shore and divides it into two unequal halves. The bay in front of us, which is surrounded to the north and south by wooded hills, reminded us much of Lake Patzcuaro, and may be about the same size. Towards the east the heights yield to a swampy, level, reed covered tract of country that stretches for many kilometers along the lake, far beyond La Barca. This is where innumerable water birds, wild ducks, geese and strange flamingo-like herons reside. These herons are often mistaken for flamingoes because of their rose-red plumage. During the Pre-French period, I myself had hunted many flamingoes on the Tunisian lakes and did not let myself be deceived by the appearance of these herons. When, after one hour, we had reached the middle of the labyrinth of islands that cover the center of the Bay of Jiquilpan, the magnificent fauna of this beautiful lake became even more striking. We were very unhappy that our travel revolvers were the only guns we possessed. As we approached, countless birds rose in a mass from each island; there were different varieties of ducks, snipes, storks etc. while others such as the pure white herons and the dignified culeberos (snake fishers) remained quietly in the reeds, paying no attention at all to us. What a paradise for hunting is this big lake, what a research opportunity for the naturalist who has time to spend a few months or even weeks here! The boatmen assured us that the lake was full of small alligators, probably similar to the *babas* [name used in Colombia and Venezuela] of the South American lakes. Unfortunately, we did not get a good sighting of an alligator, though here and there the heads of those worst enemies of fish bobbed above the blinding mirror of the water surface, only to disappear quickly again.

Hesse-Wartegg, Ernst von. 1890 *Mexiko, Land und Leute.*

Five years after Hesse-Wartegg visited the lake, the Chapala Shooting Club was formed in 1891 to purchase land adjacent to Lake Chapala on the Guadalajara branch of the Central Railway, for the purposes of shooting duck, snipe and geese. The 25 founder members included Thomás Braniff, whose family would later own the distinctive residence near the church in Chapala, which today houses the Cazadores restaurant.

34

Agriculture, trade, potential summer resort
1888
Mariano Bárcena

Born on July 22, 1842, in Ameca, Jalisco, Mariano Bárcena studied geology, botany and chemistry in the National Preparatory School in Mexico City, before becoming an engineer in 1871. He had a distinguished scientific career, making contributions to several subjects, including botany, geology, paleontology and cartography.

In 1876, he represented Mexico at the Philadelphia World Fair, and he represented his country again at the New Orleans exhibition in 1885. On the death of Ramón Corona, he served briefly as Governor of Jalisco, from November 1889 until October of the following year.

Bárcena recognised the importance of preserving Mexico's lakes: "In a country with a scarcity of water and territory as large as Mexico's, we should be trying to create lakes, rather than destroy them." He is perhaps best remembered today as the founder of the National Meteorological and Astronomical Observatory in 1877. He oversaw its move to a permanent home in Tacubaya, Mexico City, and remained its director until his death in 1899.

Bárcena's Statistical Essay on the State of Jalisco *is a systematic account, including detailed descriptions of agriculture and crops of potential importance. The author places considerable importance on the state's agricultural potential, but also mentions mineral possibilities. He foresaw a bright future for tourism in Chapala, and discusses the value of a railway link to the main line serving Guadalajara (inaugurated in 1888, the year his book was first published).*

The lake we are discussing is already the site of some commercial traffic between various parts of Jalisco and Michoacán. This trade is carried by means of a mid-sized steamboat and a multitude of canoes that ply the waters in all directions. The steamboat "Libertad" makes regular weekly trips between the city of La Barca and Chapala, touching various points in Jalisco and Michoacán, and taking passengers and varied goods, like livestock, wood, grain, sugar, etc.; the canoes carry similar cargoes, as well as fresh and salted fish. It is to be hoped that an increase in traffic will be seen with time, and even be helped by canals connected with the Lake.

Another thing worth mentioning in the region we are discussing is the existence of large deposits of sand composed of hyaline quartz which are found on the northern shores and which could be used in the manufacture of glass and crystal; rash attempts previously made in this regard, without the elements necessary for a successful business, have rapidly failed.

Lastly, we predict a prosperous future, in a time not too far away, for the settlement of Chapala, which spreads along the northern shore of the lake, at a distance of about 50 kilometers from Guadalajara. When the proposed railroad linking the state capital with the port is carried out, a town will grow there, or, better said, the small already existing one there will increase in size, filling with country homes, parks and gardens, in a similar way to some of the settlements in Switzerland, the United States and other countries that lie on the shores of lakes, affording all the beauty and attractions that are associated only with such locations. Chapala will, without doubt, become the summer resort for Guadalajara, and perhaps for all the country's inland areas.

Bárcena includes a veritable catalogue of every city, town, village and hamlet of the state, each entry following a set pattern, and based on information from a network of local informants.

For example, the entry on Ajijic reads:

Village of the 1st Cantón. The land is mixed in kind and appearance. Rains are moderate from June to October. Frosts are rare. Corn and beans are cultivated; they are sown in May and harvested in October. Chickpeas, watermelon and cantaloupe are planted in December and harvested in March. Rarely are crops lost through a lack or an excess of water. The fruit trees grown, on a small scale, are: peaches, quince, pomegranates, oranges, mangos and tunas. The commonest wild plants are: chaste tree, morning-glory, guamúchil, mesquite, kidneywood, madrone and sunflower. Skimpy woodlands, comprised of oaks and tepehuaje. Water comes from the lake, and from a permanent spring of little importance.

Chapala and Jocotepec have a much greater variety of crops, including chiles, onions, wheat, tobacco, bananas, coconuts, mamey, black zapote, mangos, chirimoyas, limes and guavas.

In San Luis Soyatlán, tobacco is also mentioned, along with sugarcane.

The rich, fertile soil around Tizapán el Alto produced corn, beans, wheat, barley, potatoes, camote, jícama, chiles, watermelons, cantaloupes, sugarcane, vegetables, coffee and a long list of fruit trees.

Elsewhere, Bárcena includes a detailed description of agave-growing, and of the processes used to make tequila.

No mention is made, in his otherwise seemingly comprehensive listing of local flora, of either the water hyacinth or marijuana. The former was probably not present at that time; it is thought to have been introduced to the Lerma river and Lake Chapala at about the turn of the century. The latter, however, would have been present, but goes unremarked.

The population figures given in the text (all for 1885) are Chapala 5,197; Jocotepec 10,913; La Barca 21,533; Ocotlán 7'033; Jamay 3,374; Tizapán 6,919.

Bárcena, Mariano 1888 *Ensayo estadístico del Estado de Jalisco.*

35

On board a paddle-steamer
1883-1889
"A. Gringo"

"A Gringo", an English traveler about whom very little is known, arrived in Mexico in 1883. "A Gringo" is believed to be the pen name of Charles Manwell St Hill, born in Trinidad in 1849, who died in Mexico between 1891 and 1901. In the preface, he states that "my object is simply to give a plain account of several years experience in the country, to show its recent progress and to enable the reader to judge the future." He also writes that "prolonged periods of travel over the greater part of its territory, by rail, stagecoach and steamer, on horseback and in canoes have afforded me exceptional facilities for studying the country and all classes of the people."

One reviewer described this as an "interesting little book descriptive of life and travel in Mexico from 1883 until a recent date". He continued "We congratulate the author on the felicitous manner in which he has performed his task" in presenting the "Mexico of today" to us. "His work is a pleasantly written handbook, its only defect is the want of a map, and this is really unpardonable."

"A. Gringo" was an observant and enthusiastic visitor. He even saw fit to remark on the ready availability of lottery tickets "at every corner" with prizes from one to 100,000 dollars". His acceptance of lottery tickets is in sharp contrast to the stance that Terry later felt obliged to adopt in the first edition of his famous handbook, when he wrote that, "mention of lotteries has been omitted intentionally because of the circulation of the Handbook in the United States–where anything in the nature of an advertisement of these games of chance is forbidden". (Terry, 1909, p iv)

"A. Gringo"'s visit to Chapala definitely took place prior to 1889, though he did not write about it until later.

Taking a carriage, which ran weekly between Guadalajara and Chapala, a town on the border of the lake of that name, I set forth one morning, and, after climbing a hill, from which a grand view of the city and surrounding countryside was obtained, I reached Chapala.

Chapala lies at the foot of a hill, overlooking the lake, the waters of which lapped the little garden of the inn where I put up. After a supper, with the agreeable addition of a bottle of lager beer, I spent the evening chatting with the pleasant old people who kept the inn, and enjoying the still night as I watched the moonbeams playing on the lake, on which loomed the black shape of the paddle steamer that was to take me tomorrow across its waters.

It was a wonderful old tub, evidently built in the days when shipbuilding was in its infancy, judging from its uncouth shape and old timbers, that creaked at every movement of the paddles. Our voyage took in several villages round the lake. At each stopping place we would land on the little mud jetties to suck a piece of sugar-cane or quaff a festive glass of tequila. At one of the villages a sad accident has since occurred; the crazy old steamer toppled over with her living freight of over two hundred passengers just as she reached the landing-stage, nearly all being drowned.

One heroic American, employed on the Central Railroad, who was on board at the time, succeeded in saving the lives of sixteen by his pluck and great swimming powers. [see "Steamboats on Lake Chapala" box]

At one place the captain called my attention to a spot where the water was bubbling, and told me that at the bottom of the lake there was a petroleum well. Although efforts had been made to utilize it, they had hitherto been unsuccessful.

In the evening we reached our destination, La Barca, where I engaged a guide, and horses to carry me to the camp, just outside the town of La Piedad, from which the Construction train was to start at 4 p.m. the next day.

"A. Gringo." 1892 *Through The Land of the Aztecs
Or Life and Travel In Mexico.*

Steamboats on Lake Chapala

In 1868, the Compañía de Navegación por Vapor en el Lago de Chapala (Lake Chapala Steamboat Company) was formed and the paddle steamer *Libertad* (Freedom) was launched on the lake. The company's director was Mr. Duncan Cameron, referred to in Rose Kingsley's write-up of her 1872 visit. *Libertad* offered regular sailings, leaving Chapala at 6.00 a.m. on Saturdays for La Barca, Ocotlán and Jamay. It returned on Monday, leaving in the evening. On Wednesdays, it sailed to Tuxcueca, Tizapán and La Palma, returning the following day.

Libertad remained in service for many years, as evidenced by the brief reference in Bárcena (1888) and the evocative short description by "A. Gringo" of a trip aboard the steamer, and of its eventual tragic demise. On Sunday March 24, 1889, *Libertad* capsized at Ocotlán, only six meters from shore; 28 people were drowned. The American referred to by "A. Gringo" was the Railway Superintendent, Mr. C.E. Halbert. The state government later decorated several people for saving lives. In the U.S., medals for bravery were awarded to five "gallant Americans"—C. E. Halbert, C. E. Shackford, L. Rosenthal, H. R. Cornforth and Joseph H. Feehan.

The following year, *Libertad* was refloated, and renamed *Ramón Corona*, for the state governor. In November 1889, Ramón Corona was assassinated. The boat was taken to Lake Pátzcuaro and renamed *Don Vasco*.

A character in the story by Frances Fisher (1893) says that *Libertad* was brought by an enterprising Scotsman more than thirty years ago from California to San Blas, and thence over the mountains here.

Besides mentioning *Libertad,* Rogers (1893) also describes another vessel: "The steamer "Chapala" is a flat bottom stern wheel boat, very like those that are common on the shallow rivers of the West; the only boats adapted to shoal water service. Everything about the steamer appears new, but one of the things not new on the "Chapala" is Juan Perez, the pilot. He is not necessarily old, but he is a veteran in service."

Gibbon (1893) describes the *Chapala* as 80 feet in length by 20 wide, drawing only three feet of water, and used for both passengers and cargo. Gibbon also took a trip on the *San Francisco*, which appears to have been usually used only for regular daily cargo voyages between Ocotlán, La Barca and Tizapán. It is possible that Romero's trip in 1897 was also aboard the *Chapala*.

Not everyone enjoyed their trip on the lake. Kirkham (1909) experienced the full force of a storm, and Dollero (1911) found himself uncomfortably close to a waterspout while on the deck of the *Raúl* in 1907.

36

Chapala? Sí, señor!
1892
Thomas L. Rogers

L *ittle is known of the life and works of Thomas L. Rogers, the American author of* Mexico? Sí, señor. *His book on Mexico was written for the Mexican Central Railway. It provides an accessible account of all the places and regions that the then-expanding railway network was opening up for travelers.*

The Mexican Central Railway was the principal railway of the Republic, with 1,846 miles of line, and the only standard gauge line connecting Mexico City and the U.S. The book covers all the network: the main route from Ciudad Juarez to Mexico City, together with the major branch lines to Tampico and Guadalajara via Irapuato. One map shows the proposed extension of the Guadalajara branch to San Blas on the Pacific coast.

Rogers provides several examples of the price of first class rail fares. For instance, El Paso to Mexico City return (2450 miles) cost 50 dollars; Chicago to Mexico City return (5700 miles) was 88.60 dollars; even New York or Boston to Mexico City return (7800 miles) cost only 135 dollars!

Rogers' writing style is informal and chatty, with detailed descriptions of places interspersed with conversations. The book is well illustrated, with numerous small photos and several maps. Rogers' visit to Mexico was made in July 1892.

The work is upbeat and positive, as might be expected from a work designed to promote the advantages of the Central Railway system.

The introduction emphasizes the low cost of traveling in Mexico, and reassures potential clients that a knowledge of Spanish is not essential:

The impression has gone abroad that the traveler in Mexico cannot get enough to eat. Doubtless many of the natives of the country do not have four, or even three "square meals" a day, but the reason is not a lack of plenty in the country. The average tourist keeps to the line or spends his time in the large towns, and no one with money enough to pay for meals need worry at all about lack of satisfactory provision for his wants... as for the cities and towns, it may be said that they have been slandered by those who expected too much, and so were, of course, disappointed. The wonder is, taking all things into account, that the traveler can fare so well, for so little money, as in Mexico.

And, further, don't worry about the language. You don't speak Spanish? Well, no matter, the Mexicans will speak it for you... A little knowledge of the Spanish language is a very valuable thing in Mexico for the traveler from the States, but even this is not indispensable.

Rogers' book has numerous illustrations, including this sketch of the steamboat "Chapala". The chapter also includes what may well be the earliest published photos of Lake Chapala. One photo (untitled) shows Ocotlán, one shows a single home (hut) on Lake Chapala, and the third photo, On the Lake Shore, signed by A. Briquet, is of a village of similar homes. Abel Briquet was a famous French photographer who was commissioned in 1876 to record the construction of the railway line between Veracruz and Mexico City. Over the next 30 years, assisted by the patronage of President Díaz, Briquet produced a series of commemorative albums, including Vistas Mexicanas, Tipos Mexicanos and Antiquedades Mexicanos. He was one of the first commercial photographers to work in Mexico.

The description of Lake Chapala comes from chapter XVI which covers the route from Irapuato to Guadalajara.

"Gems of the Sunland, never yet
Were lakes in lovelier valleys set."

Ocotlán is situated on a plain which slopes southward a few miles into the shore of the lake. With its pretty plaza, beautiful church spires, its portales, and its two bridges (one over the Sula, south of the village, and one west over the Lerma), Ocotlán is very picturesque.

The water front of the city is on the Sula, just above the bridge. Here a novel sight is seen on the levee. No great steamers are moored there, but scores of great canoes are loading and unloading, or waiting for the spirit of their captains to move. These canoes have hitherto done all the business on Lake Chapala.

The water works of Ocotlán are not extensive, but such as they are, they can be seen at the bridge across the Lerma, over which passes the highway to Guadalajara. They consist of one large wheel and a pump. The wheel is on a frame under one of the arches of the bridge. The current of the river runs the wheel, and the wheel, of course, runs the pump. But rivers in this region rise and fall, and there are times when this wheel is six feet above the water. Whenever the current cannot reach the wheel, the people of Ocotlán get their water by carts and carriers....

In a few minutes they were in sight of the lake. From the upper deck the party took in the extended view. On the left the great lagunas or swamps east of the lake, green as a meadow in June, extend for miles; directly ahead is the broken range of hills forming the southern shore, and to the right the bold Cerro Chiquihuitillo. Behind is the plain reaching away to the distant hills on the north, and from this beautiful plain rise the graceful white towers of Ocotlán church....

One of the cast of characters in the book explains that:

"Chapala is nearly the highest navigable body of water on the globe, and now that it is so easily accessible it is destined to become a great pleasure resort for very many people. You can see how beautiful the surroundings are; the climate is all that can be desired, and everything about the lake is attractive to the lover of fine scenery. A day may be spent most pleasantly in an excursion about the lake."

Mescala is the first landing place; not much to be seen here, village itself being hidden in the trees on the hillside....

The sail along the north shore from Mescala to the town of Chapala is delightful. We seem, at times, to be shut in, but the pilot finds a way out and duly brings us to a pretty little city which nestles at the base of a sugar loaf mountain, and which is the largest town on the lake. A fine old church is one of the attractions of the town for visitors, but the hot springs which boil up not far from the plaza have given Chapala fame as a health resort. The springs, although not numerous, remind one of those at Aguas Calientes; they have made Chapala a favorite resort of the people of Guadalajara and vicinity, and when better known will attract people from a greater distance. "Charming" is the word to describe Chapala; I doubt if there is another town in Mexico more prettily situated. A short distance from shore is a large island, which is made use of as a picnic ground. The view from the hill immediately back of the town is one of great beauty.

It is an interesting sight to see the water works of Chapala in operation. No wheels, no pumps, no fountains; only dippers. The lake is the reservoir, and women are the dippers. They wade out as far as they please, fill their jars as full as they please, shoulder them and march home. No scooping with gourds as at Zacatecas, for water is plenty, and no one has to wait for another.

Chapala is sure to become more and more a favorite watering place. Already there are some fine summer "seaside" cottages there, and in the offing you can see a yacht! With a combination of delightful climate and hot springs, with mountain climbing, boating, bathing, and fishing as recreations for visitors, why shouldn't charming Chapala become the finest health and pleasure resort in Mexico?

The next port is Xocotopec, at the extreme western end of the lake. The town lies in a pretty valley three miles back from the lake, and is the center of an extensive rural trade. Returning along the south shore we find no towns of commercial importance, but do find a succession of beautiful views which charm by their variety. We pass San Martin, San Cristobal, Tuscueca, and see, partly hidden by groves of orange and lemon trees, the flourishing city of Tizapan which reposes on the hillside two miles from the lake, along the little Rio de la Pasion.

We sail over what is supposed to be an oil well, some signs of which appear on the surface of the lake; we touch at the fisherman's village with the pretty name, La Palma, and thence complete our eighty mile circuit of Lake Chapala by a direct return to Ocotlán, where we resume our railroad journey.

Rogers, Thomas L. 1893 *Mexico? Sí, señor.*

37

Lake Chapala—a major attraction
1893
Eduardo A. Gibbon

*E*duardo Gibbon y Cárdenas, (1845–1897) was a 19*th* century
Mexican art critic, journalist, writer and diplomat. He wrote several
books, including La catedral de México (1874) and Reflexiones sobre arte
nacional (1892), and a Spanish translation of Felix de Salm's memoirs
about the final days of Emperor Maximilian.

*Gibbon's Guadalajara, (La Florencia Mexicana) is essentially a popular
guide to the author's chosen trilogy of major attractions in Jalisco: Guadalajara, Juanacatlán Falls (the "Niagara of Mexico") and Lake Chapala.
Gibbon's writing is poetic, verging on flowery, but despite that many of his
descriptions make for interesting reading.*

*Gibbon's romantic, poetic prose about his trips to Lake Chapala, in 1893
or earlier, includes one of the earliest detailed accounts of a boat trip on
the lake. He also mentions the fact that deposits of petroleum have been
located under the lake, and that studies are being undertaken to see if the
deposits are large enough to be worth exploiting.*

*Gibbon stayed in a simple hotel; this is at least five years before the
famous Arzapalo hotel opened. The author also describes the chalet built
on the shore by an Englishman.*

*Though apparently not very impressed by some of the statistics quoted
by Bárcena (1888), Gibbon makes several egregious errors concerning
distances himself! Like Bárcena, Gibbon clearly recognized the tourist potential of the area and outlines a prosperous future for tourism in Chapala.*

*To reach the lake, Gibbon traveled by Central Railway train to Atequiza,
and then on horseback from there, with a* campesino *as guide. Gibbon
considered himself an observant and knowledgeable traveler. He was not
impressed by those who had little or no interest in nature:*

A lack of appreciation of the beauties of nature, whether in the mountain, valley, river or lake, comes, in my judgement, from a very imperfect
intellectual organization.

In Chapter XV, Gibbon recalls his first view of Lake Chapala:

"*Señor, señor*, there is Chapala!"...

We entered along a straight and long road, like those that form the main street of every village. The houses were of a single story, with white or colored facades. The doors and windows of wood; the latter without bars or glass, showing that in the honored home of the fisherman, they are safe even without these luxuries. So it is just as easy to enter one of the homes here, through the windows, often obstructed by the pots full of flowers or the large cages of melodious birds, as it is through the doorway.

A soporific silence, that in this village of fishermen! So quiet that, at mid-day, only the buzz of the clouds of gnats, and the beating wings of the gulls crossing the sky can be heard.

But the great luminous place was at the end of this street: Lake Chapala. A fishing boat, with its lateen sail, was approaching the port. Apart from that, nothing was in sight on the immense surface of the water, on which the afternoon sun shone, producing lights and shadows like those made by marcasite....

The bells of the poetic parish church that rang on the shores of the lake-sea, brought all the village's inhabitants to their feet. On the rustic wharf, very close to the hotel, one of those regular-sized vessels, called here canoes, but which are really flat-bottomed launches, was already anchored. The unloading of the domestic merchandise that had been brought for sale, had begun; later these would be sold in the Sunday *tianguis*, [street market] so common in these villages. With a slight following wind, three canoes came through the small waves, which, with sails slightly filled, came towards the beach. The rowers were working to propel the slow advance of these such primitive vessels, which, in rough waters would tip over very easily, and which only progress in their race when the wind is really strong and favorable....

What I do find difficult to believe is that there is any lake more beautiful in our country than Chapala; since if Lake Pátzcuaro, for example, is idyllic, and Cuitzeo a verse of vast horizons in which the immense solitude is the favorite theme of the poet, the Chapalic Sea is a poem of singular and imposing grandeur, whose verses are formed by its storms and its calms, its mountainous tropical shores and its patriotic history....

But, returning to the wharf; a heavy net full of fish of various sizes was being unloaded. From the investigations I have made with respect to the growth and varied types of fish typical of the Chapalic sea, they can be classified and divided as follows:

There is the fish called whitefish, and this is the one that is most prized.

Its flesh is very white and sweet to the palate; its scales are also white, and glisten like silver, it is up to a third of a vara in size, and is very similar in flavor to a fish from the Atlantic Ocean, known as sole in England and *lenguado* in Spain. There are three or four types of this fish.

The catfish, less spiny than the whitefish, and with flesh not so white, tending more towards a purple; the skin, thick, dark in color and very smooth, without any scales. It is good in taste, but on the other hand somewhat harmful to health, being by nature cold, and also phlegmy....

Another abundant small fish, the largest of which does not exceed a sixth of a vara, is one known here by the name charal. Of the same color and scales of the whitefish, it is just as valued in the market, being of almost the same species.

There is a very spiny little fish, called the Chapala sardine; its size at best is a quarter of a vara. With an agreeable taste, it is not injurious to health; it has scales of a dark, faded color. The sardine belongs to the Atlantic and Mediterranean seas, where it remains at depth most of the year, until in autumn (according to zoological observations), it approaches the coasts to spawn. It is to be supposed, given that the sardine is a small little fish belonging to those waters, that the kind found in these fresh waters of the Chapala Sea is a special breed, belonging to the biology of the country. That is to say we consider it a species special to Chapala, given that it lives in fresh water, and the other, on the other hand, in saline sea water. There are other fish in these waters, such as the *popocha*, much valued in Toluca (according to reliable reports), and whose sale brings lots of money. Finally, the mojarra is also an abundant fish; and the *chuimé* or *boquinete*, which is a very similar fish to bass....

Gibbon takes an afternoon boat-trip on the lake:

The canoe in which we went weighed about ten tons; without doubt one of the larger vessels used in trade and navigation along these very lovely shores. Covered astern by a canopy made of thick petates, a product of the country, it was necessary in order to enjoy the views to crawl on the box at the helm, or sit on the prow. This vessel had the unmistakable odor of fish; the truth is that the fishermen are accustomed to hang the charales and sardines that were mentioned earlier on the rigging lines. These fish, cooked in the sun's rays and fried by them, served as food for the mariners on their long and uncertain voyages on Chapala's waters....

I will also say that the very lovely estate that can be seen from the sea on a hill, a quarter of a league from the village of Chapala, is the work and property of an English gentleman, who with his love for Mexican nature, and a culture only proper for one of his education and social standing, has brought much life to this region, and has also stimulated others to build holiday homes and with them give life and civilization to this very beautiful region.

It is unclear which estate Gibbon is referring to, since it is sometimes claimed that the first modern villa built in Chapala was the Villa Ana Victoria, belonging to the Collignon family, in about 1896. The first Englishman to arrive on the scene appears to have been Septimus Crowe (page 157); most sources date his arrival as 1895. Crowe made his home where the Montecarlo Hotel is today, which (ignoring the disparity in date) fits Gibbon's description. That Crowe or other foreigners may have arrived much earlier than 1895 is supported by the brief references to country houses in Rogers (1893) and in an 1896 article by Matias Romero, published in the Journal of the American Geographical Society.

The village of Chapala offers the visitor, not only the pleasures of bathing in the waters of the inland sea, but also in the springs of excellent medicinal pools. I regret not having been able to get the desired analysis of such important pools; the only thing I can claim is that they are good for rheumatic diseases and some skin ailments, their water containing a preponderance of sulfur and some very beneficial salts. As far as the water temperature is concerned, this varies greatly according to the pool where the bath is taken. In the trench or spring, the water has a very high temperature, some 100 degrees Fahrenheit; but in the last of the small pools, where the water is tepid (some 73 degrees F.), it is delightful to bathe, without running any risk of weakening the system too much, as happens here with those pools (so hot), indiscreetly bathed in by many.

Gibbon, Eduardo A. 1893 *Guadalajara, (La Florencia Mexicana). El salto de Juanacatlán y El Mar Chapálico.*

38

A quaint inn and romantic beauty
1893
Christian Reid

Christian Reid was the nom de plume chosen by Frances Christine Fisher (later Tiernan). As a woman writing in a man's world, presumably she felt that her pen name would enable her to better compete with her male counterparts. Fisher (1846-1920) was born in Salisbury, North Carolina. Her father invested in mining ventures and was the president of the North Carolina Railroad. The family was left penniless in the aftermath of the Civil War, so she began writing for money at quite an early age.

Among early pieces was *Regret*, a poem written "in memory of Julian Fairfax, MA, University of Virginia", in 1861, when Fisher was about 15 years old. Her first book was *Valerie Aylmer*, published in 1870, when she was 23. She was a prolific writer, especially of very popular and financially successful light romances. In all, she had almost fifty novels and travel narratives published. In several cases, the books used material that had been previously serialized in magazines. Her best-known book is *The Land of the Sky* (1876) set in the now homonymous western part of North Carolina. Many believe the region took its popular name from the book.

In 1887, Fisher married James M. Tiernan, a widower who had interests in silver mines in Mexico. In letters to her, Tiernan describes meeting President Díaz, and is critical of Americans who displayed prejudice against Mexicans. He also related his problems involving an embezzling official and a recalcitrant British engineer. It is unclear if the couple actually lived together in Mexico for any extended period, but she certainly must have visited frequently. The couple traveled widely, and Fisher used the knowledge she gained to write novels set not only in Mexico, but also in New York, the West Indies and Europe.

After her husband's death in 1898, Fisher turned to the church. She continued to write, in her hometown of Salisbury, until her own death in 1920. Frances Fisher (aka Christian Reid) was inducted into the North Carolina Literary Hall of Fame in October 2002.

Prior to writing the article The Land of the Sun. On Lake Chapala *from which these extracts are taken, Fisher had already used Atequiza as the setting for* A Cast for Fortune: A Story of Mexican Life *(1890).*

The protagonists in this travel story agree that Mexico's constant sunshine makes any discussion of the weather irrelevant, unlike north of the border. They are on their way from Guadalajara to visit "Don Rafael's hacienda." After taking the train to Atequiza, they ride horses to Chapala. The horseback ride, about four leagues in distance, takes longer than they expected since, as one of the characters aptly comments, "Leagues in this country are very elastic."

So talking, they rode slowly along through the golden light of afternoon, until finally they found themselves in the streets of Chapala. The little town did not altogether disappoint the expectations raised by its appearance from afar. Its streets, lined by the usual flat-roofed adobe dwellings, were moderately clean, and along them ran merrily a stream of bright water...

"It flows from the hot springs which gush forth at the foot of the mountain. Very hot springs they are, and of great medicinal value. It is only a question of time when this place becomes a great health and pleasure resort."

"The wonder is that it should not be so already,"said the general, looking around with deepening surprise and admiration.

Certainly a more beautiful spot could not be conceived. Beside the little town lying on its wave-washed promontory rose a bold and splendid height, the mountain from which gushed forth the hot springs of which Russell spoke, while before them spread the romantic beauty of the lake, a noble expanse of water, with abrupt, mountain-clad shores, save where the rich valley across which they had journeyed opened inland. The town narrowed with the promontory to a point, and at this point, within a few yards of the water, stood the church, with the tall, slender tower that had shone before their eyes all day. Opposite was the hostelry to which they were bound, and where they now dismounted, more tired, they all agreed, than if they had ridden three times the distance on good animals.

Very quaint and altogether Mexican was this inn. A low, broad passage that led from the wide street door to an inner court, around which were grouped all the domestic offices, kitchens, stables, etc., was evidently sitting and dining room in one. Wooden benches were placed along the sides, and several of the distinctively Mexican and very comfortable chairs, formed of bamboo and pig-skin, were grouped around the entrance. At the farther end a long table was a stationary feature. From this passage-way on both sides opened chambers not more scantily furnished than is usual in Mexican inns, and scrupulously clean—the small single beds being not harder than one finds them in more pretentious places. But everything had a very primitive flavor....

Mrs. Langdon and Dorothea, attended by Russell and Travers, strolled down to the edge of the softly lapping water and stood lost in admiration of a picture so lovely that they were tempted to declare that they had never seen it equalled. Before them spread the lake, a sheet of shining silver, while the mountains on its shores, clearly revealed by the brilliant radiance, were yet so ethereal and unearthly in tint that they looked like hills in a dream. On one side the lake seemed completely enclosed by these heights that rose immediately from its margin and formed a frame, with their crests against the hyacinth-blue sky, for the silver water washing their feet. In reality, however, it extends many miles beyond its seeming end in this direction—the irregularity of its form causing the deceptive appearance. On the other side it stretched away into remote distance, a shining expanse that finally melted into the sky, together with the misty heights which lined each shore. Near at hand a dark, bold shadow was thrown over the water from the mountain that rose immediately above the town—the abrupt and rocky face of which, owing to the humidity of the air, was covered with a wealth of tropical vegetation. Below, the town lay bathed in moonlight—its rows of flat, Oriental houses with their barred windows, and its church with the graceful campanile, suggesting a blending of Italy and the East.

The scene when they came out to embark the next morning was hardly less beautiful. The lake lay sparkling in the sunshine, and its surrounding heights clothed in green near by wore, as they receded away, the dimmest tints of color which imagination can conceive. The atmosphere was like an elixir of vitality, so fresh yet so balmy. In the mere act of breathing life seemed to become a thing of greater worth. "What an air!"said the general, expanding his lungs. "And this is the month of December, and we are more than six thousand feet above the sea! Where else will one find a climate so perfect?"

"Nowhere else, I think,"answered Russell. "And I have known many lands."...

And so the day went on—a journey through enchanted scenes, leisurely enough for perfect enjoyment. They sat on the decks idly talking, watching the fairyland-like beauty of the distant shores, the varying yet ever exquisite outlines of the mountains, the play of light and color on the water, and the successive villages embowered in shade at which they paused.

Reid, Christian. 1893 *The Land of the Sun. On Lake Chapala.*

39

Giant Whirlpool—a startling spectacle
1896
Anon

Its Waters Swallowed by a Subterranean Cave.
Several Pleasure Boats and Their Occupants Engulfed.
A Heavy Rumbling Sound in the Earth's bowels Accompanies the
Phenomenon - Natives are Intensely Terrified.

SAN DIEGO, Jan. 12.—(Special dispatch.) Prof. E. H. Coffey of this
city, has just received a letter from a correspondent. living near Lake
Chapala, State of Jalisco, Mex.. which describes some startling phenomena
occurring. Lake Chapala is a sheet of water fifty miles long and ten miles
wide. The formation of the country around it is purely volcanic.

On the forenoon of January 8 residents in one of the small settlements
near the western end of the lake were terrified to see a gigantic whirlpool
raging far out on the water. The waters rose in great serpentine movements, and from all directions rushed toward a common center, where a
vast cavity seemed to exist. At the same time a heavy, rumbling sound,
apparently in the bowels of the earth, took place. The whirlpool was
caused by the sudden sinking of a large portion of the lake's bottom, and
before the disturbance subsided several pleasure-boats were drawn into
the whirlpool and disappeared with their occupants. It is estimated that
a score of lives were lost.

The whirlpool continued for nearly twenty minutes, and when the
inhabitants of the surrounding territory turned their eyes from the overwhelming sight they saw that the lake had receded several feet from its
former shore line. As the lake is about fifty miles in length, with an average
width of ten miles, the enormous amount of water that was swallowed up
by the earth may be imagined. After the whirlpool subsided the surface of
the lake resumed its placid aspect, and the subterranean rumblings ceased.

There was the greatest excitement among the people for miles in the vicinity of the western end of the lake, the most ignorant and superstitious natives being beside themselves with fear. Years of familiarity with volcanic eruptions and terrestial disturbances did not seem to reassure them during this dreadful experience.

Prof. Coffey is well acquainted with Lake Chapala and its surroundings, having explored much of its coast line. He found petroleum and coal in quantities that proved the existence of vast wealth in that region. Since the strange occurrence on the lake last Wednesday, petroleum has been found running in small streams above the surface on the southern shore. The Lerma River empties into Lake Chapala on the western side and flows out in a west-northwesterly direction under the name of the Colotlan River.

Lake Chapala is in the center of a distinctly volcanic district, and it is not far from the volcano of Colima, which is always active. It is also near the Jorullo volcano, which rose in a night from a level plain in 1789. After the strange sinking of Lake Chapa!a on Wednesday, no unusual activity was noticed in the volcano or in that region.

Anon. 1896 *A Whirlpool—Startling Spectacle at Lake Chapala.*

40

The little pottery objects of Lake Chapala
1895–6
Frederick Starr

Frederick Starr (1858-1933), born in Auburn, New York, was an American anthropologist who was Associate Professor of Anthropology at the University of Chicago from 1892 until 1923. Starr, whose primary scientific experience was in geology, graduated from Lafayette College in 1882 and was appointed as a biology professor at Coe College. In 1889, as his academic interests shifted towards ethnology and anthropology, he accepted a post at the American Museum of Natural History. A few years later he was asked to organize anthropological teaching at the University of Chicago. Starr died in Tokyo, Japan, on August 14, 1933.

A passionate anthropologist, with a particular enthusiasm for fieldwork, his research on several continents led to such diverse works as *The Truth about the Congo* (1907), *In Indian Mexico, A narrative of Travel and Labor* (1908) and *Japanese proverbs and pictures* (1910).

In Indian Mexico has extensive descriptions of Lake Pátzcuaro, Uruapan, Zamora and many smaller villages. A contemporary reviewer described this book as: "the work of a keen observer, whose description of the picturesque customs of the Mexican Indians has a deeper significance than a mere collection of interesting details. Combining the qualities of the trained ethnologist with a rare sense of the picturesque, he has given us an altogether admirable book." American novelist Charles Embree (chapter 43) wrote an appendix to *In Indian Mexico*.

Prior to *In Indian Mexico*, it had been assumed that traditional methods of making paper from tree bark were extinct in Mexico. Starr, however, discovered that the ancient craft was still practised (as it is even today) in the Otomi village of San Pablito in the state of Hidalgo.

Starr's short research paper The Little Pottery Objects of Lake Chapala, Mexico *has descriptions and illustrations of* ollitas *and other pottery items dating back at least as far as the sixteenth century, found near Jocotepec, at the western end of the lake.*

My attention was first called to the little potteries of Lake Chapala by Francisco Fredenhagen of Guadalajara. Mr. Fredenhagen showed me a string of little ladles and *ollitas* found at Chapala, either in the lake or washed up on the shore. He suggested that they might come from the site of some ancient town built over the water, analogous to the well-known Swiss lake-dwellings. Since then I have attempted, with no success, to find any signs of such pile-structures. The fishermen of the neighborhood deny the existence of any stumps of posts or piles in the lake, and at the times of my visits the water has been too high for satisfactory examination. The question is not decided.

The occurrence of these little terra cotta objects—vessels, ladles, sinkers, spindle-whorls, and figures—in the lake is curious. Archaeological objects abound in the district, and pottery vessels and figures of characteristic types are common all around the lake. But they are all large, and the vessels were serviceable for daily use. These larger objects appear to be rare or quite absent from the lake itself; on the other hand, the little objects which are about to be described are so rare as to be practically unknown at all the land localities with which I am acquainted.

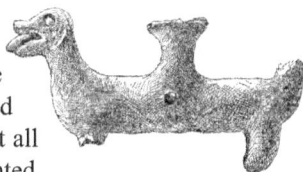

There are several points in the western part of the lake where these little objects are found. Chapala is by no means the best locality, though the first I knew. They are found again about four miles west from it. But the best of the known localities is Ocotepec. At all these places the specimens may be found, though rarely, along the shore, where they have been washed up by the waves. Such specimens usually show signs of wave wear. The most numerous and finest specimens are found when the water of the lake is at its lowest level. They may then be taken out or dug from the lake bottom at a spot where the water often stands from one to two fathoms deep. Many of the specimens are coated with a lime deposit or with slimy vegetable growth.

I divide the specimens in my own collection into five groups—ollitas, ladles, sinkers, spindle-whorls, and figurines. Far the larger number of them are of a dark gray—almost black—or grayish ware, fairly fine-grained and pretty well baked, but easily broken. The ollitas are the commonest of all the types. Out of a collection of 261 specimens there are 181 ollitas, 15 sinkers, 48 whorls, 11 ladles, 6 figurines. The ollitas are really more common proportionally than this, for in collecting I have often rejected them, while I have never refused specimens of the rest, if they were at all good....

How are they to be explained? Were they toys for children, miniatures of objects used by adults in daily life? That is the most natural first suggestion; but if so, why are they only in the lake and not on the land? If the specimens came—as Fredenhagen suggested—from a pile-dwelling village site, the theory of their being toys gains in probability; but why are not larger objects found more commonly with them?

That the perforation was of importance seems certain. The sinkers and *amphisbœna* (together with one little jar and one human figure) are the only specimens not perforated. They are grooved. So all (with the exception of two out of 261 specimens) could have been easily attached to a cord or string. That they were not all simply sinkers for fish-lines is plain enough from their forms.

So far as their presence in the lake is concerned it is *possible* that the lake's level may have risen, covering an original place of deposit on the dry land. The spot is almost within sight of the active volcano of Colima, and changes of level, through volcanic or other igneous agency, in the waters of the lake are not improbable. The old schoolmaster at Chapala insists that the town of Chapala has long been slowly sinking, and that half of it has already been engulfed by the lake. He also claims that the god formerly worshipped at Chapala was a little god, a child god, and that the little vessels were offerings to him. Mota Padilla in speaking of this town says: "Chapala is at ten leagues' distance from Guadalajara, to the southeast, and the lake is named from the pueblo, because it was perhaps in its ancient days the most populous of those which surrounded it, although today it is almost destroyed by various increases of the lake, especially those of 1555 and 1577;" further on, in the same passage, he states that Fr. Juan de Almolon threw into the lake idols of flint, greenstones, and clay, which he took from the natives.

Taking all points into consideration, with some hesitancy, the following suggestions are made: May not these small objects be offerings made to the lake itself or some spirit resident therein? They may have been let down carefully into the water by means of cords, rather than thrown in haphazard. May not resin, or gum, have been burned, or offerings placed, in the little vessels and ladles and in the cups on such specimens as those shown in [the figure, previous page]? Their miniature size, the forms, the location, the fact of perforation, or grooving, would all be thus explained. It is perfectly realized that these hints demonstrate nothing; further explanation will be welcomed.

Starr, Frederick. 1897 *The Little Pottery Objects of Lake Chapala, Mexio.*

41

Across the lake by steamer
1897
José Ruben Romero

Mexican writer José Rubén Romero (1890-1952) was born in Cotija de la Paz, Michoacán. Cotija de la Paz is about thirty kilometers from the village of La Palma on Lake Chapala's south-eastern corner.

Romero's father, an outspoken liberal, had been forced to leave the very conservative village of Cotija de la Paz, and the family home, and travel to Mexico City.

Six months later, he sent for his wife and two children, Rubén (aged seven) and his younger sister. Their journey, by horseback, steamer and train, is described in Romero's *Apuntes de un lugareño* (*Notes of a Villager*), published in 1932, by which time Romero was the Mexican Consul in Barcelona, Spain.

He was later appointed Mexican ambassador to Brazil (1937-1939) and Cuba (1939-1944).

Besides his diplomatic career,

Romero worked in a variety of fields, such as journalism and as a university dean.

He is best remembered, though, as a writer whose vivid depictions of the people and customs of his native state make him an outstanding exponent of the modern *costumbrista* novel. The *costumbrista* genre focuses on regional life, customs and manners. Romero's lasting legacy of fine works include *Desbandada* (1934), *El pueblo inocente* (1934), *Mi caballo, mi perro y mi rifle* (1936) and *Rosenda* (1946). But by far his best known book is the picaresque tale of a lovable rascal: *La vida inútil de Pito Pérez* (The Futile Life of Pito Pérez), published in 1938. A best-seller in innumerable editions, this book was turned into a movie starring Ignacio López Tarso in the early 1970s. One of Mexico's best-loved writers ever, Romero died on July 4, 1952 in Mexico City .

In his autobiographical novel, Romero describes Lake Chapala on two occasions. The first time he encounters the lake is in about 1897, on his way to Mexico City with his mother and sister at the age of seven. It includes

Romero's impressions of the steamer trip from La Palma to Ocotlán, a
regular route at the time.

We arrived at nightfall at Rancho de la Palma on the shores of Lake
Chapala.

To sleep, we threw our bedding on the ground inside a wooden hut,
but we had to get up shortly after lying down because the odor of our
provisions attracted uncountable armies of ants. Red, diminutive ants
that on being killed exuded the repugnant odor of excrement; great black
mule ants, huge of head, that crawled up my legs and bit me unpityingly.

The dawn came upon us as we lay, tired and groggy, without having
been able to sleep a wink.

At eight in the morning we got on the steamboat that would take us
to Ocotlán.

I began to run around the boat without paying attention to the excessive
cautions of my mother, who cried out for fear I would fall in the water.

The steamboat was large, with two decks and some cabins that on our
voyage were occupied by the relatives of the owner, Don Diego Moreno,
and some three or four nuns in black habits with white hoods.

During the crossing, the nuns never stopped praying and I twisted
myself into every position to see if I could see their legs because I doubted
that they had them like ordinary people.

Just past the halfway point in the lake a ruined tower appeared that
was said to have been a prison in the old days. I straightened myself to
see and began to pester all those within my reach with questions which
when all was said and done, no one could answer.

We arrived at Ocotlán, disembarked, wandered through some streets
full of dust and went to the station to await the train. The train that I
thought was a precious toy turned out to be something heavy and ugly,
full of smoke, with an intolerable odor.

"I'm not going to Mexico City in this," I told my mother, half scared
and half curious, but I was taken aboard anyhow and placed near a little
window in a seat of worn plush, where I had no alternative but to entertain
myself with the movement about the station: well-dressed travelers from
Guadalajara who strolled in the sun; others buying jugs of plum wine,
fresh cheeses, or fruits. Groups of farmers arrived, the men with valises
of striped chintz on their shoulders and full baskets in their hands; the
women dressed in brightly colored percales, with squeaky new shoes
that caused them to walk as if on thorns. They conducted, almost by
force, sunburned children as open-mouthed before the novelty of the
train as I was.

They spent that night at a hotel in Irapuato:

We dined in the hotel of a very fat, blond French woman who was highly recommended to us. Enveloped in a white dressing gown, she jiggled her opulent flesh throughout the house. Her husband, also quite obese, never stopped writing in a large book.

"Do you like the hotel?" my mother asked me.

"Yes, mamá, it's like a fattening pen for people," I answered her, very seriously.

As Dr. Wolfgang Vogt has pointed out in his article entitled El lago de Chapala en la literatura, *Romero makes good use in this passage of the juxtaposition between the horrible night in La Palma and the steamboat trip across the lake the following day. As Vogt observes, most visitors, even including D.H. Lawrence, became well acquainted only with the Chapala-Ajijic section of the lakeshore, and learned very little about the "real life of the lakeside inhabitants".*

Romero's second encounter with Lake Chapala comes a decade later, when he was living in Sahuayo between about 1907 and 1910. By this time, the Cuesta Gallardo scheme to drain the eastern portion of the lake was well under way.

Some friends invited me to hunt in the swamps that border the edges of Lake Chapala, a diversion that recommended itself very little to me since I was a bad shot, but they were very insistent in spite of the risk of receiving a stray shot from my hand.

"Go by yourselves," I told them, "for the devil loads guns and fools shoot them." The saying had no effect.

As to the spectacle, I enjoyed it: great bands of little ducks with the silky finish of children's toys; herons that resembled lilies; geese that balled themselves among the water hyacinths, like cushions in a coquette's boudoir. And the hunters, at point-blank range, had a great time pinning roses of blood on the nuptial dress of those birds without blemish.

Romero, José Rubén. 1932 *Apuntes de un lugareño.*

42

The new, revised complete guide
1899
Reau Campbell

Reau Campbell's first two books, both relatively short, were published in 1889. They were *Around the corner to Cuba* and *Rides and rambles on Staten Island.* They were quickly followed by a short work on Mexico: *Mexico: Tours through the Egypt of the New World* (1890).

Campbell had begun traveling in Mexico around 1885, and his interest in the country continued to grow. In 1892 he wrote *Mexico and the Mexicans, the material matters and mysterious myths of that country and its people*, published by the Sonora news company.

After a decade of visits to Mexico, Campbell appears to have come to the realization that a guide might be a good idea, and that it might be a lasting legacy:

"I have known these difficulties as an early traveler in Mexico, and, while I rejoiced in seeing what others had not seen, I have wished for the book that might guide me over untraveled roads, till I have come to believe that he who writes the book leaves a legacy to him who comes after."

In 1894, he undertook an "exploring expedition" to check facts and personally visit uncharted corners. Of the places "not found in other books", "none are more important or more interesting than the prehistoric Ruins of Mitla, visited first by my exploring expedition of 1894, and which are here written of for the first time since the earlier chronicles of the country."

The results of his dogged research resulted (1895) in a more definitive guide to the country than any previous effort: *Campbell's complete guide and descriptive book of Mexico*. With a special focus on railroad travel, this found a willing publisher in Chicago. By 1899, this work had been enlarged and transformed into *Campbell's new revised complete guide and descriptive book of Mexico,* which was to go through numerous editions and printings.

Campbell became the general manager of the American Tourist Association and founded his own company to run private Pullman train tours of Mexico.

Campbell's new revised complete guide and descriptive book of Mexico *is profusely illustrated by more than 200 photographs. It provides sketches of Mexico's geography and history, discusses practical matters (such as mule cars, hotels, and shopping for cigars), and offers details about amusements, railway rides, towns, cities, and natural and cultural attractions. Campbell includes two photographs of Lake Chapala, one showing a typical sail canoe, and the other a view from behind the village of Chapala over the church to the lake.*

"Libertad" was the name of Lake Chapala's first steamboat. She ran from La Barca to the towns and villages up the lake, and the voyage was one of the most delightful in Mexico, through the "floating islands" to the towering cliffs with sparkling cascades tumbling into the lake from far up the rocks, by the picturesque towns and villages, of which the town of Chapala is a resort of ancient renown, from its pure and healthful climate, its hot springs and most picturesque scenery.

The steamer "Libertad" had her machinery built in California, and was transported by piecemeal on burros over the mountains from San Blas....

Near the station, the River Lerma is crossed. Here this longest river in Mexico is crossed for the first time and the road follows its windings, and runs along the south branch for some miles, crossing it again at La Barca, a city of 10,000 inhabitants, on Lake Chapala, where the Lerma empties into it. The river is sometimes called the Rio Grande, and is referred to as the Mississippi of Mexico. It is a curious fact that this river empties into Lake Chapala at La Barca and flows out of it just below Ocotlan, fifteen miles farther on. Lake Chapala is a most beautiful body of water, on which there have been steamboats. The machinery of the first one was brought from California, by sea, to San Blas, and thence packed on burros over the mountains; the boiler lies on the beach, the rusty monument to American pluck and energy. It is not recorded that anybody else has carried steamboats over the mountains on mules. The voyage around the lake is one of seventy miles, and of many delights in the superb scenery, exceptionally beautiful. High and overhanging cliffs, reflected again in the clear waters, mountains, fertile plains, valleys with fields of fruits and groves of tropical trees. Sometimes, when a high east wind prevails, the waves loosen the vegetation growing in the shallow water of the delta, where the Lerma comes in and sends some floating islands, often an acre in extent, out into the lake. The town of Chapala, on the north shore, is picturesquely located under the towering cliffs of the mountain, and has long been a health resort of the natives, on account of the very hot springs that are there which have a high reputation for their curative properties; the waters clear as crystal, gush from under the rocks on the mountain side. Continuing the journey by rail, west from La Barca, the track comes to the river again and crosses it, after it has left the lake, near Ocotlan, the third crossing of the river. From the windows on the right there is to be seen a fine old Spanish bridge of many arches, near Poncitlan, and from the left there is another glimpse of the lake.

Campbell, Reau. 1899. *Campbell's new revised complete guide and descriptive book of Mexico.*

Therapeutic water

The therapeutic qualities of the waters of Chapala had been re-marked upon, and perhaps even enjoyed firsthand, by numerous early visitors. One of the earliest advertisements of their curative properties was placed in 1907 in *Crónica* (cited in Casillas, 2004).

The *Crónica* advertisement lauds Chapala waters as being of the highest importance for their tonic and fortifying qualities. According to the advertisement, the thermal "Sánchez" spring was at the foot of the Cerro de San Miguel, the hill which overlooks the plaza. The water originated from a depth of about 400 meters and emerged with a temperature of 35°C.

When tested in 1898, the water, once cooled to ambient temperature, was found to be colorless, transparent and odorless, with a pleasant flavor. Its calcium carbonate content was considered ideal for the digestion, serving to neutralize any excess stomach acid. Experts at the time believed that water of this type was also useful in the treatment or prevention of "impotence, sterility, amenorrhea, leucorrhoea, chlorosis, weakness and many other diseases".

The owners of the spring, Salvador Pérez Arce and his son, installed a state-of-the-art bottling machine to bottle the mineral water direct from the spring. Beginning in 1907, it was marketed using the somewhat unimaginative brand-name "Chapala".

43

A dream of a throne
1898
Charles Fleming Embree

Charles Fleming Embree was born in Princeton, Indiana, October 1, 1874, the son of lawyer David Franklin Embree, member of a prominent pioneer family, and Mary Fleming Embree. Charles was still an infant when his father died in 1877. To this day, one of the main streets in Princeton is N. Embree Street.

Charles Embree was educated in Princeton public schools and entered Wabash College in the fall of 1892. He left college after three years, without graduating, to devote himself to writing. He achieved immediate success with *For the Love of Tonita, and other tales of the Mesas (1897),* his first book.

On January 18, 1898, he married Virginia Broadwell. The young couple moved to Mexico, and lived in Chapala for eight months in 1898, before moving to Oaxaca. The precise motives behind Embree's decision to spend two years in Mexico remain frustratingly unclear.

Embree's second novel, dedicated to his wife, is set in the Lake Chapala region, but was written while they were in Oaxaca. *A Dream of a Throne, the Story of a Mexican Revolt* (1900), is illustrated with five black and white drawings by Henry Sandham (1842-1910), a very well-known Canadian illustrator of the time.

From Oaxaca, Embree penned a short newspaper piece about anthropologist Frederick Starr, who was conducting fieldwork there.

Embree's third book, illustrated by Dan Smith, was *A Heart of Flame: the Story of a Master Passion* (1901). Embree also had several short stories published in *McClure's Magazine.*

In recognition of the distinguished place he had already achieved among American novelists, Embree was awarded an honorary Master of Arts degree by Wabash College in 1903.

Embree and his wife moved to Santa Ana, California. Sadly, the couple had not long celebrated the birth of their only daughter Elinor in 1905 when Embree was taken seriously ill. He died on July 3, not yet 31 years old.

It seems a particular tragedy that someone who had produced several books, including work of this magnitude, should have died so young. In his short time in Chapala, Charles Embree had acquired an excellent histori-cal and geographical knowledge of the region at a time when American travelers to the lake were few and far between.

The publishers advertised A Dream of a Throne: the Story of a Mexi-can Revolt *in glowing terms: "A powerful and highly dramatic romance, dealing with a popular Mexican uprising half a century ago. It is a novel of adventure and of war, and its strongly contrasted characters glow with life and realism. The writer's thorough knowledge of Mexican life gives him a wealth of new material; and the descriptions of scenery at Lake Chapala are vivid, full of color, and alive with mountain air".*

The book is a remarkable achievement for the time, and for an author so young; Embree was twenty-six when the book was published. Set in the mid-19th century, it is a highly charged, gripping account of love, intrigue and treachery. In the course of the novel, Embree refers to historical events such as the Pie Claim, and to 1846 when "General Taylor crossed the Rio Grande and invaded Mexican territory."

From a geographical perspective, Embree displays an accurate and astute knowledge of all his lakeside locales. The spelling of all place-names, with the exception of Ajicjic and Tuxcueco, is exactly as it is today. Details of clothing, habits and customs all ring true. Equally, the clear parallels between events in the novel and real, historical events shows that Em-bree had a considerable knowledge of the region's 19th century history. As one small example, the story begins in the shadow of St. Michael's Hill in Chapala in May 1833, amidst fear of an epidemic of smallpox. In real life, the nearby city of Guadalajara suffered a cholera epidemic in the summer of 1833.

By the end, the novel has returned once more to St. Michael's Hill, and concludes by explaining how the cross on the hill's summit was erected in memory of the book's hero who had been executed there.

This novel is the earliest novel written in English to be completely set at Lake Chapala. Just as importantly, it is one of the earliest descriptions of everyday indigenous life in the region. As Vogt (1989) has pointed out, even by the 1920s (twenty years after Embree's novel was published), virtually no-one was observing or writing about this area from an indigenous point of view. Embree's novel has particular value since it examines the conflicts between Indians and Spaniards.

All the action in the novel takes place on and around Lake Chapala. The major locales are Mezcala Island, Chapala, Ajijic and Tizapan. Without in any way wishing to downplay Embree's abilities with dialogue, character development and storyline, the following short extracts have been chosen to highlight his depictions of landscapes.

The book opens in Chapala:

At nightfall of a day in May, 1833, there was lamentation in a fisher's hut on the banks of the Mexican lake Chapala. The shadows of St. Michael's Hill, which rises high and rocky out of the town's centre, had long since fallen across the Chapala plaza. The sun had set in red and gold, and the waves, as the darkness came on, were rising slowly...

The north shore, including Ajicjic (Embree's spelling), was the scene of considerable action, though Ajijic has changed somewhat from Embree's description:

They were riding over a rough trail with cacti and stones about, and here and there a flock of goats. To the right was a seemingly endless chain of mountains, to the left, more distant, rose St. Michael, low and round (behind whose bulk lay Chapala and the water), and the larger head, called Angostura, lying between that town and Ajicjic on the lake's edge. Between Angostura and the opposite mountain chain the road led, rising to a hill, to whose summit the little army came. They looked down on the lake and, nearer, small irregular fields, scores of them, checkering a level stretch from mountains to water. Out of these, Ajicjic's church thrust up a single gleaming tower of white. Three o'clock found the troop sweeping into the barren plaza of that fishing village.

To this day Ajicjic can claim no more than some two thousand souls. It has, even yet, no railroad, no stage; rarely has a vehicle been seen in that primitive place other than the awkward ox cart. Its low, unplastered adobe walls stand close together. The streets are alleys of extreme narrowness wherein there is mud when it rains, dust when it is dry, rocks and swine forever. Nigh every alley twists and turns, is for a block no more than a gutter, for another block a public stable for burros. Yet one may find some better quarters. The plaza, though it is only a bare, brown waste, is wide. The open court before the church, though it too is bare and dirty, with lonely, crumbling walls and pillars about it, yet has in its center a weather beaten cross that speaks of service to the Lord.

The troop filled the plaza. It was halted, and the inhabitants of the town, struck with amazement, either shut themselves up or gathered in silence round about. Groups of brown children, absolutely naked, sat down in the dirt, thumbs in mouth, to wonder in comfort. Rodrigo and Bonavidas began the inquiries, prefacing them with jocularly expressed friendship to certain storekeepers and a toss of tequila here and there down a willing throat. Boats? There hadn't come but one boat to Ajicjic the blessed day. Ajicjic was losing importance in these times. On market days everybody went to the bigger market at Chapala, where the news was dispersed. And this one boat? It had come from Tizapan with a load of wood for the lime burners...

Most of the action on the southern shore is centered on Tizapán:

The town of Tizapan lies at a short distance from the lake. The shore in that region is no such distinctly marked line of beach and rock as it is at Chapala. It is not even always easy to tell where the shore is. Between water and land there is a stretch of marsh for several hundred yards, watery, pierced by the spears of a million reeds that rise thick and green to a height of some feet. Here flock ducks in great numbers. The marsh is flat, bewildering, and dreary. Through its middle a stream, called the Tizapan River, cuts out more than one course, having formed a delta. The main course of this river, not over twenty yards at its widest part, usually much narrower, is navigable for canoes for half a mile to a point where the land is dry and from which the town lies yet another mile distant. The stream being crooked and the curves sharp, the progress from the open lake to the inner landing is usually made by poles. The lake approach to the town could be easily blocked by blocking the river. Only the one course is navigable. Nobody could cross the marshes. This fact was recognized more than a century ago.

The town itself is like the greater part of Mexican towns, narrow and crooked streets with the low houses (joined together) shutting those streets in and making them seem even narrower, and the central plaza of considerable size left vacant. That plaza is today filled with flowers and fruit and contains a band stand. In former times it was bare. The mountains rise only a little way behind the town, jagged and huge. Before them is a stretch of rolling green fields. The river, coming from the peaks, dashes down through this pastoral scene with a vivacity that has laid bare a rough and rocky bed whereon the water boils till it passes through the town. At the time when the two small armies were approaching Tizapan, much of the summer green was still on field and mountain. The unclouded sun poured his light over an emerald gem of the lake's border.

Embree, Charles Fleming. 1900. *A Dream of a Throne: the Story of a Mexican Revolt.*

An Englishman has a street named after him

Despite the fact that there is a short street in Chapala named "Callejón de Mister Crow", relatively little is known about the life of Mr. Septimus Crowe (the correct spelling of his surname). Crowe (1842–1903) was born in Kåfjord, northern Norway, and became British vice consul in Oslo on his father's retirement from that position in 1875. By then he had married Georgina Bidder, who came from a wealthy English family; the couple had one son.

It is likely that Crowe first came to Mexico in the 1880s. It is not certain when he first visited Chapala, reportedly seeking alleviation of his rheumatic ailments, but by the last decade of the 19th century, he definitely had property at the lake and was actively promoting Chapala among his circle of friends. He built his home where the Montecarlo hotel is today, and also built Casa Albión (aka Villa Josefina and Casa Schnaider) and Villa Bela. His Montecarlo property was later bought by Aurelio González Hermosillo, who asked Italian architect Ángel Corsi to build him a villa there. This villa later became the Hotel Montecarlo.

According to Jeremiah Curtin's memoirs, on November 29, 1895, he met Septimus Crowe, "one very peculiar Englishman"on the train from Irapuato to Guadalajara. "He was dressed in a Spanish Costume: a large Mexican hat trimmed with gold braid; a short, white coat; tight trousers; and a long, red sash; and white gloves. His name was Septimus Crow (The Seventh Crow). He was the youngest of fifteen Crows and the seventh male one, he informed us."

In 1898, very soon after their marriage, young novelist Charles Fleming Embree and his bride Virginia Broadwell arrived in Chapala. They lived in the village for eight months, before moving to Oaxaca, where Embree wrote *Dream of a Throne*. Embree includes an unusually specific reference in the book, which must surely allude to the Hon. Septimus Crowe: "Now, at the century's end, navigation by modern means is just beginning to appear on Chapalac. There is one old steamer full of vermin and rickety, exceedingly small. She fell over once in the water and drowned many passengers. There is a new steamer talked of. The Hon. S——— C———, Her British Majesty's ex-consul general to Sweden, has a little yacht that skims these waters. Otherwise the shipping is the same that has conducted the primitive lake commerce for hundreds of years." If not accidental, the geographic misidentification of Sweden for Norway may have been deliberate obfuscation on Embree's part.

Septimus Crowe died in Mexico City in July 1903, as he was preparing to leave on a trip to the U.K. His son became a prominent doctor, author of several works about chronic rheumatic conditions.

44

The Hotel Arzapalo and a stagecoach ride
c. 1898-1899
Owen Wallace Gillpatrick

Owen Wallace Gillpatrick (1862-1925) was an American author and playwright whose prose was very popular in his native country during his lifetime. He was a fluent Spanish speaker, and his translation "with much taste and skill" of Catalan writer Àngel Guimerà's play *Marta of the Lowlands*, was performed on Broadway in 1903. He also translated Guimerà's *La Pecadora (*Putnam, 1917).

The title of his book on Mexico, *The Man who likes Mexico*, is the byline he used as a correspondent for the *Mexican Herald*. His planned one year trip in 1898 eventually became six years in length. The book describes journeys made during the first two years of that time. He approached Mexico with a very positive attitude, summed up by the following quote from the foreword:

"Americans who visit Mexico will not fail to discover much that is likeable; and it seems only just to remark first on what is likeable, deferring adverse comment until a careful observation of life and conditions shall have rendered intelligent criticism possible."

Gillpatrick was born in New Hampshire, but lived almost all his life in California. He had always yearned to visit Mexico:

"Reared in California, where the romance of early Mexican days still lingers, and where the prodigality of nature and of life are in keeping with Mexican tradition, I ardently dreamed of this Spanish American southland".

Gillpatrick proved to be a spontaneous and adventurous traveler. Unlike many of his contemporaries, Gillpatrick positively preferred the areas away from the railroads. He stayed for a month in Guadalajara, before continuing on to Chapala. Gillpatrick's enthusiasm for Mexico never waned. He closed his book by writing that "Two ties united my heart to Mexico—first, love of friends; last and always, her mountains". He included an atmospheric photo of moonlight shining on Lake Chapala.

In a jiffy we reached the top of the hill. Before us lay the lake, with the mountains beyond and the little town of Chapala lying close to the margin...
That the manager of the Hotel Arzapalo was a man of taste, I knew when I saw the hotel, with its clambering rose-vines, its well-kept gardens and the little pier running out into the lake, with comfortable benches at either side. When he assigned me to a room, with a view of mountain and lake combined, I was doubly sure. The memories of my ride, together with a bountiful dinner, made me content to loaf the rest of the afternoon; but towards evening I started in search of the warm mineral baths, for which the place is noted. A gentleman who knows Chapala, had said to me, "Don't go to the fine-looking bath-house with the 'Baño' sign; follow the same street till you come to some old buildings and then ask for the *tanque.*" So I walked by the fine-looking baños and in an old orange orchard, I found the great swimming tank. It must be sixty feet long by twenty wide, and the bottom slopes so that at one end it is over a man's head. It is surrounded by a high wall and the palms and orange trees grow close up to it. The water is a trifle more than blood-warm, so that you feel an almost imperceptible accession of warmth in stepping into it. It is the kind of a bath that you leave reluctantly and then feel tempted to return to. The springs at Cuautla, Morelos, are nearly like these in temperature.

When I came out I asked the dueña to sell me some oranges; and she sent a boy to pick them—three big, luscious ones for two cents. An Indian was launching his canoe, and I asked him to take me in; he ran and got a little rush-bottom chair which he put in the stern, and we paddled away. There was the last flush of crimson and purple in the west and a crescent moon overhead; and I could hear the voices of the Indian boatmen, as they rowed out through the dusk to the fishing grounds.

While the lake is often perfectly still during the afternoon, a breeze comes after sunset and soon little waves are running up on the beach. The moon makes a silver track across the water; you hear a soft lapping along the shore, and the scent of flowers pervades the shaded balcony of the hotel. The despondent traveler, who has been seeing the country by day and waging fierce wars by night, in hotels where he pays for a bed and then has to fight to hold it, will hail the *Arzapalo* as a haven of rest. The beds and bed-linen are spotlessly clean and one lies down with no misgivings as to the manner of his awakening. I could tell gruesome tales of nights spent in Mexican hotels, but I won't. Perhaps the reader is tender-hearted; and for me, it would only open old wounds anew. The *Arzapalo* has some fifty rooms, a large sala and dining-room overlooking the lake, and is provided with a bar and billiard table. The cooking is excellent and the bread is all made in the house. The hotel is situated in what is, beyond doubt, one of the loveliest and most healthful spots in all Mexico. Good hotels are a crying want in the republic, and when I encounter one I sing its praises.

Circumstances over which I had no control forced me to leave Chapala. My trunk ran amuck. I found it at Silao, but I lost—Chapala. I left it when my love was at its height. It was morning on the lake. The mists were hanging on the mountain tops, the breeze was ruffling the surface of the water, and the palms and orange trees shone emerald-green in the sunlight. I rode on top of the coach and as we approached the summit of the divide, we could see a good part of the length of the lake, some thirty leagues in all...

There was a last glimpse of a great stretch of shining water, and the next minute we had crossed and were bowling down the other side to Atequiza.

If you have never ridden on a Mexican coach, you have still a new sensation in store. The Chapala coach has a cushion on top and if you are fortunate in sharing this seat, you ride *muy a gusto,* seeing the country and the manner of manipulating an eight-mule-team at the same time. There are two about the size of rabbits on the lead, a string of four in the middle, and two larger ones on the wheel. The driver has a whip, with a lash long enough to reach the leaders. His assistant has another shorter one, but his chief persuaders are rocks. The assistant earns fifty cents a day and free insurance against dyspepsia. He alights at the base of every hill and fills his sombrero full of rocks on the way up. He then shies several boulders big enough to dislocate a hip at the leaders; and when the whole team are in full gallop, he swings himself on to the box in some miraculous way—I think he stands on the hub. He could never do it if he wore shoes. When they change mules, he leads the discarded team up and down to cool them off; while the driver takes the new ones and tangles them up, so you can't tell where wheelers end and leaders begin. At last they are off again with a whoop and a yell. People talk of Mexico as slow, but the word can never be applied either to stage coaches or street cars, when they once get started.

Gillpatrick, Owen Wallace. 1911 *The man who likes Mexico.*

The Hotel Arzapalo

Prior to 1898, visitors to the small fishing village of Chapala stayed either with friends or in the one small guesthouse belonging to Doña Trini. After 1890 or so, many well-to-do Guadalajara families and some foreigners, such as Septimus Crowe, built villas on the lakeshore. The village's fame as a place to vacation grew steadily, boosted by a brief visit from President Díaz in 1896. Díaz returned in January 1904 to visit his in-laws, which only served to further boost Chapala's appeal.

In the mid-1890s, Ignacio Arzapalo Palacios, who had recognized the curative properties of Chapala's waters, and fallen in love with the natural beauty and favorable climate, began to build the village's first major hotel.

The Hotel Arzapalo opened in March 1898 with 36 rooms, and acquired its own diligences, to ensure daily service between Chapala and the Atequiza railway station. Rates at the hotel, including meals, were between $2.50 and $4.00 a day, depending on the room, more than twice the daily rate across the street at the Posada Doña Trini.

Arzapalo's businesses did so well that in 1908 he opened a second hotel, designed by Guillermo de Alba. This was first called the Hotel Palmera, later the Niza, and then the Nido hotel, before being occupied by municipal offices. Arzapalo died in 1909, leaving all his Chapala property to his seven-year-old granddaughter.

Several years earlier, Doña Trini's guesthouse had been upgraded by Victor Huber to become the Hotel Huber (later the Gran Hotel Chapala). Located immediately opposite the church, it was demolished in about 1950 when Avenida Madero, the wide boulevard leading directly to the pier, was created.

45

A famous ichthyologist visits the lake
December 1898-January 1899
David Starr Jordan

David Starr Jordan (1851-1931) was a very famous American naturalist, who specialized in ichthyology (fish).

He was a leading educator and peace activist, whose illustrious career included terms as president of the California Academy of Sciences (1896-1904), Indiana University and Stanford University.

In addition, he was president of the World Peace Foundation (1910-1914) and chaired the 1915 World Peace Conference.

In 1916, he was a central figure in Mexico-U.S. discussions aimed at re-establishing peace in Mexico during the Mexican Revolution.

His autobiography, subtitled Memories of a Naturalist, Teacher, and Minor Prophet of Democracy, *reveals that he found Mexico strangely compelling:*

In these pages I cannot attempt to do even partial justice to our varied impressions of the land with its contrasting glories and squalor, but the trip was highly interesting and instructive. Mexico's teeming millions, ignorant, superstitious, and ill-nurtured, with little self-control and no conception of industry or thrift—lacking, indeed, most of our Anglo-Saxon virtues,—had yet for me a certain compelling fascination.

On his visit to Lake Chapala, Jordan and his traveling companions, most of whom were connected to Stanford University, stayed with Señor Joaquin Cuesta on his hacienda at Atequiza.

In the course of his academic career, Jordan published several articles about fishes obtained in Lake Chapala and other nearby lakes and rivers, as well as authoring dozens of books, including Manual of Vertebrates, Animal Life, Fish Stories, Philosophy of Hope, Life's Enthusiasms, Religion of a Sensible American, The Higher Sacrifice, The California Earthquake of 1906, The Care and Culture of Men, *and* The Stability of Truth.

Jordan's visit to Lake Chapala took place in December 1898-January 1899:

During our stay in that region we were all guests for a day and a night at the ample *hacienda* of Atequiza, a great *rancho* twenty-four miles out of Guadalajara, near Lake Chapala, Jalisco; for Señor Joaquin Cuesta, head of the house, whom I had previously met in San Francisco, had invited us to visit him when in his neighborhood. The lordly courtesy and hospitality of our host we found thoroughly delightful. Going about the estate, I was much interested in the contrast between progressive American methods and the primitive customs of an unscientific people. Don Joaquin, for example, was operating a modern flouring mill stocked with machinery from Rochester, New York, but the soil was still planted with crooked sticks because the *peons* persistently refused to have anything to do with *gringo* inventions....

Leaving the party from time to time, Snyder and I made several large collections—one at Lake Chapala, famous as the choicest winter resort of migratory birds on our continent, one at Puente de Ixtla in a tributary of the Río de las Balsas, and one from the sea at Vera Cruz. Specially interesting is the fish fauna of the three volcanic lakes, Chapala, Pátzcuaro, and Zirahuen, as each separate body of water contains several species of closely related, large atherine fishes of Silversides of the genus *Chirostoma*, all of very delicate flesh and locally known as *pescados blancos*, "white fishes" or *pescados del rey* "fishes of the king." *Chirostoma* occurs only in various lakes of central Mexico, though its allies are scattered over warmer parts of the world. But the singular feature is that the dozen or so clearly defined species look very much alike, forming an apparently marked deviation from Jordan's Law. [1] A probable explanation of this anomaly is that earthquake disturbances at one time or another threw together parts of different river basins, thus mingling different faunas.

[1] Jordan's Law: a general rule governing the formation of distinct species by isolation or separation: "the nearest relative of any given form is usually not found in exactly the same region nor at a distance, but just on the other side of some barrier to distribution".

Jordan, David Starr. 1922 *The Days of a Man: Being Memories of a Naturalist, Teacher, and Minor Prophet of Democracy.*

46

Chapala the beautiful
1900
Hon. Maud Pauncefote

The details of the Honorable Maud Pauncefote's life have proved disappointingly elusive.

She was the eldest of the four daughters of Sir Julian (later Lord Julian) Pauncefote, who was the British Minister in Washington (and subsequently the British Ambassador) from 1889 until his death in 1902. He was senior British delegate to the First Hague Conference, and was nominated for the Nobel Peace Prize in 1901.

Sir Julian's major claim to fame was the Hay-Pauncefote Treaty signed in November 1901, by which time Roosevelt had succeeded the slain McKinley as U.S. President. The Hay-Pauncefote Treaty mapped out the role of the U.S. in the construction and management of a Central American canal, linking the Atlantic Ocean to the Pacific. The treaty led to the agreement in 1903, under which the U.S. and the newly established republic of Panama agreed that the U.S. should have exclusive canal rights across the Isthmus of Panama in exchange for financial reimburse-ment and guarantees of protection.

The Hon. (Selina) Maud Pauncefote (1862-1919) was born shortly after her father, a lawyer, had lost almost all his private fortune due to a bank collapse. The family sailed to Hong Kong in 1862 and stayed there ten years before returning to England. In 1889, the Pauncefotes relocated to Washington D.C., where Maud, who loved the U.S., acted as hostess, alongside her mother Selina, at the British embassy.

Besides *Chapala The Beautiful*, Maud Pauncefote also wrote *Life in Washington* (1903), an article about diplomatic life, and fiction, such as the short stories entitled "The Silence of Two" in *Munsey's* (1908) and "Their Wedding Day", published in *The Cavalier* in 1909.

In *Life in Washington*, Maud Pauncefote offers some timeless advice for improving trans-Atlantic understanding: "In England there is still a vague notion that Americans are almost English. If that impression were thoroughly eradicated we should comprehend the American nation much better."

This piece, the Hon. Maud Pauncefote's first published article, appears to be the earliest travel article dedicated exclusively to the lake area. It includes what are thought to be the first published photographs of the village of Chapala: one, taken from the wharf, shows the lakeshore with the church in the background, another shows a diligence in the high street, with the lake behind.

n the western slope of mountainous Mexico is a beautiful lake resembling in size and surroundings the Lake of Geneva. It is called the Lake of Chapala, and as it is out of the beaten track, many visitors who feel that they have seen Mexico quite thoroughly fail to see that interesting place.

To reach charming Chapala one must either take a steamer from the end of the lake, or leave the train at the station called Atiquiza, thirteen miles across the mountains. Then comes a drive over a road so full of bowlders and holes, hills and valleys, that the wonder is one has a bone unbroken in one's body at the end of the journey. A diligence awaits you such as is only seen in museums nowadays. Such a very odd old thing it is, immensely heavy, with gigantic wheels, and a body as big as a house, with leather straps inside to hold on to. It is drawn by eight mules. It goes back and forth daily to Atiquiza station to fetch the mail, passengers, and parcels. The driver, a young "peon," receives the vast wages of fifty cents per diem for driving his very refractory mules, who frequently kick and plunge and are not in any way broken. Most primitive are his methods. Those he cannot reach with his whip he corrects with a well-directed stone from a heap lying at his feet. There is also a conductor on this great conveyance. He spends his time in jumping on and off the diligence, and in killing little birds with well-aimed stones when not engaged in mending the harness or punching a slow mule—little cares which frequently interfere with his amusements. That thirteen-mile drive is an experience —over such lovely country, with sudden views of the lake on turning a corner or arriving at the top of a tremendously steep climb. The wonder is how the mules ever get the old machine up the mountains. During the rainy season it is a marvel how it ever goes at all through the mud and over the swollen streams.

Chapala is 400 feet lower than the city of Mexico. The lake is surrounded by mountains, which in that lovely atmosphere, so high and rarefied, take every shade of violet and pink and blue. The coloring is magnificent, and the sunsets and starlight nights are things to dream of. The Southern Cross is seen, and every star seems brighter and bigger and nearer, and the sky more filled with gems than one ever imagined. The little village of Chapala nestles down below the mountains on the shore of the lake. There is a small foreign settlement there whose members have discovered the charm and have built villas on the borders of the lake, the air being very good for the lungs. But the native Indians are not inclined to sell their homesteads, so it is difficult to procure land on the water's edge. Very picturesque are these Indian fishermen, who, owning the land around the lake, are able without any trouble to their lazy natures to carry on their business of supplying the market at Guadalajara, the nearest city. After a good haul they take their fish to town on mule-back—a long journey by road. The Indian's wants are few; nature has done so much for him. In that climate no fires are necessary, so their shanties are merely huts of adobe and thatch, adobe being a sort of clay plastering together a few wooden posts. Not an expensive style of building, surely, and about architecture they do not worry. Neither are they particular as to many rooms—sleeping-apartments or parlors or kitchens—so one or, at most, two compartments make a house. Sleeping in the open air wrapped around by the "serape," a striped, colored rug, is much in vogue among the men, and right they certainly are, as it is more healthy than those awful huts where, as in Ireland, the pig, the hens, and most of the live stock share the house with the proprietor. As to the necessaries of life, the lake supplies fish, banana and orange trees grow in profusion, and apparently in every one's garden, a little maize to make the pancake "frizole"—what more can one want? These supply all the native's wants. The climate is so warm and lovely that cotton clothes are all any one can wear.

Life at this rate hardly necessitates an income, so very naturally the Indians would rather keep their lovely sites down by the water than sell them, however well, and have to move off up the mountains, where they must come far to fish, and may lose their right to what living the lake supplies. As in every Mexican city, the market square or plaza is the great place of "rendezvous", and on Sunday mornings and fête-days a little fair is held, when every one, well dressed in cleanest white or blue, is to be found there buying or selling, chattering, gossiping, and flirting. Such are the charmingly, merry, picturesque scenes, for in Mexico all is color, brilliant and variegated. The Chapala "plaza" is surrounded by shady orange-trees, with a charming peep of the lake down past the lovely white church....

Lazy as the Indian of that region certainly is, and uncivilized, he has a trait in common with modern civilization—the love of bathing. He bathes and swims in the lake, and also in the many sulphur pools which abound. In riding by—for driving is out of the question, on account of the roads deep in dust or mud, according to the season—one sees a brown or black head, like a strange water-lily, appearing upon the surface of one of the pools. Here the water is warm, over seventy degrees, and the Indians stay in and stew for a long while. They are an amiable people, most grateful for any kindness, but the men are very jealous, and murders are frequent from a kind of vendetta. The frequent glass of pulque is responsible, no doubt, for many of these deeds.

Pauncefote, Hon. Maud. 1900. *Chapala the Beautiful.*

Chapala as I saw it
1900-1901

Ethel Brilliana Harley (later Mrs. Alec Tweedie)

Ethel Brilliana Harley (1862-1940) was born in England to Dr. George Harley and his wife Emma (Muspratt). Ethel, educated at Queen's College, London, and in Germany, married Alexander Leslie Tweedie (1849-1896), an insurance broker, in 1887. The couple had two sons, born in 1888 and 1890, but the family's prosperity and joy were short lived. Alexander (Alec) was financially ruined when his insurance syndicate collapsed. He died shortly afterwards in 1896, leaving nothing to his wife and sons. In the same year, Ethel's father died; he also left her nothing.

Motivated by a desire to do the best she could for her sons, Mrs. Tweedie gradually transformed her previous hobby of travel into a career. Eventually, she re-established herself as a London socialite and philanthropist, having become a Fellow of the Royal Geographical Society, an indefatigable traveler, well-known artist and one of the world's first female professional travel writers. Sadly, in the course of this process, she lost both sons, killed in the First World War.

Tweedie's philanthropy was mainly related to women and travel. She served on several committees of the International Council of Women and was a life governor of two hospitals. In 1912 she was thanked by the Italian government for having helped survivors of the powerful 1908 Sicilian earthquake in which 200,000 lives were lost.

Prior to visiting Mexico, she had already published books about Iceland, Norway, Finland and the Oberammergau Passion Play. Her books were written to appeal especially to female armchair travelers, combining a spirit of adventure with descriptions of people and places.

After Mexico, she spent two years traveling in central Asia. This trip led to numerous other books, and resulted in an exhibition of three hundred watercolor sketches at the Alpine gallery, London. This led to many other exhibitions and one woman shows, prior to her death on April 15, 1940.

Mexico as I saw it *was the product of her first visit to Mexico which lasted six months between 1900 and 1901. Five years later, she returned to "this fascinating country". When re-issued in 1911, the book reflected "the great changes that have taken place over the last ten years", and included an appendix on the conditions of the country as a result of the Revolution of 1910 and the resignation of General Porfirio Díaz.*

Tweedie's writing on Mexico was roundly criticized by Henry Baerlein, another prolific British author of the time: "Mrs. Alec Tweedie wrote in a newspaper article that it is difficult to write of a country when you are 6000 miles away; and I submit that, in everything which matters, she has never been any closer to Mexico. The lack of understanding, the nauseous egotism, the total absence of charm and of literary qualities..."

Her background inevitably gave Tweedie a rosy view of the essentially feudal system rife during much of Diaz's prolonged time in power. Like so many at the time, she considered Mexico "picturesque and quaint", seeing the peons as stupid and unable to better their positions because of such character flaws as lack of thrift. As the Mexican Revolution showed when it erupted in 1910, most peons certainly did not share this view.

Tweedie describes her visit to Lake Chapala in straightforward, direct language, suitable for a varied readership. Her writing is full of anecdotes and comparisons with other places she knew.

We stayed at Chapala, where there are sulphur baths on the lake of that name. Whether those natural springs induced the folk to wash, or whether they did so on account of its being Sunday, I know not; but everywhere was cleanliness. Spotless linen was worn on all sides; women, stripped to the waist, were washing their clothes in the stream; washing was on every side. After six months' sojourn in Mexico I can honestly say I consider the natives are most cleanly. In the country, by a lake or stream, they are always washing and bathing, and only in the squalid portions of the towns does dirt exist.

On one day of the year at least every man, woman and child in Mexico bathes, namely, the 24th of June, which, it will be remembered, is St. John the Baptist's day. This yearly bath is taken in honour of St. John, who chose baptism by total immersion as his symbol of penitence and purification. In Edward VI's first Prayer-book we read that "the prieste" had "to dyppe the child in the water thryse."

There is one part of their bodies they neglect, however, viz., their heads; they have not learnt the value of paraffin, as applied in hospitals, and five, six or even seven people will sit in a row like ninepins, searching for the animals which seem indigenous to neglected locks. It is not a pretty sketch, but so true a picture of Mexican daily life that it cannot be omitted.

Several times we passed folk riding pillion; generally the woman sat sideways, the man astride behind, and they jogged on as contentedly as did our forefathers in the Highlands of Scotland, who rode pillion to kirk to be married.

During our exciting drive to Chapala, several strange trees arrested my attention. To prevent the cattle from stealing the fodder, Indian corn is put up into the forked arms of the trees. One sees a nice large tree which looks as though it were in extraordinarily full leaf and on drawing nearer discovers that there is a hay or rather a corn-stack, among its boughs!

The waggons on the road were all drawn by ox teams such funny waggons, too; just ribs of bamboo, the sides being kept together with matting, or hairy cow-hide, yet the wheels were massive blocks of wood. The poor people cannot afford to buy wheels, spokes are difficult to make, and a good solid trunk of a tree can be sliced into a number of convenient wheels. They look heavy and cumbersome, but they work and wear, and after all that is what is wanted. "Time was made for man" suits very well in Mexico, as does the Finnish proverb, "God did not create hurry."

A family removal, and what a family! There appeared to be about fifty of them, and perhaps there were, for Mexican families—even of the highest rank—live together in a manner that is perfectly incomprehensible to English ideas. Dozens of members of this family were stowed away behind the matting walls of the cart, and as the team of oxen drew up for us to pass, every fold of matting was raised, and out popped two or three heads. It was very hot, and what the temperature must have been inside that cart we shudder to think. The few worldly goods possessed by these folk were on another waggon; men sat on the top with fowls tied by the leg, pigs or cats in their laps, and bird-cages hanging over the edge of the cart.

We passed; the waggon drivers took their long sticks with spear points at the end, prodded those handsome old oxen, and on they plodded.

Some boys were larking by the roadside over their midday meal, their horses being tethered near by. Something displeased one of them. In an instant there was a flash of steel, and each youth had drawn the sword or *machete* which he carried. The quarrel ended in nothing; but the rapidity with which swords were drawn, and the fact that each youth carried one, showed the temper of the country.

Chapala enjoys a glorious climate, tropical vegetation abounds, and birds and beasts from every clime shelter along the shores of the lake when they are driven southwards by the cold. Innumerable orchids clustered on the trees. There are great tall plants, twenty or thirty feet high, of bourganvillia—flaming red, lilac and purple—also geraniums, palms and cocoanuts.

Delicious fish abound in the Lake, which is about eighty miles long; they are caught in nets. These pescado blanco (white fish) are literally transparent when they come out of the water. They are spoken of as lake herring, though I cannot say I thought they resembled a Loch Fyne herring in taste so much as a river trout....

The black, white and red plumage of the giant woodpecker is a wonderful contrast to his ivory-like beak. It is an Indian superstition that the short red feathers from the head will cure all diseases if worn in the ears, consequently these birds fetch high prices. They are rare, and difficult to shoot, that being probably the reason why the superstition has arisen, and they are so highly prized.

In the evening we went out to look at the moon on Chapala Lake—one of those lovely moons all lakes know so well how to reflect. In front of the hotel door we saw a weird figure with a flaming torch in his hand, apparently looking for something on the ground. What had he lost?

"I am burning ants," was his reply; under a wild fig tree—as big as an ordinary horse-chestnut—these ants, big as bees, had made their home. They came out at night, whole families of them, each one carrying a little leaf he had purloined from the tree, and this dark gentleman with his torch of resin was burning them wholesale. He swept his death weapon remorselessly along the ground, and up the sides of any wall where he saw a family of ants promenading, and we heard them cremated. They looked almost as large and brown as those delicious oyster crabs which frizzle on to one's plate at Delmonico's. But these Mexican ants are really a plague, for they will strip a tree of its entire foliage in one night.

What a lovely evening that was at Chapala. How gloriously bright the moon, but I felt homesick, and Moore's beautiful lines came back to me :—

"The best charms of nature improve
When we see them reflected from looks that we love."

What truth lies in those two lines. Of course, the "strong-minded woman," the "elderly scribe," ought never to feel lonely or homesick; but I did, and in such peaceful hours as these, or in the gay throng of some large reception, trouble came upon me. The greater the crowd, the more public the moment, the more I longed for my own kith and kin to share its pleasures with me. Stupid but true!

Tweedie, Mrs. Alec. 1901 *Mexico as I Saw It*.

48

An anthropologist finds votive offerings
1902
Carl Sophus Lumholtz

Carl Sophus Lumholtz (1851-1922), born in Lillehammer, Norway, was a scientist, traveler and anthropologist in the generalist Humboldtian tradition. After graduating from the Theology department of the University of Christianía in Oslo, Lumholtz went to Australia as a naturalist. While living with cannibalistic aborigines in northern Queensland, he became fascinated by the study of primitive peoples, and spent the rest of his life enthralled by the anthropology and ethnology of native tribes in many different parts of the world.

Lumholtz made six separate trips to Mexico, with the express purpose of studying indigenous people and their beliefs and customs. This approach was in stark contrast to that adopted by previous travelers, who had tended to regard the contributions of native Indians to the overall picture of life and work in Mexico as relatively insignificant.

His visits were supported by generous, wealthy patrons, as well as by the American Geographical Society and the American Museum of Natural History in New York. Helped by letters of introduction from politicians in Washington, Lumholtz was able to obtain logistical support from President Porfirio Díaz, who Lumholtz considered to be "not only a great man on this continent, but one of the great men of our time." Díaz helped organize a translation of Lumholtz's work into Spanish. This was published, in 1904, only two years after the original English edition.

Lumholtz first entered Mexico with a team of some thirty scientists, with specializations ranging from geography to physics and from botany to mineralogy, and 100 horses. By the fourth trip, he had abandoned the team approach in favor of traveling alone, since this allowed him to explore some of the remotest parts of north and west Mexico, and live for extended periods of time with isolated Indian tribes. His respectful, patient attitude allowed him to gain the confidence of his hosts, and be permitted to take some of the earliest known photographs of them and their activities.

He was particularly impressed by the Indians' practical skills: "In all kinds of handicraft, for instance, in carving on stone, wood, and so forth, the ancient people of Mexico have no equal today for accuracy of execution and beauty of outline." His sense of priorities is best summed up by his statement that he felt he had to protect the "Indians from the Mexicans, the Mexicans from the Americans".

To his eternal regret, Lumholtz's work in Mexico was interrupted by the outbreak of the Mexican Revolution in 1910, and he felt forced to turn his attentions to other parts of the world, including India, Borneo and south-east Asia.

A prolific author, with dozens of works to his credit, Lumholtz died in 1922 while planning a research trip to New Guinea.

Unknown Mexico is an account of Lumholtz's first four trips to Mexico, representing a total of five years in the country, between 1890 and 1900. Even today, it remains a classic of anthropological literature. Illustrated with dozens of drawings and photographs, it provides a wealth of details about the lifestyles, customs, native remedies, music and beliefs of some of the indigenous tribes.

I made also an excursion to the beautiful lake of Chapala, the largest sheet of fresh water in Mexico, fifty miles long and from fifteen to eighteen broad. Its name is Nahuatl, which should really be Chapalal, in onomatopoetic imitation of the sound of the waves playing on the beach. The stage runs to a small village of the same name, lying on the shore, where some pretty country houses have been built.

The book includes drawings of two ceremonial hatchets "used at sacred sites" and found in the "neighbourhood of Chapala".

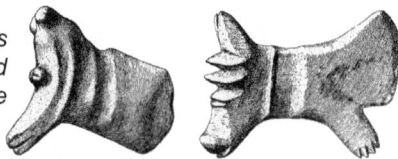

In this lake, especially at its western end, are found great quantities of ancient, roughly made, diminutive jars, and a number of other objects. Near the village of Axixic (Nahuatl, "Where water [atl] pours forth") the people make a business of diving for them, threading them on strings, and selling them to visitors to the village of Chapala. I gathered several hundreds of them, and the supply seemed inexhaustible. No one knows when or why they were thrown into the lake. Most likely they were votive offerings to the deity of this water, to secure luck and health and other material benefits.

Lumholtz, Carl Sophus. 1902 *Unknown Mexico.*

49

Two bird-lovers at Lake Chapala
1904: Charles William Beebe and
Mary Blair Rice (later Blair Niles)

Charles William Beebe (Will Beebe, as he preferred) was an American ornithologist, naturalist, explorer, and author, born in Brooklyn, New York. Beebe (1877-1962) never completed a college degree, but undertook pioneering studies in various fields of ecology, in habitats ranging from high altitude forests (in search of pheasants) to tropical rainforests, coral reefs and the ocean depths.

Beebe married his first wife, Mary Blair Rice (see below), in 1902. *Two Bird Lovers in Mexico* describes their first trip overseas in the winter of 1903-1904, when Beebe was curator of ornithology at the New York Zoological Society. Beebe went on to become director of the Society's Department of Tropical Research, undertaking work in dozens of countries, including extended stays in British Guiana (now Guyana), the Galapagos Islands, Bermuda and Trinidad. He inspired an entire generation of naturalists to explore the connections between animals, plants and their environment.

Beebe wrote dozens of books, and hundreds of magazine articles during a prolific career. His non-academic books (such as *Two Bird Lovers in Mexico*) popularized natural history, while simultaneously promoting the need for conservation. They brought the sights, sounds, thrills, and perils, of remote places into the homes of armchair travelers everywhere. Among his best-known works are *Galapagos* (1923), *Half Mile Down* (1934), and *Unseen Life of New York* (1953).

Among Beebe's many extraordinary achievements was a record descent (with Otis Barton) to 3 028 feet (914 meters) below the ocean surface in a bathysphere off Bermuda in 1934.

He also seems to have been the first person to identify the temperature anomalies that are now known as El Niño. More than 88 animal species had been named after him by the time of his death, in Trinidad, on June 4, 1962.

Armed with a shotgun, rifle, and two revolvers, the Beebes arrived in Veracruz in December 1903 and immediately took the train across the country to Guadalajara. They set off to camp on the slopes of Colima volcano, witnessing an eruption there the following January.

During their trip to Mexico, Beebe and his wife observed and collected hundreds of birds, flowers, grass-hoppers and lizards, but seem to have encountered remarkably few Mexicans, except for the ones who piled stones on their railway tracks for a prank.

Beebe and Mary Blair Rice divorced in 1913.

Mary Blair Rice (1880-1959), contributed the cover design and a chapter entitled "How We Did It" to *Two Bird Lovers in Mexico*. She also wrote several articles about the trip, as they camped their way across Mexico, for the *New York Post* and *Harper's*.

In 1913, Blair divorced Beebe, marrying architect Robin Niles (Beebe's next door neighbor) the very next day. She subsequently changed her name to Blair Niles, and had a distinguished career as a travel writer and novelist, as well as being one of the four founding members of the Society of Women Geographers. In addition to travel books on Ecuador, Columbia, and Haiti, she also wrote *Strange Brother,* a novel with a homosexual hero, and *Condemned to Devil's Island: the Biography of an Unknown Convict,* which was turned into one of the first talking movies of all time.

An ardent traveler, Blair Niles died in 1959, leaving behind a remarkable legacy of books, and having had a significant impact on 20th century feminism.

The Beebes visited Chapala in the latter half of March 1904. The following extracts reflect the situation immediately prior to Cuesta Gallardo's scheme, which drained the eastern portions of Lake Chapala.

Our visit to the oasis of *Agua Azul* was one of many delights, but when the marvel of the bird life of Lake Chapala and its marshes revealed itself to us, the feelings we experienced cannot be put into words; such one feels at a first glance through a great telescope, or perhaps when one gazes in wonder upon the distant earth from a balloon. At these times, one is for an instant outside of his petty personality and a part of, a realizer of, the cosmos. Here on these waters and marshes we saw, not individuals or flocks, but a world of birds! Never before had a realization of the untold solid bulk in numbers of the birds of our continent been impressed so vividly upon us. And the marvel of it all was the more impressive because of its unexpectedness....

One should spend a month upon the waters of the little river and the mighty lake, learning the secrets of the wild life. What things the giant catfish could reveal, feeling their way among the reed and lily stems!

At the great marsh, where the stream flows from the lake, many ebony rattlesnakes lived a semi-aquatic life, slipping, when disturbed, from the damp mounds, and undulating through the black water, like the moccasins in a Florida cypress swamp.

From their sinewy folds of death to the beauty and grace of a snow white egret is, indeed, an extreme; but here snake and bird lived in close association,—finding in the same swamp rest, shelter, and food. We in the North have neglected the egrets until well nigh the last survivor has been murdered; but here in this wild place, where, outside of the towns, a man's best law and safeguard is in his holster, these birds have already found champions. Short tolerance had the first plume hunter—an American—who began his nefarious work in the Chapala marshes. The rough but beauty loving *caballeros* who owned the *haciendas* surrounding the lake talked it over, formed—to all intents and purposes—an Audubon Society, ran the millinery agent off, and forbade the shooting of these birds. There was no fine or imprisonment for shooting egrets,—only a widespread verbal "revolver law," more significant and potent than many of our inscribed legislative enactments.

Loons and grebes delighted in the swampy end of the lake—the former shrieking and diving in the joyous abandon of their wild, unlimited lives. The great Western Grebe was especially interesting,—another species which must fight for very existence in its Northern haunts, its silky breast having found fatal favour in the eyes of milliners.

Hundreds of White Pelicans are said to make their winter home here, breeding far to the northward; but a distant glimpse of a few of the great birds is all that may be hoped for in a flying visit....

Few hunters thought of looking for sport elsewhere than on the waters of the lake itself, and so we were not surprised to find the birds tame and unconcerned at our presence. Little streams appeared, with coots and handsome little Scaup Ducks floating on their quiet surface, and sandpipers teetering along the muddy banks. At last we leaped two ditches, the guide leading the way through an opening in the willow tangle, and we found ourselves at the edge of the marshes, a vast plain, half dry, half flooded, broken here and there by patches of tall reeds, a great land expanse stretching mile upon mile to the lake toward the south west and to the barren mountains rising hazy and blue in the east.

At another time and place we have seen thousands of pelicans close together on a tiny islet; again, ducks have surrounded us in such masses that we seemed floating in a sea of birds; but all our remembrances paled before the avifauna of the Chapala marshes. Migration had already begun, and we were told that vast numbers of Pintails and Widgeons had left for the North, but untold thousands of birds were before us. As far as the eye could see, living feathered forms were scattered irregularly or massed in dense flocks. Our guide could not understand why we did not wish to shoot, but only to look, and look again, wishing we could draw out the seconds to minutes, the minutes to hours, in which to feast our eyes upon the wonderfully beautiful sight....

The air was filled with a multitude of sweet notes,—half strange, half familiar,—and the sight of scores of brilliant yellow breasts, crescent marked, turned toward us, told us that it was a hint of well known Meadowlark music which puzzled our memory....

We now came to occasional swampy places with small patches of open water surrounded by higher ground. Blackbirds, and Cowbirds with red eyes, chased grasshoppers and other insects. When an occasional hopper of unusually large size sprang up, a fluttering mass of feathers, scarlet, white, golden, and black would set upon him. But often a low browed Caracara galloped up, scattering the lesser birds and appropriating the remains of the insect for himself. It was amusing to see how these curious birds seized their small prey in the talons of one foot and lifted it toward their beak, nibbling at it from between their toes, like a cockatoo with a piece of bread.

All these scenes were noted within a few minutes, and then our attention was wholly absorbed by the wading and water birds. We rode acre after acre with Killdeer and one or two unnameable species of plover calling and dabbling for food in the moist places close to our horses' feet. Greater Yellow legs and their miniature copies—the Lesser—waded in the flooded areas. The beauties of all the long legged waders — the Black necked Stilts—were here in great numbers. In one small swamp meadow I counted more than eighty, and in all directions their striking black and white forms were visible, raised above the level of the reeds. With all their great length of legs they were graceful walkers, their movements having an easy swing which was most pleasing. From their little round heads with the long, slender, needle like bills, the bright jet black eyes kept sharp watch upon us, but they showed no fear unless we approached within a few yards, when they glided evenly but quickly to one side....

The guide pulled up suddenly and pointed ahead, and we saw a misty, dun coloured cloud slowly disentangling itself from the marsh. The glass showed untold numbers of White fronted Geese drifting slowly off toward the lake. To the left were what appeared like great patches of white sand or snow, and we galloped our horses toward these. Soon the patches enlarged, changed their relative positions, and began to ascend, and we realized that we were looking at enormous flocks of Snow Geese taking to wing,—one of the most beautiful sights in the world of birds. Reluctantly we turned backward by a new route—a short cut to the town.

But Chapala honours us with a final farewell. The sun is sinking in a cloudless sky, a wind rises from somewhere, ruffles the face of the pools and brings the scent of the marsh blooms to us. A small flock of White fronted Geese passes rapidly overhead, not very high up, when all at once there floats into view cloud after cloud of purest white, stained on one edge by the gold of the setting sun. We dismount and look up until our bodies ache, and still they come, silently driving into the darkening north. The great imperative call of the year has sounded; the drawing which brooks no refusal.

Beebe, Charles William. 1905 *Two Bird-Lovers in Mexico.*

50

Chapala—a place for the leisure class
1904-1907
Stanton Davis Kirkham

Stanton Davis Kirkham (1868-1944) was an American naturalist and the author of numerous books. He was born in Nice, France on December 7, 1868, and educated in California public schools and at the Massachusetts Institute of Technology. He lived much of his adult life in Canandaigua, New York.

His book on Mexico, *Mexican Trails. A record of travels in Mexico, 1904-1907, and a glimpse at the life of the Mexican Indian,* includes 24 of his own photos. It was "affectionately dedicated" to the memory of his grandfather, General Ralph Wilson Kirkham, who was wounded at the storming of Chapultepec Castle, Mexico City.

Mexican Trails was enthusiastically received by readers at the time of its publication. One contemporary reviewer described *Mexican Trails* as providing "a charming picture of Mexico". It is "an impressionistic painting, full of the atmosphere and color of the real Mexico". Kirkham is interested in everything and "finds continual delight". "Mr. Kirkham has succeeded in portraying the individuality, the elusive spirit of Mexico".

Kirkham liked to travel well off the beaten track. He enjoyed Mexico as a "lotus eater" which he defined as one who escaped from the rut of everyday life, "to look about a little and rejoice in a new horizon, an interested spectator merely of a quaintly fascinating life."

Though Kirkham recognized that below the quaintness was a bare, grim reality, he tended to focus on pleasurable things. Sitting in the shade, for instance, he reflected that to a peon a sombrero was a utensil through which he could strain coffee or transport meat, as well as being an element of apparel that afforded him dignity.

Kirkham is on his way from Zamora to La Barca:

Several leagues beyond we came to hot springs, whose boiling was audible some distance away. I paused before a gently simmering pool, whence arose a cloud of steam. Suddenly a great volume of water shot into the air, with subterranean rumblings terrifying to hear. The startled horse recovered his vim and we continued our journey....

From La Barca to Ocotlan is eight leagues. We were to make it in time for the boat, which leaves at ten. As we rode through the town a tremendous cannonading was going on; bombs were exploding, crackers sputtered, and rockets hissed, while the streets were as full of smoke as if a battle were in progress.

Evidently the mozo had had too much fiesta. He was a small man, who collapsed under his big sombrero, till there was little to be seen but the hat and a huge pair of spurs depending from long leather leggins. Rain fell and the wind blew. From time to time the white mule strayed off into the corn fields with the trunk, but the disconsolate mozo only retreated further under his sombrero. There was still a league to go when the preliminary whistle sounded—a shrill little pipe in the distance. *Andale! andale!* the trunk swayed and teetered, the sombrero and spurs were almost jolted out of the saddle. As the bedraggled cavalcade tore down the bank the boat was putting out; the trunk was thrown on board and we were off.

On the lake we felt the full force of the storm. The wretched little craft pitched and tossed all that afternoon like a chip on the waves, which were of astonishing size. At every roll the propeller was out of water, the engines panted, sighed, stopped — then reluctantly went on again, groaning in a new key. There were no small boats and no way of bailing out the cabin should she fill.

But I came at length, after such mild adventures, to Chapala—one of the few towns in Mexico that may be called a resort. Like Cuernavaca, it is one of the idle places of earth—a place in which to loaf and invite your soul. You may wander along the shore or float idly on the lake; you may bathe in December. But if floating and dreaming are not to your taste, Chapala is not for you. Every one there belongs to the leisure class.

Lake Chapala has a languid beauty, according with voluptuous and dreamy moods. The scenery is not "sublime" but very lovely. A railroad circular says that Humboldt considered this unsurpassed by any lake in the world, and that it has over a thousand square miles of water. But Humboldt saw it in its prime. Like Popocatepetl it has changed. When I went to school Popocatepetl was twenty one thousand feet high. Now it is less than eighteen thousand. But Chapala is still charming. The Indian canoes drift listlessly upon its bosom; the clouds—great white cumuli— float leisurely over the azure hills. Soft is the wind, balmy the air, the days idyllic.

Kirkham, Stanton Davis. 1909 *Mexican Trails. A Record of Travel in Mexico, 1904-07*

51

Chapala today
1907
Adolfo Dollero

Adolfo Dollero, a well educated Italian traveler, was born in Turin in November 1872. He moved to Mexico in 1895, but continued to make regular trips back to Europe. In 1898, he married Maria Luisa Paoletti, countess of Rodoretto. Eight years later, the couple, now with two children, Ernastina and Lamberto, and a Mexican servant, are named on the passenger list of a boat back from Europe. The couple added twin boys to their family in 1912. Towards the end of 1914, the difficult political circumstances in Mexico caused the family to relocate to Cuba.

They remained in Cuba until 1921, before returning to Mexico. The family also lived for periods of time in Colombia and Venezuela. Dollero died in Mexico City in September 1936.

In migration records, he described his profession variously as "publicist", "publisher", "author" or "press." On one passenger list, his twin sons, then aged 5, are listed as married!

A Colombian book, by Rito Rueda Rueda, describes Dollero as a historiographer who, he says, agreed with the geographer Eliseo Reclus "that all the native Americans belong to the same ethnic group despite their diversity of customs and their four hundred languages."

The details in México al día (Mexico Today), *published in 1911, relate to travels in Mexico in 1907. This large volume, almost a thousand pages long, covers the entire country fairly comprehensively. It provides a detailed look at ranches, villages, towns and cities, and includes a partial listing of hotels.*

Dollero considered that many parts of the country were in desperate need of improved transport routes which would allow the nation's natural wealth, mines, caves, lakes, coast and rivers to be fully exploited.

The title page of México al día *refers to future English, French, Italian and German editions of the book. However, only the Italian edition ever saw the light of day, and that was not until 1914. Dollero, did, though, write several other books, on Cuba, Colombia and Venezuela.*

Dollero's account of the Lake Chapala area includes descriptions of several towns, the climate and fertility of the lakeshore, the gold and silver mines in the area, and even the names of the major landowners. The only hotel listed for the "bathing resort of Chapala", with its 3000 inhabitants, is the Hotel La Palmera, owned by Francisco Mántice.

Chapala is a village of no more than 3,000 inhabitants, but its privileged location and truly unbeatable climate have made it the meeting place for the most important Mexican families, especially those from the Republic's capital and Guadalajara.

On the shores of the lake, or at the foot of the hills that are reflected in its water, are magnificent chalets. The President of the Republic General Porfirio Díaz himself likes to spend some vacation time here at the end of Lent in the company of his close friends.

Then the lake acquires a special liveliness: hundreds of steam launches and boats plough through the water in every direction; everywhere there are high society parties and lots of money is spent.

It is a shame that this liveliness has been, up to now, very short lived; it has always been restricted to a few months of the year, perhaps on account of the communication difficulties.

From the station at Atequiza, we were shaken for more than two and a half hours in an uncomfortable diligence, which was certainly not very agreeable. They assured us, however, that within a short time a branch line of the railroad would be started to remove the only obstacle which up to now has prevented Chapala from being a place of happiness year round.

We were staying in the hotel La Palmera, belonging to a congenial Italian citizen Mr. Francisco Mantice. The hotel was first rate and the cooking, distinctly French and Italian, was therefore very satisfying.

Chapala has, in general, good land, especially that which is on the shores of the lake; some fields are less fertile than others.

Besides dedicating themselves to agriculture, the inhabitants also fish; fine fish are abundant, as are turtles and various species of aquatic birds, some of them valued highly for their very fine feathers.

Lake Chapala measures some 100 kilometers in length and its maximum width is 24 kilometers.

There are some mines for gold and silver in Ajijic, but judging by what has been discovered in them up to now, they are not very rich. Some traces of petroleum have been found in the lake, but tests have shown it to be insufficient for exploitation.

The sand of the lake contains lots of quartz and silica and could be used for the manufacture of glass: there was already one bottle factory, which was closed down for lack of capital. Several thermal springs also exist in Chapala: one of them is ferruginous and another one sulfurous.

We stayed two days in Chapala and afterwards, crossing the length of the lake, we went to Ocotlán, on board the very small steamship Raúl. Our voyage lasted four hours and proved extremely interesting.

Black storm clouds were gathering on the horizon, and from time to time a ray of sunshine shone through them for a few moments to fleetingly illuminate the top of this or that greenish hill before becoming hidden again behind other clouds, still blacker and heavier....

Only a very short time after we had passed Presidio Island we saw a huge vertical column shaped like an enormous serpent appear on the horizon.

We had the opportunity to see for the first time the phenomenon of a waterspout, which greatly interested us, though we would have preferred to meet it on board a large steamer rather than the extremely fragile Raúl. However, the little steamer's owner who had not put down the telescope, calmed us down shortly afterwards, assuring us that the wind from the North that was blowing strongly at the time would have changed the direction of the water spout or would have destroyed it. In fact, some twenty minutes later, the column of water became less dense, becoming gradually like a bow before disappearing completely.

Without delay, the water of the lake became calm, and shortly afterwards, the last clouds clearing, the sun allowed us once again to contemplate the beautiful blue of the sky.

The left bank gradually acquired an extraordinary liveliness: house followed house; then came ranches and haciendas which they told us belonged to American citizens who had changed them into poetic residences with an abundance of flowers, fruit and cattle.

A more enchanting landscape could not be planned. At last, we entered the River Zula and then clearly saw the small churches of Ocotlán and to the right the Hotel Rivera [Ribera] Castellanos and the haciendas of El Fuerte, also extremely pleasant places, and very popular with North Americans, great lovers, as is known, of the beauties of nature.

Ocotlán is a small town of 5,000 inhabitants with a lot of commercial activity. The products of all the lake arrive here. Given this, it attracted our attention that there was no wharf and that the small steamers and different vessels had to moor alongside the trees on the banks! We were told, however, that a Mr. Ramón Flores, a person of initiative and capital, had requested authorization from the Secretariat of Communications and

Public Works to build a suitable one within a short period of time.

Ocotlán is a true granary: since all the region is fertile, canoes come here from all directions with loads of cereals, fruit, matting of *tule* (an aquatic plant that is very abundant in these parts). On some occasions, the dozens of warehouses belonging to the Railway Company and private owners, and the wagons of the Tram Company, which sometimes transport up to 3,000 loads a day, an enormous quantity considering that Ocotlán is more a town than a city, are not sufficient.

The countryside is splendid: irrigation, already practiced on a vast scale, will soon be on an even larger one, once the magnificent project of Mr. Manuel Cuesta Gallardo, for which the Federal Government has made important concessions, has been carried out.

The project consists of reducing the basin of the lake and making channels on all the surrounding areas to receive, by means of the most modern systems, a portion of the basic liquid.

Being thereby exposed a belt of land of superior quality which the Government cedes to the irrigation company, the latter will get a fairly good profit by selling parcels of the previously mentioned belt.

Several lakeside property owners had been opposed at the time to the Cuesta Gallardo project, alleging previous rights over the lake shores. The concession holder has now reached extra-judicial agreements with the most important of them, so no doubt therefore remains that the company will have concluded by achieving its objective, resulting in great benefits for all....

Ocotlán also has the advantage of the water of the Lerma; on leaving Lake Chapala the river receives the name of Río Grande: the River Zula joins this river forming a small bay for loading and unloading, precisely where the construction of the wharf is planned. The climate of Ocotlán is mild: however, during our stay there, the huge number of flies bothered us greatly; the loathsome dipterans left nothing untouched and every once in a while... we would have the disagreeable surprise of finding them on the plates and in the glasses!

Dollero, Adolfo. 1911 *México al día. (Impresiones y notas de viaje).*

Schemes which changed the lake

In the 19th century, most of the proposed schemes to change the course or nature of the Lake Chapala area were never carried out. Of those that were implemented, the most significant was the construction in 1883 of the Presa Corona. This dam facilitated the construction of a hydro-power plant at the Juanacatlán Falls. Associated irrigation channels allowed much of the Santiago valley to be farmed all year.

At the eastern end of the lake, farmers had tried several times to gain permanent additional land by draining parts of the lakeshore. Calls for more land, and more control over the position of the edge of the lake were renewed following a drought in 1896, and the very low lake level the following year, when the hydro plant had to be taken out of service for lack of water. Engineers decided to build a dam at Poncitlán to regulate the Santiago river, and conserve water in times of plenty.

A few years later, in 1904, very high floods following the rainy season made landowners even more unhappy. The inauguration of the Poncitlán dam in 1905 ironically meant that water levels remained high each year for longer than usual in the much-coveted eastern marshes. In several places, including Jamay and La Palma, local landowners constructed dykes to prevent the water from covering their fields. Levées were built along the Lerma and its tributary the Duero.

Manuel Cuesta Gallardo (a native of Guadalajara) had a much bolder vision, which reflected how successfully Europeans had increased their areas of farmland through drainage and reclamation schemes. He convinced President Porfirio Díaz to award him a concession for the 50 000 hectares of land that would be gained by constructing an 80-kilometer-long earth bank from La Palma to Maltaraña, to completely amputate the eastern end of the lake, the area known as the Ciénega of Chapala. The scheme, designed by engineer Luis P. Ballesteros, also involved digging major drainage channels. All the work was done by hand. By 1908, the work was complete. Cuesta Gallardo went on to become the Governor of Jalisco, albeit only briefly, for a few months in 1911.

The following year, disastrous floods overwhelmed the earth banks, destroyed bridges and wrecked crops. Further floods in 1913 caused further damage, but all the dykes were rebuilt by the following year. While the scheme has certainly not prevented occasional flooding, it has increased the agricultural area in the region. But at what cost? Critics say that the delicate ecological balance of the lake was destroyed for ever. The marshland's natural sponge-like ameliorating effect, soaking up excess rainfall to make it available again in times of drought, was gone for good.

52

A place of contrasts
1909
William English Carson

Very little is known about the early life of British-born journalist William English Carson (1870-1940) though it appears that, accompanied by future tabloid pioneer Alfred Harmsworth (later Lord Northcliffe), he toured the Outer Hebrides in 1897, keeping a diary (unpublished) of the trip.

Carson later made his home in New York and became a naturalized American citizen in 1920. He wrote three books. The best known is his first: *Mexico, the Wonderland of the South* published originally in 1909, just before the revolution began. It was based on four months residence over a winter and covers familiar ground, since Carson did not venture far from the railway.

A contemporary reviewer wrote that "Some of his remarks are amusingly naïve, such as: "Few Mexican women are domesticated, and everything is left to the servants" or "fevers and malaria are certain to result from exposure to the rains or the intense heat of the midday sun."

A revised, second edition of *Mexico, the Wonderland of the South* was published in 1914.

Carson also wrote *The marriage revolt; a study of marriage and divorce.* (Hearst's International Library Co., 1915) and *Northcliffe, Britain's Man of Power* (Dodge Publishing Co., 1918).

Carson was an enthusiastic traveler, described by one academic as a "tour promoter". Many of his views about Mexicans will strike modern readers as stereotypical. He dedicates an entire chapter to The Mexican Woman, which makes for fascinating reading despite many statements which read today as outrageous over-generalizations, such as "As a rule, the Mexican women are not beautiful"; "no foreigner, unless he be associated with diplomacy, is likely to have any chance of studying and judging the Mexican women"; "the Mexican girl has but two things in life to occupy her, love and religion".

He tells of clerical restrictions becoming more lax, with bells ringing at all hours. He attributes progress (as evidenced by the bustling city and high costs of living) in Mexico City, and elsewhere, to American influence. He considers "Americanization" has made such an impact that he even projects the possibility of Mexico being "peacefully annexed to the United States."

Carson arrived in Guadalajara in November and stayed over the New Year before visiting the village of Chapala for a few days. He includes an interesting account of a water-weed infestation in the lake, but his description, if accurate, refers to a "yellow lilly", which seems unlikely to refer to the violet-flowered water hyacinth described at about the same time by Terry. If it is meant to refer to the water hyacinth, it would be the first detailed reference to the problems caused by the lirio, planted by an "imbecile", and to possible methods of combat.

There are three hotels at Chapala, all very much alike. I found quarters at the Arzapalo, a rambling stone building of two stories, a few feet from the lake and commanding some beautiful views. Although somewhat crude in a few minor particulars, the place was comfortable and, for a Mexican hotel at least, unusually well managed.

Very few Americans have ever heard of Lake Chapala, although it is one of the largest lakes in the world....

All along the shores of the lake, and in the Lerma River which runs into it, hundreds of peons are employed in gathering and burning yellow water-lily which has invaded the waters. A few years ago, some imbecile planted a quantity of the lily in the river, thinking it would look pretty. In an incredibly short time it spread like wildfire; some of the streams were completely choked with it, and when I visited Chapala the river was covered in places with green masses of the plant. It had spread all along the lake when the Mexican government took the matter in hand and appropriated a large sum of money for its destruction. At night, fires can be seen blazing along the shores of the lake where the peons have collected and are burning large piles of the noxious weed.

The village of Chapala is built upon the northern shore of the lake, where a sloping, sandy beach makes a capital bathing place. The narrow streets center at a tiny plaza adorned with orange trees and other tropical vegetation. Here on Sundays the market is held, and picturesque natives from the surrounding country pour into the little town and gather there. A number of pretty villas are dotted along the lake's edge, embowered in bougainvillea and hibiscus, palms and orange trees. On a hill a short distance from the shore some land has been divided into building lots for villas, with the idea of starting a model American summer village; but the price of the ground is so high—about $1000 per lot—that very few purchasers had been found.

A rude pier of rough stones extends into the water, and here one can embark in a rowing or sailing boat or a naphtha launch and take trips up and down the lake. There are one or two old-fashioned steamers on it, but they do not make regular runs and have to be chartered for special trips. There are also a number of small fishing schooners. The little village, with its big white church and mountainous background, bears a wonderful resemblance to some of the lake villages in northern Italy, and makes a most beautiful picture. This little bit of lake might be taken for a scene on Como; but the waters of Chapala are slightly yellowish instead of blue. The lake, too, is very shallow, and for this reason the government has prohibited its waters being used for irrigation.

In the lake there are some small white fish (pescados blancos) which are caught with nets, but there is nothing to tempt the angler. The Mexican government is now stocking the waters with trout, bass, perch and other game fish, which may eventually make the lake more attractive to lovers

A great architect leaves his mark

Guillermo de Alba (1874-1935) was the architect of many of the finest buildings in Chapala. Originally from Guadalajara, de Alba graduated as an engineer-surveyor before undertaking a trip to Chicago. Soon after his return, he began to build houses in Chapala. In 1906 he completed his family residence, Mi Pullman, and was then commissioned by Ignacio Arzapalo (owner of the eponymous hotel) to design a second major hotel, the Hotel Palmera. By this time, de Alba had become the favored architect of many wealthy families from Guadalajara and designed several more noteworthy homes, including Villa Niza (1919).

However, de Alba's architectural masterpiece in the Chapala area is not a villa but the beautifully proportioned Chapala railway station (1920), now a museum and cultural center.

Guillermo de Alba married Maclovia de Cañedo y González de Hermosillo, who was 15 years his senior, in Chapala in 1900. They were blessed with one child, Guillermina, born in 1902. In 1933, when it was her turn to get married, Guillermina insisted on having the civil ceremony on board a steamboat out on the lake.

De Alba was also a distinguished photographer, to whom we are indebted for many of the finest pictures of Chapala during the early years of the 20th century, a time when the resort was, in many ways, enjoying its finest hour.

of the road and reel; but the Indians along the shore are such inveterate netters that it will be very difficult to breed the fish.

For the sportsman Chapala is far more attractive. Lying along some parts of the lake are extensive flats that are overflowed at high water. During the winter months these swamps are favorite resorts for myriads of feathered visitors from the north, ducks of all kinds and sizes, snipe, plover, geese, swans, and in fact all varieties of birds that like muddy creeks and shallow waters here congregate and fatten. While I was in Chapala a retired English naval officer, who had been cruising about the lake, brought in thirty geese one evening, the result of only one day's shooting. He said that Chapala afforded the finest wild-fowl shooting that he had ever enjoyed in his travels.

Chapala is beautiful at all times, but is particularly charming as the day wanes; in fact, it is famous for its sunsets. The great expanse of waters with its mountainous background then becomes a thing of wondrous beauty. As night falls a stiff breeze generally springs up, which makes the air very fresh and invigorating. Then the waters of the lake dash on the shore and break over the pier in marked contrast to their placid appearance in the daytime.

A short distance along the shore, within sight of the beautiful electric-lighted villas, there is another of those queer contrasts so often met with in Mexico. Here is a little village of Indian fishermen who live in huts or wigwams of rushes and adobe, some of the fishing houses being built on piles in the lake like those of the prehistoric lake-dwellers in Switzerland. These Indians are descendants of the fierce Chapaltecos, one of the last tribes subdued by the Spaniards. At sunset these wild-looking creatures, in very scanty raiment, can be seen casting their nets in the lake and catching the small white fish, which they sell in the neighborhood. To visit this place when the sun is setting, and see the weird figures flitting about beneath the semitropical foliage, conversing in low tones in their ancient dialect, living the most primitive of lives, makes it almost impossible to realize that hardly a mile away are comfortable hotels, a railway, Pullman cars and other adjuncts of latter-day civilization.

Carson, William English. 1909 *Mexico: the wonderland of the south.*

53

Lake Chapala, a travellers' handbook
1909
Thomas Philip Terry

Thomas Philip Terry (1864-1945) was born in Georgetown, Kentucky. Working as a journalist for various U.S. newspapers, he visited several countries as a foreign correspondent. These extended stints abroad included one in Japan from 1890-1895. He served as an Asian correspondent during the Russia-Japan war, and returned to Japan numerous times between 1919 and 1937.

Terry first visited Mexico in 1885. From 1905 to 1910, he lived in Mexico City and was the administrator of the Sonora News Company, a prominent publishing house.

He wrote many magazine and newspaper articles, but is best remembered today for his tourist and language guides.

His earliest recorded book (1891) was *Spanish English pocket interpreter, with a figurative pronunciation...* His first country guide was *Terry's Mexico handbook for travellers*, published in 1909. This encyclopedic guide, thoroughly good reading, covers much ground that is hard to find elsewhere. The description of Chapala in the handbook convinced British writer D. H. Lawrence to visit the lake, which became the setting for his great novel *The Plumed Serpent*.

Terry's research was meticulous and his informative guide delves into everything from history to hotels, and from shopping to excursions. It was reprinted in numerous editions as *Terry's Guide to Mexico*, with later editions fully revised by James Norman.

In 1914, Terry produced another book on Mexico: *Mexico: an outline sketch of the country, its people and their history from the earliest times to the present.*

He also wrote books on learning Spanish, Japan and Cuba. Terry died in Hingham, Massachusetts in 1945.

The map in Terry's handbook shows the lake as being much larger than it really was in 1909, following the draining of the eastern swamps. Terry describes the rail journey from Irapuato via Lake Chapala to Gua-

dalajara, and thence to Colima and Manzanillo. As the train approaches the lake from the east:

154 Km. **La Barca** (the barge), a sun-baked town four miles to the south of the station (left) on the **Lerma**. Tram-cars meet all trains, 10 c. *Gran Hotel Berlin,* facing *the Plaza Principal;* $1.50 to $2.50 American Plan; English spoken. Trunks may be sent up to the hotel (which faces the tram-line) for 10-25 c. according to weight. At the railway station there is a refreshment room (meals $1); good roast wild-duck (from the near-by marshes) and buttermilk *(leche de mantequilla).*

A quaint, weather-beaten old parochial church and a crumbling *Palacio Municipal* are the chief buildings of the town. Fine fruits are specialties of the region and many varieties are offered for sale at the railway station — along with cheese, milk, butter and similar products. The adjacent marshes are usually alive with water-fowl. 158 Km. Feliciano. 167 Km. Limon.

In the summer and early fall when ploughing for the winter wheat is underway, many white-trousered *peones,* with oxen and primitive wooden plows, are seen at work in the adjacent fields. The red blankets (usually tucked in the branches of mesquite trees) of the workers form strong color notes in a landscape where the herbage is nearly always a vivid green. The land is dotted with cane-fields which usually show a lighter green—a mere lightening of shade—against the deeper hues of alfalfa, corn, wheat and barley.

180 Km. **Ocotlan**, where west-bound passengers for **Lake Chapala** descend from the train. Tram-cars to the town (visible in the distance), 10 c.; trunks, 15-25 c. A runner of the *Hotel Ribera Castellanos* usually meets trains.

Ocotlan (Nahuatl = place of the pines) lies in the earthquake belt and the town has suffered repeated shocks during its existence. The brown-stone *Parochial Church* (uninteresting), which faces the small, tidy *Plaza Mayor,* and the quaint old Spanish bridge hard by are badly cracked. The church has been twice destroyed completely....

El Lago de Chapala. Chapala Village, at the N. end of the lake, is reached in 3-4 hr. by a steam launch which plies between the village and Ocotlan. A popular method of reaching **Chapala** is to descend from the train at **Atequisa** station and travel thence by diligence *(diligencia,* stage-coach). Distance about 16 kilometers; time about 1½ hrs.; fare $1 each way. A special conveyance *(guayin)* can be had for a small party (about 4) at an inclusive charge of $5 for the journey. During the rainy season (June-September) horses are sometimes substituted for the *diligencia,* because of bad roads....

The *diligencia* generally draws up in front of one of the several hotels at **Chapala Village**.

Hotels *Hotel Arzopala,* facing the lake; $2.50 to $4 American Plan, according to location of room. The upper rooms command better views than those on the ground floor. Spanish cooking and management.— *Hotel Victor Hugo,* $2 to $2.50 American Plan—*Hotel de la Palma,* $2 to $2.50 American Plan. Lower rates for a prolonged stay in all the hotels.

Boats. Launch on the lake (consult the hotel manager), $5 an hour, inclusive charge for a party of 10 or less. To *Ocotlan,* $3; round trip, $5. Row-boats, 75 c. an hour. Each boat will hold three or four persons comfortably. The above rates also apply to boats at other towns on the lake. *El Viento* is the name given by the fishermen to a sudden squall that sometimes breaks over the lake. In a steam-launch one is generally protected, but one is usually in for a fright and a wetting if caught out in

The Chapala Development Company

One of the most dedicated promoters of Chapala as a resort was Paul Christian Schjetnan (1870-1945). Schjetnan, from Kristiansund in Norway, had several business enterprises in Mexico City, including the Norwegian-Mexican Company in 1901, prior to moving to Chapala in about 1908. His home in the village was the Villa Aurora.

Schjetnan later formed the *Compañía de Fomento de Chapala*, a company to promote and develop the village. He also hoped to export agricultural produce grown on the newly drained farmland at the eastern end of the lake. The export business came to nothing but by 1911 Schjetnan and his partners had completed and opened a yacht club in Chapala. Unfortunately, this coincided with the Mexican Revolution, which put paid to many investors' dreams. By 1914, the yacht club had been abandoned; in 1916, it was accidentally burnt down.

But Schjetnan was not to be deterred for long. In 1917, Schjetnan announced plans to launch two new steamboats on the lake: the *Viking* for passengers, and the *Tapatío* for freight. Even more ambitiously, he spearheaded the task of completing a railway line from Chapala to link with the Mexican National Railway at La Capilla, near Atequiza.

The Chapala railway station, designed by Guillermo de Alba, was one of the most beautiful ever constructed in Mexico. It was inaugurated in 1920, with twice daily service. It reduced the travel time between Guadalajara and Chapala from the 5 hours or more by diligence to 3 hours each way. Sadly, even the railway failed to make any profit, and in 1926, following severe floods, rail service to Chapala came to an end. Happily, the restored railway station has found a new lease of life as a cultural center.

an open boat. Excursions should always be planned with the assistance of the hotel manager; he should also be asked to fix the boatmen's fees....

Ribera Castellanos (often spoken of as the *Riviera of Mexico),* the most popular resort on the lake shore, 3 miles south of **Ocotlan**, with a good hotel and attractive scenery, is perhaps destined to become a celebrated tourist resort. Boating, fishing, riding, driving and hunting excursions are planned by the hotel management at reasonable rates. *Ribera Hotel,* on a high hill immediately overlooking the lake, $3-$5 American Plan, American cooking and management. The hotel courier meets all trains, and the company's gasoline launch conveys passengers (and luggage) along the lake shore to the hotel. Fare, 50 c. Trunks, 50 c. The Ocotlan *tranvia* carries the passenger (5 c.) from the railway station to the little orange-crowned *plaza* in the centre of the town. Thence it is 2 minutes walk to the boat-landing, near a quaint old stone bridge, built by the Spaniards. Hand-bags by *cargador* 12-25 c. between car and landing.

We follow the course of the **Rio Zula** and soon turn into the **Rio Santiago**, which flows out of the lake. At certain seasons of the year the narrow river is almost choked with floating *lirio acuático.* The ½ hr. ride on the water is very attractive. The company rents row-boats and launches. The smaller boats, manned, cost about $1 a day per passenger. Sail-boats holding about 6 persons, $1 an hour; $2 to $5 the hour for short trips in the launch holding 6-15 passengers. Horses at reasonable rates. Good swimming from the end of the pier. Excellent fishing everywhere in the lake. Good hunting (ducks, geese, etc.) within a mile or more of the hotel....

Jamay... (3 miles from **Ribera Castellanos)**, is noted for fine *petates* — a species of mat made of palm leaves. The industry gives employment to nearly all the inhabitants, from the toddling tots to the sturdy centenarians. It is also celebrated locally for a crude, but curious, monument erected (about 100 years ago) to *Pio Nono.* It is the work of local craftsmen and was constructed with funds subscribed by the mat-makers. Although made of a cement-like clay, and repeatedly joggled by earthquakes, it still stands; its quaint carvings recall certain of the Jat temples of British India.

In these sequestered spots, far from the destructive complexities of modern life, almost every man lives his allotted threescore years and ten, while many of them pass the century mark with a springy step and a resolve to make the next decade unusually depopulating for the piscine denizens of the lake.

Terry, Thomas Philip. 1909 *Terry's Mexico Handbook for Travellers.*

The water hyacinth or *lirio*

There is no evidence for Lake Chapala having an aquatic weed problem prior to the story published by Christian Reid (aka Frances Fisher) in 1893. Reid included lengthy descriptions of floating islands at the eastern end of the lake which complicated navigation by boat. It is unclear, though, whether she was referring to the water hyacinth (*lirio*) or to some other aquatic plant, when one of her characters says: "It is brought down by the river in great quantities—a kind of aquatic plant—which is Nature's first step toward the formation of islands and marshes."

According to Antonio de Alba (1954), the *lirio* was introduced to the lake, together with a new species of carp, in 1905 by Manuel Cuesta Gallardo who was also responsible shortly afterwards for draining the eastern end of the lake, If de Alba's assertion is correct, then the *lirio* multiplied extraordinarily rapidly. By 1907, the April edition of *El Mundo Ilustrado* (cited in Casillas, 2004) says that, "among the photographs we include today, thanks to the kindness of Eduardo Orrin Jr., are some very interesting ones which show the advances made so far in the invasion of the terrible aquatic *lirio*. In some places, this plague has completely blocked some docks, and in others it has appeared in such large masses that the Indians have been forced to suppress their trips, damaging trade, scared that they will be caught up in the wave of green. Fortunately, the Development Ministry has now taken charge of ridding the lagoon of this famous lirio, and to that effect, has commissioned very competent individuals to study the best way of achieving this without harming the spawning of fish which are abundant in the lake and which constitute, we might say, the main patrimony of the region's residents."

Carson, who visited the area in about 1908 or 1909, described how hundreds of peons are employed in gathering and burning yellow water-lily which has invaded the waters. The description of this plant as a "yellow water lily" leaves some room for doubt since the water hyacinth has purplish-blue flowers with yellow stamens.

But, by the time Terry's handbook is published in 1909, all doubt is removed. Terry describes a serious *lirio* problem, especially along the river Santiago which exits the lake: "At certain seasons of the year the narrow river is almost choked with floating *lirio acuático*." Downstream, the situation sounds even more serious. The lowlands and marshes near Ocotlán are "blue with the tints of the *lirio acuático*". At nearby San Jacinto, "When the river runs full, a myriad of water-hyacinths float down on the turgid waters, and at certain points almost choke the stream." A short distance upstream of the Juanacatlán Falls, "The lowlands are covered with the bright green of growing hyacinths".

54

Notes on some water-fowl
1909
Charles Bernard Nordhoff

Charles Bernard Nordhoff (1887-1947) was born in London, England, to well-to-do American parents. The family moved to Berlin, where his mother wrote in the family diary that, "Charlie undoubtedly began his study of water fowl, as his daily outing in a small pram or push cart led him first to the bakeries for a supply of stale buns and back to the lake to feed the ducks."

The family also lived on a ranch near Todos Santos in Baja California, where as a young child, Nordhoff learnt to hunt, sail and fish. Later, the family moved to California.

Following in the footsteps of his grandfather, a journalist and author, Nordhoff wrote his first article, for publication in an ornithological journal, at age fifteen.

He studied briefly at Stanford University, but left in the aftermath of the serious earthquake and fire of 1906. After completing a B.A. at Harvard University in 1909, he moved back to Mexico, to work as a supervisor on a sugar plantation in Veracruz. Unable to win the heart of the plantation owner's beautiful daughter, and with the Mexican Revolution breaking out around him, Nordhoff left Mexico in 1911, and never returned.

In 1917, Nordhoff joined the French Foreign Legion as a pilot, eventually winning the Croix de Guerre for his efforts. After the war, he wrote a history of the Lafayette Flying Corps. with James Norman Hall (who later updated *Terry's Guide to Mexico*). The two men later moved to Tahiti to write travel articles for *Harper's,* where Nordhoff married a Polynesian woman, Pepe Teara; they had six children.

While Nordhoff wrote several books of his own, including several novels, he is best known for his collaboration with Hall on the *Mutiny on the Bounty* trilogy about the famous 1789 mutiny in the South Seas. The novel was the basis for three movie versions, the first of which, released in 1935, won an Oscar for Best Picture.

Tragically, following a severe depression and heavy drinking, Nordhoff committed suicide on April 10, 1947.

More than a decade after leaving Mexico, Nordhoff wrote up his notes on a November 1909 visit to Lake Chapala, as a brief ornithological note to Condor Magazine.

The fresh water marshes of Lake Chapala, in the state of Jalisco, Mexico, form another haven for waterfowl. At one end of the lake there is a great area of flooded land cut by a veritable labyrinth of sluggish channels, 400 square miles, I should say. The far interior of this swampy paradise, reached after three days' travel in a native canoe, is a vast sanctuary for wildfowl, a region of gently rolling damp prairies, set with small ponds, and traversed by a network of navigable channels leading to the great lake. I saw as many geese, White-fronted (*Anser albifrons*) and Snow (*Chen hyperboreus*), as I have ever seen in the Sacramento Valley, and the number of ducks was past belief, with some interesting species like the Masked and Florida Black or Dusky, to lend variety. A more thorough investigation of this field would be worth while for I have reason to believe that several species of northern ducks breed there, and breed at a much later season than in our country. On November 20 (1909) I found a brood of young Shovellers (Spatula clypeata) unable to fly, and the natives told me that hundreds of ducks nested there, among them Gadwall, Dusky, Sprig, Shoveller, and Cinnamon Teal.

Nordhoff, Charles B. 1922. *Notes on some water-fowl.*

RC

55

Holy Week and the elite of Mexican society 1909-1910

Vitold de Szyszlo

Witold, later Vitold, de Szyszlo (1881-1965), was born in Warsaw but lived part of his early life in Paris, where he studied natural sciences and became a member of the Paris Society of Geography. His first visit to the U.S. is recorded as taking place in 1904. The passenger list says he was 23 years old, single, of "Polish-Russian" nationality, and a book-writer.

He lived in Mexico for almost twelve months, from 1909 to 1910, making astute observations on the eve of the Mexican Revolution. Shortly after the Revolution began, he moved to Peru. By 1925, he was married to Rosa Valdelomar; had a young son, Fernando; and was functioning as the Polish Consul in Lima.

Rosa came from a distinguished Peruvian family. Her brother Abraham Valdelomar (1888-1919) was, briefly, a Peruvian diplomat in Italy, besides being one of his country's most famous authors, crafting everything from short stories and novels to poetry, essays and theater plays.

De Szyszlo's son, Fernando, clearly inherited some of the family's artistic genius since he has become one of Peru's best known modern artists.

In an interview in 2005, Fernando attributed his success to the inspiration of Picasso and Mexico's Rufino Tamayo. He recalled that his father considered painters to be drunks and impoverished, and had been disillusioned when he had abandoned formal studies of architecture to dedicate himself to painting. Fernando's recognition by the art world came too late to be enjoyed by his father, who died in Lima in 1965. (Some sources suggest 1963)

Besides *Dix mille kilomètres à travers le Mexique, 1909-1910*, Vitold de Szyszlo also wrote *La Naturaleza en América Ecuatorial* (1955), a book based on forty years of research and exploration in the Amazon rainforest. He was a remarkable man, described in promotional material as a "geographer, biologist, zoologist and pioneer."

Dix mille kilomètres à travers le Mexique, 1909-1910 contains excellent descriptions of some parts of Mexico, such as Chiapas, Oaxaca and Baja California, which were decidedly lesser-known at the time Vitold de Szyszlo was writing.

Despite including some poetic descriptions of Lake Chapala and towns like Ocotlán, de Szyszlo was somewhat disappointed with the reality of the lake, since he felt that the available maps had made the surrounding scenery seem much more Alpine.

At eight in the morning we arrive at Ocotlán, where a streetcar takes us to the landing dock for the little steamboat on Lake Chapala. Ocotlán is the center of all commercial activity for the region....

Nowadays, gigantic works are under way, on account of a firm, the "Irrigation and Electricity Company of Chapala", headed by the restless Don Manuel de la Cuesta. It is carrying out neither more nor less than the desiccation of more than a third of Lake Chapala by means of a cement dam, channeling the water to 250,000 hectares of the surrounding countryside. The idea is to obtain thus 13 million *piastres* by the sale of 60,000 hectares of land won from the waters of the lake.

The capital available to the society will probably reach 14 million *piastres*. A driving force of 100,000 horse power, sufficient to supply Guadalajara with electric power, will contribute to stimulate the establishment of the most varied industries. The government has loaned the company three million *piastres* to help initiate this undertaking....

According to geographical maps, often inaccurate, I had come to imagine Chapala as a real alpine lake, of imposing and severe stature. I experienced a strong disillusion.

The mountain range, rising up on the southern shore, is too distant to give relief and color to the scene. The sheet of water, of a milky green, lacks luster; the sun has burned the grasses and brush, stripped the leaves off shrubs, leaving only the thorns; the monotonous succession of flat and naked shores deprived of tropical plants tires the eye. The impression of a mud pond is too strong to consider making comparisons with the natural marvels glimpsed in other parts of the country. Nowhere do we find the picturesque charm of details nor the harmony or majesty of the whole.

Chapala, the most frequented settlement of the lake of the same name, serves as a meeting place during Holy Week for the elite of Mexican society. Elegant villas line the edge of the lake, surrounded by colorful gardens, created at great expense on the rocky soil of the beach. One of the prettiest, "El Manglar", belongs to Mr. Elizaga, the brother-in-law of ex-President Diaz, who gives, in this enchanting setting, splendid Mexican fiestas, where nothing is lacking: cock fights, balls and joyous dinners.

The village of Chapala itself leaves a lot to be desired regarding its viability and resources. Built without a street plan, offering only shadeless stony roads in poor condition, it will never be able to compete with Tehuacán, Cuernavaca, Cuautla and other places renowned for the mildness of their climate. Whoever visits Chapala, seeks to enjoy aquatic sports, swimming, canoeing and fishing. The neighboring hills, studded with cacti, rattlesnake lairs and scorpions do not tempt the walker....

Chapala possesses a ferruginous spring at 37 degrees and another, sulphurous, at 33 degrees Celsius; the water is brought in from a nearby hill. The ferruginous water is used to make refreshing drinks, the quantity of solid corpuscles that it contains not altering the taste. Aside from commercial baths, there are others that are free, in open air basins, where the Indian women come to bathe their children who collaborate happily.

Taking advantage of my stay in Chapala, I decided to go hunting and climbed in a tiny canoe with a young Indian. On arriving in a cove which had a quartz rich sandy bottom, I was surrounded by hundreds of galaretas,

President Díaz and Lake Chapala

Porfirio Díaz had been President of Mexico for more than fifteen years when he visited Chapala in December 1896. When he revisited Chapala in January 1904, he stayed with Eduard Collignon, while his wife stayed with Lorenzo Elizaga, her brother-in-law. By this time, Díaz was in the twilight of his military and political career. Since he had first taken office in 1877, economic boom times had returned and the national budget had been balanced. Agricultural production had risen. Massive investments, many of them emanating from foreign countries, had been made in mining and infrastructure, particularly railways.

Politically, though, the country was in the hands of a dictator. Elections were rigged and public opinion ignored. A restricted, select group of advisors—called the científicos, but actually a group of lawyers and economists—had assumed more and more power. Nepotism was rampant. Massive land concessions had been made to foreign speculators and personal friends.

After his 1904 visit, Porfirio Diaz returned to Chapala at Easter time in 1905, 1908 and 1909, always staying with his in-laws at El Manglar. By that time, in gratitude for being given the concession of recently drained land, Manuel Cuesta Gallardo was reportedly planning to make a gift of Villa Tlalocán (designed by George Edward King) as a residence for the President and his family. However, when Díaz visited Lake Chapala in 1910, he did not stay at the town of Chapala but in several haciendas at the east end of the lake. In 1911, Díaz went into exile in Paris, never to return.

gallinules with pretty blue feathers, who had only their heads sticking out of the water. I fired into the middle and felled a large number. As a hunting trophy, I brought a live gallinule with a leg wound back to the hotel. When the bird saw a lighted candle, it sprang to it and threw it down, a manoeuver that was repeated several times. Each time that it wanted to peck me violently with its beak, it first leaned its head backwards so as to hit more forcefully.

The lake waters are home to a large variety of aquatic birds of all kinds: ducks, flamingos, egrets, herons and strange looking pililes....

I returned to Chapala in April [1909] to attend the Holy Week festivities. While all the other Mexican towns are absorbed by Lent, a large number of visitors flock to Chapala for that period. Under the auspices of President Diaz, then in power, regattas were organized in small canoes reserved for the young ladies of the best society.

The president, in a navy blue suit and wearing a panama hat, was accompanied by his wife, dressed all in black, and his daughter Luz, in an elegant outfit. Among the other representatives of the smart set, come to Chapala for the occasion, were: the eminent finance minister Mr. Yves Limantour, to whom the country owes the consolidation of its foreign credit; Mr. Braniff, a railroad king, of working class origins, and Sr. Moreno, whose revenue reached a fabulous figure. It is said, not without malice, that just the wool from his sheep's tails could be worth one million *piastres*. Also present were Mr. Landa, governor of the state of Mexico, Mr. Ahumada, governor of the state of Jalisco, Mr. Escaudon, governor of the state of Morelos, Messrs. Corcuera, Cuesta, Cosio, Hermosillo, Malo, Del Valle, etc.

Mexican millionaires make up the so called national aristocracy, but their doors are little accessible to strangers or even to their less fortunate compatriots. It is a very vain and proud circle where no one will speak to you without inquiring about your personal situation. The ladies, who make generous use of makeup, are rarely beautiful. Their annual budget for jewellery, toiletries, trinkets and trips to Europe amounts to hundreds of thousands of *piastres*. Some families own private hotels on the Champs Elysées, villas in Switzerland, on the Côte d'Azur, and at popular beaches and the fancy resorts of the good life.

Szyszlo, Vitold de. 1913 *Dix mille kilomètres à travers le Mexique, 1909-1910*

Glossary

Units of measurement:

carga: load of 2 *fanegas* or about 91 kilograms (200 pounds).

estado: a Spanish unit of distance, usually vertical, the average height of adult men: about 1.672 meters or 1.83 yards.

fanega: both a dry measure (about 1.5 bushels or 46 kilograms of maize) and an area of cultivation (about 3.58 hectares in the case of maize).

fathom: as used by Narváez, this equals a depth of 1.67 meters (6 Spanish feet).

league (legua): a variable measure of distance, from 4.180 kilometers (the legal league) to 6.687 kilometers, depending on the region. To add to the imprecision, it is also sometimes used to represent the typical distance that could be covered in an hour, a distance which depended on the nature of the terrain.

milla: the traditional Spanish mile (5 000 Spanish feet, or 8 estadios) , equivalent to about 1.392 kilometers or 0.865 statute miles.

mille: the traditional French mile, equivalent to about 1.949 kilometers, or 1.211 statute miles. In modern France the mille is sometimes used for the nautical mile of 1.852 kilometers.

miglio: the Italian mile (5,000 Roman feet), equivalent to about 1.5 kilometers, or 0.931 state miles.

vara: a variable unit of length, equivalent to about 83.82 centimeters or 33 inches. 5,000 varas = 1 league.

Other:

corregidor: district magistrate, Royal magistrate, governor of a district or province.

doctrina: Indian community converted to Christianity but lacking a parish; similar to a curacy.

encomienda: grant by the Spanish Crown of the right to collect tributes and labor from Indians within a specified area.

estancia: grant of land, often for a livestock estate - usually 1,756 hectares in the case of cattle, or 780 hectares in the case of sheep or goats.

hacienda: landed estate; large rural estate, usually based on a mix of grain and livestock farming.

monte: open scrubland or woodland, often on a hillside.

vecino: householder or citizen (the number of vecinos is therefore approximately equal to the number of households or families, rather than number of individuals).

visita: small chapel or church ministered by nonresident clergy.

Visitador: investigator; a royal Visitor, appointed by the King (through the Council of the Indies or the Audiencia). The Visitor often had the power to execute justice on the spot.

Sources of extracts

Acuña, R. (ed) 1987 *Relaciones geográficas del siglo XVI: Michoacán.* Volume 9 of *Relaciones geográficas del siglo XVI.* Mexico City: Universidad Nacional Autónoma de México.

———— (ed) 1988 *Relaciones geográficas del siglo XVI: Nueva Galicia.* Volume 10 of *Relaciones geográficas del siglo XVI.* Mexico City: Universidad Nacional Autónoma de México.

Anon. 1832 From an Unpublished Journal. *The Episcopal Watchman,* Mar. 27, 1832 and *The Episcopal Watchman,* Apr. 3, 1832.

Anon. 1868 *Colección de Acuerdos, Ordenes y Decretos sobre Tierras, Casas y Solares de los Indígenas, Bienes de Comunidades y Fundos Legales de los Pueblos del Estado de Jalisco.* Guadalajara: Tip. De J. M. Brambila. Cited in Talavera Salgado, 1982.

Anon. 1896 A Whirlpool—Startling Spectacle at Lake Chapala, *Los Angeles Times,* Jan. 13,1896.

Balbuena, Bernardo de. 1622 *El Bernardo.* Madrid. Lines translated from Pedro Vargas Avalos, 1984, Chapala, afán de Jalisco, *Chapala, ayer y hoy.* Guadalajara, Mexico: Sociedad Mexicana de Geografía y Estadística de Jalisco.

Banda, Longinus. 1873 *Estadística de Jalisco: formada con vista de los mejores datos oficiales y noticias ministradas por sujetos idóneos en los años de 1854 a 1863.* 2nd edition, 1982 Guadalajara, Mexico: Gobierno de Jalisco, Secretaría General, Unidad Editorial.

Bárcena, Mariano. 1888 *Ensayo estadístico del Estado de Jalisco: referente a los datos necesarios para procurar el adelanto de la agricultura y la aclimatación de nuevas plantas industriales.* Second edition: Guadalajara, Jalisco, México: Gobierno de Jalisco, Secretaría General, Unidad Editorial, 1983. Serie Estadísticas Basicas #6.

Beebe, Charles William. 1905 *Two Bird-Lovers in Mexico.* New York: Houghton, Mifflin & Company.

Beltrami, J.C. (Spanish: Giacomo Costantino) 1830 *Le Mexique.* Paris: Chez Delaunay, 2 vols. Translation by Brigitte & Bob Plummer.

Bullock, afterwards Hall, William Henry. 1866 *Across Mexico in 1864-5.* London and Cambridge: Macmillan and Co.

Campbell, Reau. 1899 *Campbell's new revised complete guide and descriptive book of Mexico.* Chicago: Rogers & Smith Co.

Carson, William English. 1909 *Mexico: the wonderland of the south.* New York: Macmillan.

Castellanos, I. 1867 Request to drain part of the lake, a letter published in Armando Hermosillo Contreras. 2001 Urge secar el Lago de Chapala. Un documento de 1867. Chapala, Jalisco: *El Charal, Periódico semanal,* 28 de julio de 2001.

Ciudad Real, Antonio de. c.1590 *Tratado curioso y docto de las grandezas de la Nueva Espana: Relacion breve y verdadera de algunas cosas de las muchas que sucedieron al padre fray Alonso Ponce en las provincias de la Nueva Espana, siendo comisario general de aquellas partes.* 3rd ed, 1993. Mexico: UNAM Instituto de Investigaciones Historicas. 2 vols.

Conkling, Alfred Ronald. 1886 *Appletons' Guide to Mexico, including a chapter on Guatemala and an English-Mexican vocabulary; with a railway map and illustrations.* New York: Appleton, 3rd edition.

Dollero, Adolfo. 1911 *México al día. (Impresiones y notas de viaje)* Paris-Mexico: Librería de la Vda. de C. Bouret.

Embree, Charles Fleming. 1900 *A Dream of a Throne: the Story of a Mexican Revolt.* Illustrations by Henry Sandham. Boston: Little, Brown and Company. London: Gay & Bird.

Fossey, Mathieu de. 1857 *Le Mexique par Mathieu de Fossey de L'Académie de Dijon.* Paris: Henry Plon, 2nd edition 1862.

Galeotti, H. G. 1839, Coup d'oeil sur la Laguna de Chapala au Mexique, avec notes géognostiques, *Acad. Roy. Soc. Bruxelles, Bull.,* 6, pt 1: 14-19. Translation into Spanish: Descripción de la laguna de Chapala, con notas geognósticas, *El Mosaico Mexicano, ó colección de amenidades curiosas é instructivas,* c.1840, vol 6: 337-348. Mexico: Ignacio Cumplido..

Gibbon, Eduardo A. 1893 *Guadalajara, (La Florencia Mexicana). Vagancias y Recuerdos. (1893) El salto de Juanacatlán y El Mar Chapálico.* Guadalajara, Jalisco. 1992 reprint: Guadalajara, Jalisco: Presidencia Municipal de Guadalajara.

Gillpatrick, Owen Wallace. 1911 *The man who likes Mexico. The spirited chronicle of adventurous wanderings in Mexican highways and byways.* New York: The Century Co.

Hesse-Wartegg, Ernst von. 1890 *Mexiko, Land und Leute. Reisen auf neuen Wegen durch das Aztekenland. Mit zahlreichen Abbildungen und einer Generalkarte Mexicos.* Wien und Olmütz: Verlag von Ed. Hölzel. Translation by Marianne Davey.

Humboldt, Alexander von. 1811 *Political essay on the kingdom of New Spain: With physical sections and maps founded on astronomical observations and trigonometrical and barometrical measurements.* Translated from the original French by John Black. London: Longman, Hurst, Rees, Orme, and Brown, 1811. 1966 reprint: New York: AMS Press, 4 volumes.

Jordan, David Starr. 1922 *The Days of a Man: Being Memories of a Naturalist, Teacher, and Minor Prophet of Democracy.* New York: World Book Company. 1922. 2 vols.

Kingsley, Rose Georgina. 1874 *South by west or winter in the Rocky Mountains and spring in Mexico.* London: W. Isibister & Co.

Kirkham, Stanton Davis. 1909 *Mexican Trails. A Record of Travel in Mexico, 1904 07, and a Glimpse at the Life of the Mexican Indian.* New York & London: G.P.Putnam's Sons. The Knickerbocker Press.

Lázaro de Arregui, Domingo. 1621 *Descripción de la Nueva Galicia.* Edited by François Chevalier. 1946 Sevilla.

López Cotilla, Manuel. 1843 *Noticias Geográficas y Estadísticas del Departamento de Jalisco.* Guadalajara: Imprenta del Gobierno. 3rd edition 1983, Guadalajara, Mexico: Gobierno de Jalisco, Secretaría General, Unidad Editorial.

Lumholtz, Carl Sophus. 1902 *Unknown Mexico. A record of five years' exploration among the tribes of the Western Sierra Madre; in the Tierra Caliente of Tepic and Jalisco; and among the Tarascos of Michoacan.* 2 vols. 1973 reprint: New Mexico: Rio Grande Press.

Lyon, G.F. 1828 *Journal of a residence and tour in the Republic of Mexico in the year 1826, with some account of the mines of that country.* London: John Murray.

Menéndez Valdés, José. 1980 *Descripción y censo general de la Intendencia de Guadalajara, 1789-1793.* Preliminary study and version of the text by Ramón Maria Serrera. Guadalajara, Jalisco: Gobierno de Jalisco, Secretaría General, Unidad Editorial.

Mota Padilla, Matias de la. 1742 *Historia del reino de Nueva Galicia en la América Septentrional.* Modern edition: 1973 Guadalajara, Mexico: Universidad de Guadalajara– Instituto Jalisciense de Antropología e Historia.

Mota y Escobar, Alonso de la. 1605 *Descripción geográfica de los Reinos de Nueva Galicia, Nueva Vizcaya y Nuevo León.* 1940 edition, intro. by Joaquin Ramirez Cabañas. Mexico D.F.: Editorial Pedro Robredo.

Narváez, José María. 1817 *Plano del lago de Chapala, Guadalajara de la Nueva Galicia.*

Nordhoff, C. B. 1922 Notes on some water-fowl. *Condor,* 24: 64-65.

Ornelas Mendoza y Valdivia, Fr. Nicolás Antonio de. 1719-1722 *Crónica de la provincia de Santiago de Xalisco, escrita por Fr. Nicolás Antonio de Ornelas Mendoza y Valdivia, 1719-1722.* Modern edition: 1962 Guadalajara: Instituto Jalisciense de Antropología e Historia.

Oswald, Felix Leopold. 1880 *Summerland Sketches; or, Rambles in the Backwoods of Mexico and Central America.* Philadelphia: J. B. Lippincott.

Pauncefote, Hon. Maud. 1900 Chapala the Beautiful, *Harper's Bazar,* Volume XXXIII #52, December 29, 1900.

Reid, Christian. 1893 The Land of the Sun. On Lake Chapala. *The Catholic World, A monthly magazine of General Literature and Science.* 186. June 1893. 381-395. Reprinted as chapter XII of *The Land of the Sun: Vistas Mexicanas.* 1894. New York: Appleton.

Roa, Victoriano. 1825 *Estadística del Estado Libre de Jalisco: formado de orden del Supremo Gobierno del mismo Estado con presencia de las noticias que dieron los pueblos de su comprensión en los años 1821–1822.* Guadalajara, Mexico: Imprenta del C. Urbano Sanromán. 1981, 2ⁿᵈ edition Guadalajara: Gobierno de Jalisco, Secretaría General, Unidad Editorial.

———— c.1836 La Isla de Mescala en el Departamento de Jalisco, *El Mosaico Mexicano, ó colección de amenidades curiosas é instructivas.* Mexico: Ignacio Cumplido, vol. 2: 422-425.

Rogers, Thomas L. 1893 *Mexico? Sí, señor* Boston: Mexican Central Railway Co.

Romero, José Rubén. 1932 *Apuntes de un lugareño.* Translated by John Mitchell and Ruth Mitchell de Aguilar as *Notes of a Villager: A Mexican Poet's Youth and Revolution* 1988 Kaneohe, Hawaii: Plover Press. Translation quoted by kind permission of

Ms. Margo C. Mitchell of Plover Press, with minor revisions based on Shirley Ballard's article, Romero's Michoacán: One Woman's Odyssey, *Travelmex* #123, Guadalajara.

Sámano, Juan de. c 1530 *Relación de la Conquista de los teules chichimecas que dió Juan de Sámano*, in volume 2 of García Icazbalceta, Joaquín. 1866 *Coleccion de documentos para la historia de México*. Mexico: Antiguo Librería. 2 vols.

A Gringo. 1892 *Through The Land of the Aztecs Or Life and Travel In Mexico*, by 'A Gringo' (pseud.) London: Sampson, Low, Marston & Company.

Starr, Frederick. 1897 *The Little Pottery Objects of Lake Chapala, Mexico*. Department of Anthropology Bulletin II. University of Chicago Press, Chicago.

Szyszlo, Vitold de. 1913 *Dix mille kilomètres à travers le Mexique, 1909-1910*. Paris. Plon-Nourrit et Cie. Translation by Marie-Josée Bayeur.

Tapia de Castellanos, Esther. 1869 *A orillas del lago de Chapala*. Fragments of the poem are quoted in Vogt, 1989.

Tello, Antonio. 1891 *Libro segundo de la Crónica Miscelánea, en que se trata de la conquista espiritual y temporal de la Santa provincia de Xalisco: en el Nuevo Reino de la Galicia y Nueva Vizcaya y descubrimiento del Nuevo México*. Guadalajara: Impr. de "La República Literia" de C.L. de Guevara, 1891.

————— 1942 *Crónica Miscelánea de la Sancta Provincia de Xalisco. Libro tercero*. Guadalajara, Jalisco: Ed. Font.

————— 1945 *Crónica Miscelánea de la Sancta Provincia de Xalisco. Libro cuarto*. Guadalajara, Jalisco: Ed. Font.

Terry, Thomas Philip. 1909 *Terry's Mexico Handbook for Travellers*. Mexico City: Sonora News Company and Boston: Houghton Mifflin Co.

Torres, Francisco Mariano de. 1755 *Crónica de la sancta provincia de Xalisco*. Modern edition: 1965 Guadalajara,: H. Ayuntamiento de la Ciudad de Guadalara, Inst. Jalisciense de Antropología e Historia, INAH.

Tweedie, Mrs. Alec. 1901 *Mexico as I Saw It*. New York: Macmillan; London: Hurst and Blackett.

Velázquez de Lara, Antonio Manuel. 1768 Unpublished census and map from Chapala parish records cited in Antonio de Alba, 1954.

Villa-Señor y Sanchez, Joseph Antonio de. 1746-1748 Theatro Americano, descripción general de los reynos y provincias de la Nueva España y sus juridicciones. Mexico: Imprenta de la Viuda de D. Josef Bernardo Hogal, 2 vols.

Ward, Henry George. 1828 *Mexico In 1827* London: Henry Colburn.

Ximénez, J. Antonio. 1847 Letter to the State Governor, following the earthquake of 1847, cited in Antonio de Alba, 1954.

206

Illustrations

Illustrations are by Rosemary Chan, except for those on the following pages:
48 map from Talavera, 1982: 74;
110 portrait from Tapia de Castellanos, Obras poéticas, 1905;
119 illustration from Oswald, 1880: 84;
132 illustration from Rogers, 1893:222;
145 illustration from Starr, 1897: 52;
165 portrait by Stiletto from Frank Leslie's Illustrated Weekly, July 20, 1893;
165 decorated drop capital from Pauncefote, 1901: 2231;
173 illustration from Lumholtz 1902: v2, 450.
Images not by Rosemary Chan are copyright unknown or believed to be in the public domain.

General Bibliography

Alba, Antonio de. 1954 *Chapala*. Guadalajara, Jalisco: Banco Industrial de Jalisco.

Barker, Nancy N. 1979 *The French Experience in Mexico, 1821-1861*. Univ. of N. Carolina Press.

Casillas de Alba, Martín. 2004 *¡Salvemos a Chapala! Breve historia del lago y de la villa de Chapala: desde sus orígenes hasta dentro de diez años, cuando pueda volver a ser un recurso natural sustentable.* Mexico City: Editorial Diana.

Castañeda, Carmen. 1997 Bienes, libros y escritos de Domingo Lázaro de Arregui. *Estudios del Hombre,* Guadalajara: Univ. de Guadalajara, num 6, 1997, pp 111-114.

Chevalier, François. 1963 *Land and Society in Colonial Mexico - The Great Hacienda.* Univ. of California press.

Cole, Garold. 1978 *American Travelers to Mexico, 1821-1972; a descriptive bibliography.* Whitson Publishing Company, Troy, New York.

Fernández, Rodolfo. 1994. Latifundios y Grupos Dominantes en la Historia de la Provincia de Ávalos. Mexico City: INAH / Guadalajara: Editorial Agata.

Fernández-Armesto, Felipe. 2003 *The Americas; the history of a hemisphere*. London: Weidenfeld & Nicolson.

Ferrer Muñoz, Manuel. *(*ed) 2002 *La imagen del México decimonónico de los visitantes extranjeros: ¿un Estado Nación o un mosaico plurinacional?* UNAM: Instituto de Investigaciones Jurídicas. Serie Doctrina Jurídica, Núm. 56.

Iturriaga de la Fuente, José. 1988 *Anecdotario de Viajeros Extranjeros en México Siglos XVI-XX.*

James, George Wharton. 1909 (ed) *The California Birthday Book. Prose and Poetical Selections from the Writings of Living California Authors with a Brief Biographical Sketch of each.* Los Angeles: Arroyo Guild Press.

Lozoya, X 1984. *Plantas y luces en México, La Real Expedición Científica a Nueva España (1787-1803)* Barcelona: Ediciones del Serbal.

MacLeod, Murdo J. 1986 The "Matlazáhuatl" of 1737-1738 in Some Villages in the Guadalajara Region. *West Georgia College: Studies in the Social Sciences* 25, pp7-15.

McDowell, Jim. 1998 *José Narváez. The Forgotten Explorer. Including his Narrative of
a Voyage on the Northwest Coast in 1788.* Spokane Washington: The Arthur H. Clark
Company.

McHenry, J. Patrick. 1962. *A Short History of Mexico.* New York: Dolphin Books.

Melville, Elinor G. K. 1994 *A Plague of Sheep. Environmental consequences of the conquest of Mexico.* Cambridge University Press.

Meyer, Michael C. & William H. Beezley. (eds) 2000 *The Oxford History of Mexico.*
New York: Oxford University Press.

Moreno García, Heriberto. 1988 *Geografía y paisaje de la antigua ciénega de Chapala.*
Instituto Michoacano de Cultura, Morelia, Michoacán.

Morin, Karen M. 1999. Surveying Britains' Informal Empire: Rose Kingsley's 1872 Re-
connaissance for the Mexican National Railway. *Historical Geography* Vol. 27, pp 5-26.

Matthew, H.C.G. and Brian Harrison. (eds) 2004 *Oxford Dictionary of National Biography.* Oxford University Press.

Parkes, Henry Bamford. 1950. *A History of Mexico.* Cambridge, Mass: The Riverside
Press.

Peregrina, Angélica. 1994 *Chapala visto por viajeros.* México: El Colegio de Jalisco
Oficina de Comunicación del Lago, Comisión Nacional del Agua.

Poblett Miranda, Martha. 2000 *Viajeros en el siglo XIX.* Consejo Nacional para la Cultura
y las Artes. México D.F.

Simpson, Lesley Byrd. 1941 *Many Mexicos.* Fourth edition, 1969. University of California Press.

Suárez, G., V.García-Acosta & R. Gaulon. 1994 Active crustal deformation in the Jalisco
block, Mexico: evidence for a great historical earthquake in the 16th century. Elsevier:
Tectonophysics 234 (1994) 117-127.

Talavera Salgado, F. 1982 *Lago Chapala, turismo Residencial y Campesinado.* Mexico
City: INAH.

Van Young, E. 1981 *Hacienda and Market in Eighteenth Century Mexico. The Rural
Economy of the Guadalajara Region, 1675-1820.* University of California Press.

Vogt, Wolfgang. 1989 El lago de Chapala en la literatura. *Estudios sociales: revista
cuatrimestral del Instituto de Estudios Sociales.* Guadalajara: U. de G. Year 2, Number 5:
1989, p 37 47.

————— 1993 Chapala en los años veinte. *Latinoamérica, México, Guadalajara. En-
sayos literarios.* Guadalajara, Jal., H. Ayuntamiento de Guadalajara/Editorial Agata.

Note: References used in compiling the biographical sketches are available on-line at:
www.sombrerobooks.com/biographical_references.html

Index

A

Acknowledgments

That this book is finally published is more of a testament to the interest and encouragement of the many people who assisted me at various stages, than to my own determination.

Besides the constant support of my wife Gwen, I have always been able to count on advice from David McLaughlin, the Publisher of MexConnect (mexconnect.com), and Carol Wheeler, the Editor-in-Chief.

My appreciation goes to the outstanding librarians at The Royal Geographical Society and the British Library, both in London, England, and at the New York Public Library, where Amy Azzarito was particularly gracious. Margo Gutierrez, Assistant Head Librarian, at the Nellie Lee Benson Latin American Collection of The University of Texas at Austin kindly unearthed various hard-to-locate items. Closer to home, the staff at Vancouver Public Library deserve a special vote of thanks, as do my local librarians Barbara Kerfoot and Lynne Starbird of the Vancouver Island Regional Library, who helped facilitate inter-library loans from across Canada.

Additional material was ably located by Sra. Maricruz Ibarra in Mexico and Dick Perry in California. Glenn Burgess kindly sent me a copy of the article by the Hon. Maud Pauncefote. Dr. Wolfgang Vogt, of the University of Guadalajara, kindly provided copies of his own excellent articles focussing on the literature of the Lake Chapala area. In France, Msse. Anne Le Berre spent many hours pursuing a potential lead which sadly proved to be a dead-end. Dr. Karen Morin, of the Geography Department at Bucknell University, graciously sent me her own thorough and fascinating article about Rose Kingsley.

My heartfelt thanks to several people who assisted with translations. Marianne Davey's ability to read 19th century Gothic German script proved quite remarkable. Marie-Josée Bayeur, and Brijitte (and husband Bob) Plummer tackled French passages with verve and sensitivity. Lorenza Castiello responded quickly and amicably to a barrage of Spanish language queries.

Several people helped search for material related to Charles Embree, whose life and work now hold a particular fascination for me. They include Elisabeth Swift, Archivist of Wabash College in Indiana, Becky Cape, the Head of Reference and Public Services at The Lilly Library, University of Indiana, and Florrie Kichler of Patria Press.

Those faults or oversights which remain are my own.

The Author

Geographer Tony Burton, born in England in 1953, is an author and educational consultant with graduate degrees from Cambridge and London Universities. He is a Fellow of the Royal Geographical Society.

Tony lived 18 years in Mexico, teaching, lecturing and leading specialist cultural and ecological trips, while writing hundreds of articles on natural history and ecotourism for a variety of publications, in both English and Spanish. He is the only three-time winner of ARETUR's former annual international travel-writing competition for articles about Mexico.

His previous book, *Western Mexico: A Traveller's Treasury* (Perception Press, 2001), explores towns and villages within easy driving distance of Guadalajara and Lake Chapala. He is also responsible for the best-selling "Lake Chapala Maps", first published in 1996, and the innovative interactive maps on Mexico Connect website: www.mexconnect.com.

He and his wife Gwen have two grown-up children and live on Vancouver Island with a cranky cat.

The Illustrator

Rosemary Chan (Melbourne, Australia, 1947) has had a passion for all kinds of art for as long as she can remember. She has combined the acquisition of new forms of art with a varied teaching career spanning all age ranges and abilities. An accomplished weaver, quilter, calligrapher and photographer, her favorite media are pen-and-ink drawings and Chinese brush paintings, which she finds to be both relaxing and rewarding. This is the first book she has illustrated.

www.ingramcontent.com/pod-product-compliance
Lightning Source LLC
LaVergne TN
LVHW011222080426
835509LV00005B/272